Nehemiah

Man's Place in God's Plan

Nehemiah inspects the walls and gates of Jerusalem.
—*Neh. 2:13*

Nehemiah
Man's Place in God's Plan

Pastor Melissa Scott, Ph.D.

Published by Dolores Press, Inc., Glendale, CA

DoloresPress.com

For additional teaching, please visit PastorMelissaScott.com.

ISBN 978-1-60670-010-5

Contents

INTRODUCTION

When we talk about a man or a woman who has the call of God on their life, there are a few things that are, or should be, self-evident. The difficulty arises when people start making their own opinions and depart from what is clearly laid out in the Scriptures. The apostle Paul wrote to the Ephesian church about the gifts that God gave to the church, saying that God gave some apostles, prophets, evangelists and pastoring-teachers for the perfecting of the saints *to* the work of the ministry. That passage is often misinterpreted to put all of the responsibility on the minister's back, and many people mistakenly believe that they can travel carelessly along their pathway while the minister does everything for them.

When a person is called of God, there are certain traits that you can be absolutely sure of, based on the pattern that is given in the Bible. First, the majority of the people whom God called never wanted the position. They did not volunteer themselves. If you genuinely understand the precariousness of handling God's word and talking to His chosen ones, you might be less inclined to run out and declare that you are starting a ministry. In fact, the chances are that if God puts a burden on your heart, the first thing you will want to do is to fast and pray about it. And if it is truly a burden from God, it will be a burden that is unique to you. It will not be an imitation of someone else's ministry. It will be a unique burden that God has placed on your heart and it will consume all your waking hours. Further, we know from God's word that when He places a burden on someone's heart, it will be a burden to pick up what has been ruined and to restore what has been destroyed. When God calls a person, He always calls them to build up. He will not call you to tear down or predict doom, unless you are called like the prophet Jeremiah. God's people are called to build up. When God raised up the apostle Paul, He called him to build up the New Testament church so that it should not be a mere splinter of Judaism.

So we know that when people are called of God, they do not start out by volunteering themselves. And even though you might say, "Lord, what can I do?" that only comes after much trepidation, because when you step into the realm of desiring to be used of God, it is going to come at a price. I may be the most unpopular person in Christendom today for saying that; so many ministers want to tell you how wonderful everything will be when you come to the Lord. The reality is that if you really step out for Christ and stand on His word, you are a marked man or a marked woman. The enemy does not care how he takes you out or takes you down, cripples your mind or hinders your acting in faith. That is a reality which is seldom talked about.

There are some who have been called of God and yet they do not want to assume their responsibility and fulfill that calling on their life. But God works on their hearts and minds, and eventually, like a horse wearing a bit and bridle, they will come to accept it. They come to embrace the fact that God has called them for a certain position.

All of this is a foundation to say that God has chosen some very unusual characters. And most of them had no special training or a background in theological studies. Not many are called by God to preach, but if you are going to go out and start preaching on a street corner, you had better have a message from God's word. All of those gift ministries named in Ephesians 4:11—apostles, prophets, evangelists, pastoring-teachers—relate to the word of God. You had better have a burden for the word of the Lord. Ephesians 4 states the purpose: that we might all come to the unity of *the* faith, which is in Christ Jesus. You will not have a "ministry" of throwing stones at one another or boasting "I'm better than you" or "I'm more equipped" or "I'm more knowledgeable." A true God-called ministry will be carried out with great humility.

My burden is for people to draw closer to God. John 17:3 says, "This is life eternal, that they might know thee the only true God, and Jesus Christ," His Son, "whom thou hast sent," which brings us to the principle of drawing close and abiding in Him. I desire to bring you to a closer relationship with the Lord through His word, so that your relationship will be fortified, even if you have been walking in the faith for forty years. I also desire that you not get complacent about the things of God. Sometimes the word should make you uncomfortable, but that is still part of growth. The day that you can no longer be made uncomfortable or that you no longer are ministered to, even if it is just from Bible reading, is the day you have disconnected yourself from the Lord.

The truly called man or woman of God does not enter into the ministry to elevate themselves. Paul, writing to the Corinthians, said, "God uses the base things to confound the wise," so that the wisdom of the world is not vaunted before men. But God uses those base things, those things that are of lowly estate, to build up. Why else would the Scripture say that when Christ came, He took on the form of a servant? He did not take on the form of a king; He did not establish a palace for Himself on earth. Jesus said, "The Son of man has nowhere to lay his head."

There are many who would like to tell you that they are called, but they do not study the word of God; the Spirit is not even remotely active in them. There are multitudes who will follow them and say, "Well, that sounds about right." Then there are others who think they have a ministry, when the only "ministry" they are performing is like that of Sanballat and Tobiah. And that brings us to the book of Nehemiah.

The books of Ezra and Nehemiah, along with the books of Esther, Haggai and Zechariah, tell us about what happened to God's people who were carried away into captivity, and what happened when the decree was issued for the people to return to Jerusalem. Only a small portion of the people returned; most of the people chose to remain in Babylon.

Ezra and Nehemiah were originally one book in the Hebrew canon, but they became separated in the Latin Vulgate. In terms of their content, Nehemiah devotes six chapters to the reconstruction of the walls. The last seven chapters deal with the reinstruction of God's people, for the people had forgotten much while they were in bondage. Ezra is also divided into similar sections of building and restoring. In the first chapters of Ezra, the altar is rebuilt and the book of the law is read. When Nehemiah opens, the walls and the gates have not yet been restored.

The book of Nehemiah can be understood in a historical sense, but there is also a practical application for the church today. And there is another application that is seldom pointed out: the city had to be restored before the coming of Christ. God orders all things perfectly, yet if we were to take a page out of history and only read the opening of Nehemiah, it would not seem like God was very much in control, because the city was still in ruins. I am going to transition at many points in our study from the historical to the practical: Many times this situation in Nehemiah is where we find ourselves as Christians. We cannot understand why something is still lying in ruins. We wonder why a problem is not yet fixed, because we cannot see the big picture. We cannot see the whole plan unfolded, but God can. When you come to trust God, you realize that He will even enter into the messes (whether you made them or not) and work them out for His purpose and for His glory.

CHAPTER 1

GOD'S PERSON AND THE BURDEN THEY CARRY

Nehemiah 1 begins, "The words of Nehemiah the son of Hachaliah." Nehemiah's name means "Whom Jehovah comforts," and Hachaliah means "He who waits for Jehovah." "And it came to pass in the month Chisleu," which corresponds to either November or December in our calendar, "in the twentieth year, as I was in Shushan the palace, that Hanani, one of my brethren, came, he and certain men of Judah; and I asked them concerning the Jews that had escaped, which were left of the captivity, and concerning Jerusalem."

There are many lessons that we can glean out of this passage. I want us to notice that Nehemiah enquired about God's people and about God's place. Some of us need to ask ourselves, when was the last time that we enquired about God's people around us, or God's place? Nehemiah cared enough to ask, even though he was living in a palace far away. Jerusalem and the people who had returned were still a part of his heritage, even though he was serving under a heathen king in a distant land. And when men came from Judah, he cared enough to enquire. "And they said unto me, The remnant that are left of the captivity there in the province are in great affliction and reproach: the wall of Jerusalem also is broken down, and the gates thereof are burned with fire."

It is easy for us to read this passage simply as history, without putting flesh and blood on it. Think for a moment about Nehemiah as a man who could have easily lost his grip on God while living in the palace of a heathen king. We could title the first chapter of the book of Nehemiah "Piety in the Palace," because it is rare for people to understand this principle that Jesus picks up and heralds to His disciples: "If you were of the world, the world would love its own; but you are not of the world; for I have chosen you out of the world." Nevertheless, we still have to be in the world. So even though Nehemiah was in a palace, he still had a powerful reaction to the report about the conditions in Jerusalem.

I want us to see Nehemiah's compassion as he enquired after God's people and God's place, and I want us to see his care: "It came to pass, when I heard these words, that I sat down and wept, and mourned certain days, and fasted, and prayed before the God of heaven." We know that this weeping, mourning, fasting and praying lasted at least four months, because this chapter begins in Chisleu, around December, and the second chapter picks up in the month of Nisan, which is either March or April, when Nehemiah was about to appear before the king.

Nehemiah was not the first person to ever react to the condition of God's people and His place, nor was he the last. What was he weeping, mourning, fasting and praying over? Over the condition of Jerusalem. In the New Testament, we see Jesus weeping and lamenting over Jerusalem. Some people casually say, "I'm praying for you," which has about as much meaning as someone in Hollywood saying, "Let's do lunch." You will even meet people who say that they belong to God, but when they see your burden, they only say, "Hey, good for you. I'm glad. Take care." But we can see the profound impact that the report of the conditions in Jerusalem had on Nehemiah, and how self-denying he was, that without any self-serving or self-pity, he would take it upon himself to weep, fast and pray.

It is too bad that the body of Christ today is so busy about things that never build up the body, so busy about things that have little or no relevance. The church gets worked up about things that comprise only a very small percentage of what the Bible addresses, or things that are not even mentioned, and people spend their whole lives railing, "You ought to live a better life" or "You ought to do this" or "You ought to do that." But what does any of that have to do with our relationship with Christ? Exposure to God's word and exposure to the risen Christ through this word, through His Spirit, brings a changed life that will dedicate itself with complete willingness, without needing any coercion.

Nehemiah had a heart that God prepared for a specific call, and he was moved so much that he prayed for four months. When he heard the report from his brethren, he didn't just burst into the king's presence and put on a sad face, hoping that the king would ask him what was wrong. He earnestly petitioned God about His place and His people.

This is a lesson that we need to apply to ourselves today. Too often, people come to church with the thought, "It's all about *me.* I need a word from the Lord. I need the pastor to minister to *my* needs today." They expect the church to work like a thirty-minute television program: first there is a crisis and then the problem is solved and everybody is happy at the end of the thirty minutes. Unfortunately, it doesn't work like that. You might say, "But I need a quick fix!" Then that is about all you will get, because the problems will still be there. Without faith, it is impossible to even address our problems with a lasting solution that Christ presents to us through His Resurrection power. So if you are looking for a quick fix, I cannot help you. But if you want to understand God's ways through His word, then see this man who has a burden, see his compassion and his care, and listen to his profound petition.

We read starting from verse 5, Nehemiah said, "I beseech thee, O Lord God of heaven, the great and terrible God, that keepeth covenant and mercy for them that love him and observe his commandments: let thine ear now be attentive, and thine eyes open. . . ." God, I don't want You to only hear me, I want You to see me too. Let Your ear be attentive, "that thou mayest hear the prayer of thy servant." Notice that Nehemiah did not simply rush into

God's presence to dump all of his requests onto Him. He started by expressing his need for God to listen and see him. Nehemiah knew the word, and he did not pray a random prayer. He said, "Let thine ear now be attentive, and thine eyes open, that thou mayest hear the prayer of thy servant, which I pray before thee now, day and night, for the children of Israel thy servants."

Notice also how self-denying Nehemiah was, for his prayer was first "for the children of Israel thy servants." He didn't begin by saying, "I have a prayer request for me." He came into God's presence with a burden for God's people. A true burden from the Lord starts with God's people, God's word and God's place, which for us is the church.

Nehemiah asked God to hear his prayer "which I pray before thee now, day and night, for the children of Israel thy servants, and confess the sins of the children of Israel," as a body, "which we have sinned against thee." Notice that he included himself, saying, "*we* have sinned." That is another trait of a godly leader, not someone who boasts, "I don't drink, I don't smoke and I don't cuss." He said, "We have sinned, we have fallen short, we have missed the mark." Think about that. "We have sinned against thee: both I and my father's house have sinned. We have dealt very corruptly against thee, and have not kept the commandments, nor the statutes, nor the judgments, which thou commandedst thy servant Moses. Remember, I beseech thee, the word that thou commandedst thy servant Moses, saying, If ye transgress, I will scatter you abroad among the nations: but if ye turn unto me, and keep my commandments, and do them; though there were of you cast out unto the uttermost part of the heaven, yet will I gather them from thence, and will bring them unto the place that I have chosen to set my name there. Now these are thy servants and thy people, whom thou hast redeemed by thy great power, and by thy strong hand. O Lord, I beseech thee, let now thine ear be attentive to the prayer of thy servant, and to the prayer of thy servants, who desire to fear thy name: and prosper, I pray thee, thy servant this day, and grant him mercy in the sight of this man. For I was the king's cupbearer."

Again, the person called of God will not rush out without taking the time to pray, to dedicate, to understand, to meditate and to ask God for understanding and to open up a pathway. This is an absolute law in the spiritual realm. In Nehemiah's case, his prayer was not "God, build me a kingdom. Make me famous. Give *me* something." This is the person of God. This is the clay that God will use to minister to His people.

There are many who do not understand this, and they will try to tell you what a person of God should be like, just as there are many who are quick to offer their opinion of what a Christian is. They will tell you that a Christian does this and doesn't do that, or a Christian should look like this and should talk like that. I want us to see what a person of God looks like in His book. Some people say that they have a ministry to one particular group of people or to a different faith. But if we are a people called of God, called to His purpose, true ministry will always bring you back to the word of God. You will never build something for God if you are trying to build something man-made for some random purpose, unless you want to be like those who built the Tower of Babel.

I want us to see the elements of Nehemiah's reaction, his weeping and mourning. There are many passages in the Bible where people are said to have wept bitterly. In Psalm 137, when God's people had been carried away into captivity, they were asked to sing the songs of their land, but they hung their harps and wept bitterly, saying, "How shall we sing the LORD'S song in a strange land?" Jesus said in the Beatitudes in Matthew 5, "Blessed are they that mourn: for they shall be comforted." That does not speak of human comfort; it speaks of the comfort of God.

Jesus taught about fasting and prayer. We can never pray too much. Andrew Murray said, "Prayer is not monologue, but dialogue; God's voice in response to mine is its most essential part." John Bunyan said, "Prayer will make a man cease from sin, or sin will entice a man to cease from prayer." Charles Spurgeon said, "Prayer can never be in excess," you can never pray too much. And Søren Kierkegaard said, "Prayer does not change God; it changes . . . the one who prays." Martin Luther is said to have prayed three hours a day, or more by some accounts. The man or woman of God will be praying.

It is surprising how many people I encounter who do not know a thing about what the Bible says about a person who has been called of God. But they start following someone, and then they become delusional. The Bible speaks of people who get turned over to a strong delusion; they believe a lie and are damned. I cannot fix that. I cannot help someone who will never even open up the Bible and read. But I can tell you what I *can* fix: I can declare, "This is what God's word says."

Let's look at the characteristics of Nehemiah's prayer: it is reverential and full of adoration, it has elements of confession and pleading, and it has definiteness. Nehemiah did not just vaguely say, "Oh, Lord, I pray for this people, amen." But there is first a humble confession, that "we have sinned: both I and my father's house." I do not mean to condemn anyone with this remark, but if we are really honest with ourselves, we know that at times we are busy trying to tell God how much we have turned to Him or how much we have changed. But when you come into His presence with humility before Him, it is only you and God. No one else is listening, and you can just lay your heart open to God. This is not limited to a man or a woman who has been called to lead; it is for every child of God, for every person following. We should open our hearts bare before God in our prayer closets and in our private time. And let there be soul searching, let there be stirring, let all of those things come that can make us more malleable. Isn't that the whole purpose? We come to God and He knows our frame; the word of God says He knows what we need before we even ask Him, but we still come to Him like children asking their father.

So the lessons of Nehemiah's prayer apply to all of us, but I am specifically looking at this man of God and I see his compassion, his care, his call to God and his confession. And in verse 11, there is also an interesting confidence displayed here when he says, "O Lord, I beseech thee, let now thine ear be attentive to the prayer of thy servant, and to the prayer of thy servants, who desire to fear thy name: and prosper, I pray thee, thy servant this day, and grant him mercy in the sight of this man. For I was the king's cupbearer." As we continue reading in Nehemiah 2, we see that four months have elapsed. Someone might ask, "Should you really keep petitioning and praying for so long?" Sometimes that is what it takes when God gives you a burden.

It starts with someone who cares about the word of God and the health of His church. I believe it is possible for God's people to turn around. There has to come a moment of recognition that you are going to serve someone. Get on the Lord's side, and begin to follow Him. Find someone who is opening up the word faithfully, week in and week out, and not someone leading you on rabbit trails and taking you down pathways that may be interesting but bear no fruit for the kingdom of God. Get right with God and begin by taking these steps.

If listening to a sermon does not bring you closer to the Savior, then you have wasted your time. Jesus said that if you are not gathering with Him, you are scattering. If you are not building up, you are tearing down. The message should be designed to bring people closer to God, not closer to the preacher. I believe it is a natural spillover that you will begin to love the one who is leading you and who desires to bring you closer to the Lord, but the focus of the message must draw you closer to Christ until you can say, "Who shall separate us?" Someone will say that the devil indeed has the power to pry someone away, by exploiting people's self-pity or even their lack of prayer. But the question remains, "Who shall separate us?" The answer is *no one can* if you stay connected by faith. And as faith comes by hearing God's word and you are fortified, you will begin to develop deep roots. It is a lot harder to chop down a tree when the roots are very deep, than it is to chop down a young tree.

Let's read on in Nehemiah 2: "It came to pass in the month Nisan, in the twentieth year of Artaxerxes the king, that wine was before him: and I took up the wine, and gave it unto the king." As the king's cupbearer, Nehemiah was in a very trusted position, because the cupbearer would taste the wine first to ensure that the king would not be poisoned.

"I took up the wine, and gave it unto the king. Now I had not been beforetime sad in his presence." We know the danger of this situation from the book of Esther. To come into a king's presence unbidden, or to show sadness or make a personal request, could result in death. But we see the Lord's favor in the king's response to Nehemiah after four months of praying and fasting: "Wherefore the king said unto me, Why is thy countenance sad. . . ?" It is remarkable that Nehemiah did not even have to ask the king. The king spoke to *him* and said, "Why is thy countenance sad, seeing thou art not sick? this is nothing else but sorrow of heart. Then I was very sore afraid, and said unto the king, Let the king live for ever: why should not my countenance be sad, when the city, the place of my fathers' sepulchres, lieth waste, and the gates thereof are consumed with fire?"

Nehemiah was very daring to say that to the king. But amazingly, the king replied, "For what dost thou make request?" In other words, "What is it that you want? State your request!" Now look at Nehemiah's response. He said, "So I prayed to the God of heaven." Later Nehemiah will say, "God's hand was upon me." God's hand was on this man, leading him. But not only that, God's hand was also on this heathen king to cause him to ask Nehemiah the question that opened the door. The king did not punish him, and he granted Nehemiah's request. But we need to see this in the context of Nehemiah's prayer and remember that his request was made to the king only after four months of petitioning God.

"And I said unto the king, If it please the king, and if thy servant have found favour in thy sight, that thou wouldest send me unto Judah, unto the city of my fathers' sepulchres, that I may build it. And the king said unto me, (the queen also sitting by him,) For how long shall thy journey be? and when wilt thou return? So it pleased the king to send me; and I set him a time. Moreover I said unto the king, If it please the king, let letters be given me to the governors beyond the river, that they may convey me over till I come into Judah."

There are three things I want us to see here: he asked to be sent, he asked for letters of safety, and lastly he asked for "a letter unto Asaph the keeper of the king's forest, that he may give me timber to make beams for the gates of the palace which appertained to the house." He asked the king for supplies. And the Scripture says, "The king granted me, according to the good hand of my God upon me." All of Nehemiah's requests were fully met.

I am not saying that when we come into God's presence that we can ask Him for anything we want and He will give it to us right away, like some kind of genie-in-a-bottle. But we certainly can petition God concerning the welfare of His church. All too often we want to give up because our prayers are not answered instantly, because things don't happen quickly enough. I am also not saying that if you haven't received a response from God, it is because you haven't prayed or fasted enough. I am just saying that no one knows God's timing, except God. God has perfect timing. I know now that He led me a certain way, although I didn't know that He was leading me at the time. God's timing was perfect in that my heart was ready to hear and my eyes and ears were opened. And we know that there are seasons like that for every person.

The person of God must be prayerful and their focus must be on the welfare of the church. I have heard people say, "But you are asking me to do something that God has not asked me to do. In fact, I don't have to 'do' anything." Let me tell you something: when you have a bad attitude like that, I cannot fix it. I believe that your correction might come when you are standing before the Lord, being judged for your bad attitude because you were not willing. Jesus lamented over Jerusalem, saying, "How often I would have gathered you, but you would not." I say these things to get us to think about how we treat the church of Jesus Christ. We do not know how much time God will give us. God does all things perfectly, so I cannot lament about the brevity of time we are allotted, because in reality all of our lives are very brief. That is why I live every day for Christ, as God gives me the strength. I open my eyes in the morning and say, "Thank You, Lord, for the breath in my lungs." I do not know if

I will be here next year, and neither do you. You must act on certain things and not put them off; you must seize opportunities in the kingdom of God.

But I want us to notice God's ways. Nehemiah was a man of God who was raised up for a purpose, but he didn't just rush out the door. He didn't make himself an enemy of the king, nor did he make enemies of the people who would be performing the work of building up Jerusalem. He had a mission, he prayed, he fasted and he was grieved.

Any person who cares about the church should have a mourning spirit. I do not mean a spirit of gloom and doom, rather I am talking about grief for the state that the churches have fallen into, where the word of God has either been censored or put in the back seat. Too many churchgoers no longer have a hunger for the word of God. They just want something to tantalize them; and God forbid if the sermon is longer than twenty minutes, because their attention span is so short that they could not bear to sit through an hour-long message, as though an hour's investment of time in preparation for eternity is too great a sacrifice.

When we look at Nehemiah's life, it should inspire us. I do not mean that we should try to imitate it; rather we should prayerfully consider it. You see, Christ sends us, He orders our steps, and sometimes He orders our stops. Nehemiah will certainly encounter many bumps in the road. I heard a preacher talk about how easy it was to plant a church and how they now have so many members, but God is not impressed with sheer numbers. I would rather pastor a church with only a hundred people who desire God and have a burden to be closer to Him, people who want to have their hearts operated on by the Great Physician, and who are constantly being drawn towards Him and not away from Him. Give me a hundred of those people, rather than the thousand or ten thousand who are indifferent. There are people who only come to church for some auxiliary reason; they have no part in the church of Jesus Christ. Give me the hundred people who will say, "The most important thing in my life is Jesus Christ and His word being a beacon of light until He comes again." Those are the type of people through whom God will carry out His will.

The next thing I want us to see is that we only have to read two more verses before Nehemiah encounters opposition, right at the beginning of his journey, right at the beginning of his ministry. We read, "Then I came to the governors beyond the river, and gave them the king's letters. Now the king had sent captains of the army and horsemen with me. When Sanballat the Horonite, and Tobiah the servant, the Ammonite, heard of it, it grieved them exceedingly that there was come a man to seek the welfare of the children of Israel."

Any time God sends a man or a woman who seeks the welfare of His people, His place or His church, there will always be people who will be angry about it. "It grieved them *exceedingly* that there was come a man to seek the welfare. . . ." Some of God's people need to wake up to this fact and recognize that many people are grieved when a pastor preaches the gospel. The enemies of the gospel will harass, gossip, lie and bring pressure; and they would like nothing better than for the pastor to leave.

Any pastor should take comfort in the knowledge that he or she has enemies, though that is nothing to boast about. I have taken the words of Christ and applied them to my heart. My enemies have taught me how to love them, which is impossible. Your enemies are impossible to love, but Christ commands us to love our enemies for a reason. He said that He is going to make them His footstools. I would not want to be under Jesus' feet. I want to be in His arms, and not under His feet.

There will always be adversaries who are grieved when someone has committed themselves to the Lord's work to resurrect and rebuild and repair. They will mock and say, "What can these people possibly do?" I will tell you what the people did in Nehemiah's day: they built the wall! I get frustrated when dealing with people who refuse to see what building up the work of God entails. And they defensively avoid their responsibility and say, "Well, since we are saved by faith alone, aren't you saying that we should go out and do 'good works'?" Absolutely not! I am not talking about doing some kind of good work or righteous deed that could somehow merit God's approval. I am talking about rebuilding for God, and I am first talking about the people in Nehemiah's day who had to go out and physically build a real wall with their own hands. God could have said, "It's time for *Me* to rebuild Jerusalem." Then He could have waved His mighty hand and with a *whoosh!* the walls would have magically arisen. I am sure God could have instantly rebuilt the city and the walls and they would have looked pristine, but He made the workers work. And if you will read carefully, you will find that most of the people lived very close to the places they repaired, because the work of reparation, rebuilding and restoration always starts closest to where we live. It begins in the heart of man and works its way out. Anyone who says, "Well, but you still have to do certain specific good deeds" is wrong. They think you can please God by doing works. When you are doing a true work of God, it is the result of God's leading, not man's initiative. And it starts a process in you that enables you to change your direction in response to God's leading.

You can always tell when someone is truly God's person by the burden they carry and the opposition they encounter. We see Nehemiah's prayerful attitude, and even though God's hand was upon him, he still faced great opposition to God's building program. So when we face opposition, do not think that it is a bad thing. It is a good thing and it tells us that we are on the right track. The closer you get to the heart of God, the more resistance and opposition you will encounter.

Someone said to me, "You're always talking about spiritual warfare and the devil, and how the devil interferes and gets into people's hearts and minds. I never have those problems. In fact, where I go to church, we don't spend that much time talking about the devil." I believe that person was making a true confession. But the closer you press to the cross, the closer you draw near to Christ, the more you will encounter the attacks of the enemy. The devil is not going to look at someone who is not making a dent for Christ or for the kingdom of God. That is why some churches are unbothered. But the ones who are doing the most damage to the prince of the power of the air's territory are the ones who are hindered.

There are people who are committed to God who can drive their cars all week without a problem, but then suddenly on a Sunday morning they have a flat tire. Or they will go months without having a financial problem, but when they decide that they want to give an extra offering as an act of sacrificial faith, suddenly an avalanche of bills lands on them and they wonder, "How did this happen?" I don't like to blame everything that happens on the devil, but when those kinds of things happen to you, they should be a sign to say that you are important to God's plan.

You matter to God. When you forget how important you are to God's plan, the devil can easily pick you off. It is very easy to forget that there is a battle going on. Ephesians 6 declares that our warfare is not against flesh and blood, but against the prince of the power of the air. Satan sends missiles: he sends people to discourage and disappoint, and he spreads propaganda and negative things. But when someone comes to build up God's work, they will always come with this mindset: I will first pray about it and lay it before God. I will not rush in hastily. I will delight in the fear of God, and will seize the opportunity of faith that is afforded me. And if I fail, that is okay. God will let me get up again and again as long as I am looking unto Him who is indeed not only the Author and Finisher of Faith, but He is also the Rewarder of those who diligently seek Him.

Let me close with Ephesians 4. God gave ministers as a gift to the church to build up the body to bring us to the unity of the faith, that we be henceforth no more like children tossed to and fro with every wind of doctrine, but that we may stand firm in the unity of the faith, resilient against all of those things that will come against us. But to those who understand what Nehemiah understood, God's hand is upon His church and upon each of us individually as more than conquerors in Christ. I want us to keep our eyes focused on the kingdom of God and the great honor that we have. There is power. We are not helpless; we are not standing alone crying out, "What shall we do?" We have great power when we come to Him and we lay it all before Him in prayer.

To the heavy soul coming to God, unloading his burden and giving it all to Christ, Jesus said, "Come unto me, all you that labor and are heavy laden, and I will give you rest." You find peace with Him when you place your burden with Him. Keep going. Like the woman who kept knocking, you keep going. But eventually, when you are petitioning God about His plan and His purpose, He answers, because it is according to His will. If you come to church expecting an instant magical deliverance, I cannot help you. But if you will keep knocking on heaven's door, I tell you that God is faithful; His ears are open and His eyes are looking at His treasures, knowing what it is that you are asking for, but waiting for you to keep petitioning. And He is faithful to bring it to pass.

God has great plans for His church, and the enemy is not ignorant of that fact. Many things have come against the church, especially a lack of faithfulness on the part of the people. Satan is very crafty in what he does, and he knows how easily people can be lured away. So I am asking you to pray for this work. This is the most important work we will ever touch. We must keep the message of Jesus Christ going out to a world that certainly needs the message of light and hope that He brings to those who will come, those who can hear and those who will respond. I am asking you to claim that with me, in Jesus' name. Amen.

Chapter 2

CONCERN FOR GOD'S WORK

We have looked at the character of Nehemiah and the burden that he carried. He was serving as the cupbearer to a heathen king, and when he heard the report about the conditions in Jerusalem, he sat down and wept, fasted and prayed for four months. Then he made his request to the king to be allowed to go there and rebuild. I would highlight Nehemiah's words in Nehemiah 2:5: *"Send me, that I may rebuild it."* And the king not only granted him leave, he also gave him letters for safe passage and a letter for supplies. Nehemiah attributed his success to God, for we read in verse 8, "The king granted me, according to the good hand of my God upon me."

It is easy to read the Bible without putting flesh and blood on the people whose lives are recorded on its pages. We sometimes wonder, because the book is so old, "How can this apply to me?" How could we possibly say, "According to the good hand of my God upon me," when sometimes it feels like God's hand is *not* upon me, or like God has even turned His back on me? I know the power of discouragement; the problem is that we keep falling into the trap. Jesus warned us, saying, "If you were of the world, the world would love its own; but because you are not of the world, but I have chosen you out of the world, therefore the world hates you." He also said, "In the world you will have tribulation."

The battles will never end; there will always be enemies both inside and outside the church, and they will always have the same traits. That is one of the ways you can know that they are not from God and that they come from the spirit of the world, the flesh and the devil. The devil likes to use the same methods over and over again. It is as though Satan is saying, "That one worked really well in the past. I am going to keep using that one, because you keep stumbling over it!" We may foolishly keep stumbling over the same things, but if God's hand is upon us, then He will indeed make a way to raise us up again. Maybe we will have to go through certain things, but we *will* go through them, because the Lord is leading us.

I am sure that when Nehemiah set out on his mission, he never imagined that there could be so much opposition to someone whose only intention was to do something for God's people and His work. Yet almost immediately after he set out, he encountered the first battery of opposition. We read in Nehemiah 2:10, "When Sanballat the Horonite, and Tobiah the servant, the Ammonite, heard of it, it grieved them exceedingly that there was come a man to seek the welfare of the children of Israel." In the Hebrew, there is a double expression of grief. It deeply disturbed and distressed them that someone had arrived who cared about furthering God's work. And today it is no different: you will always encounter spiritual warfare whenever you are doing something to help send forth the gospel message.

Nonetheless, Nehemiah said, "I arose in the night, I and some few men with me; neither told I any man what my God had put in my heart to do at Jerusalem." That sounds like Paul addressing the Galatians when he says of his calling, "I conferred not with flesh and blood." In other words, when God is really doing something, it will not only be God-inspired, it will be God-led. Like Paul, Nehemiah didn't tell anyone what God had put on his heart. And like Paul, Nehemiah did not receive his leading from flesh or blood; *God* gave him his instructions. Nehemiah said that he only took a few men with him, "neither was there any beast with me, save the beast that I rode upon. And I went out by night by the gate of the valley, even before the dragon well," or *jackal* well, "and to the dung port, and viewed the walls of Jerusalem, which were broken down, and the gates thereof were consumed with fire. Then I went on to the gate of the fountain, and to the king's pool: but there was no place for the beast that was under me to pass. Then went I up in the night by the brook, and viewed the wall, and turned back, and entered by the gate of the valley, and so returned. And the rulers knew not whither I went, or what I did; neither had I as yet told it to the Jews, nor to the priests, nor to the nobles, nor to the rulers, nor to the rest that did the work. Then said I unto them, Ye see the distress that we are in. . . ." The King James Version translators chose too mild a word; the problem was much deeper than just *distress*. "Ye see the distress that we are in, how Jerusalem lieth waste, and the gates thereof are burned with fire: come, and let us build up the wall of Jerusalem, that we be no more a reproach."

It is interesting to compare how certain Hebrew words are used in these passages. One of the challenges in translating the Hebrew language is that one word can have many different meanings, and there can be ambiguity in the shades of meaning. We saw in Nehemiah 2:10, concerning the enemies, that "it grieved them exceedingly." Now in Nehemiah 2:17, we read that Nehemiah said, "Ye see the distress that we are in." The same Hebrew word is used in both instances, which shows that the same situation affects some people in one way and other people in another way.

"Then I told them of the hand of my God which was good upon me; as also the king's words that he had spoken unto me. And they said, Let us rise up and build. So they strengthened their hands for this good work. But when Sanballat the Horonite, and Tobiah the servant, the Ammonite, and Geshem the Arabian, heard it, they laughed us to scorn, and despised us, and said, What is this thing that ye do? will ye rebel against the king?"

Opposition is not always a bad thing; it is actually a good thing. It is part of God's plan that we should encounter people just like this. God does enter in to all things to work His good, and by the very opposition, we know that we are a part of His plan. Notice that Sanballat and Tobiah are introduced in verse 10, and suddenly in verse 19, there is a third person, Geshem the Arabian. Geshem most likely would have started out as an enemy to Tobiah and Sanballat, but the three of them have banded together here. People who would normally be each other's enemies will not hesitate to gang up against God's people. They may even claim to be Christians, but the things that they do are for their own selfish interests, and are never for the betterment of the church.

These enemies came together and they "laughed us to scorn and despised us." This is typical of what happens to God's people in every age. In Genesis 21, shortly before Abraham cast out Hagar and Ishmael, Ishmael was mocking Isaac. Galatians 4 describes this episode as an example of the children of the flesh persecuting the children of promise, those born of the Spirit. When Jesus was hanging on the cross, the chief priests, scribes, and elders mocked Him, saying, "See, He saved others, but He can't save Himself." The apostle Paul was ridiculed by people who said, "Isn't he the one who persecuted the church?" In the Corinthian letters we read that some were accusing Paul and treating him like he wasn't really who he said he was. Verse 18 of Jude warns of a future time when men will be mockers. They will make a mockery of anyone who takes a stand for the cause of Christ. And if you keep walking towards the Lord and away from the world, the flesh and the devil, you will soon find this kind of opposition, or rather, it will find you.

Some people say that when you are in the body of Christ, everyone should love each other; but it is normal to have enemies. It is not a sign of a lapse of faith or a lack of understanding. If we were not going to have enemies, then why did Jesus teach about loving and praying for our enemies? He understood that the same words that bring life and light and the reality of His presence to some, also bring death to others. It is a double-edged sword.

As we study these verses in Nehemiah 2, I would like us to make note of a few key concepts. First, when Nehemiah went out to survey the walls of Jerusalem by night, he went out with concern. He did not go to serve his own ego; he did not go to cater to his pride. He did not say, "Hey everyone, I am going to be the best builder in Jerusalem!" He simply went out with concern, assessing the ruins to get a real picture of the situation.

The next thing I want to point out is Nehemiah's call. After he assessed the situation, he exhorted the people, saying, "Ye see the distress that we are in, how Jerusalem lieth waste, and the gates thereof are burned with fire: come, and let us build up the wall of Jerusalem, that we be no more a reproach," that is, a reproach concerning the things of God. Notice that he said, "Ye see the distress *we* are in." He did not say, "Ye see the distress that *you* are in." To make an application to the church today, the problems facing the church are the responsibility of every individual in the family of God. No one should come into the church and say, "It is someone else's problem." Those who have the spirit of Nehemiah are the ones who will roll up their sleeves and say, "What can I do?" and "What more can I do?" Start first, like Nehemiah, by having a concern for what is in ruin. Nehemiah said, "Send me," and he went out and investigated the damage, and his concern was to rebuild the wall of Jerusalem. Our concern should be for maintaining the integrity of the church, which is a concern that has been lost by much of the church world today.

Next I would like to point out Nehemiah's confidence. He said in verse 18, "I told them of the hand of my God which was good upon me; as also the king's words that he had spoken unto me. And they said, Let us rise up and build. So they strengthened their hands for this good work."

Now immediately, when everyone decided to be of one mind and one accord, here come the enemies again. This is speculation, but Sanballat most probably had a political interest that might have been hindered by Nehemiah's appearing. Tobiah may have had some kind of religious position, and his situation would be at risk if the gates were put back up and proper worship practices were restored. And

Geshem was likely a businessman who profited from the trade that would pass by, so Nehemiah's rebuilding would adversely affect his business. So these three banded together to falsely accuse Nehemiah, saying, "You are trying to rebel against the king," even though Nehemiah had letters from the king that authorized this very work. These enemies come straight from the devil, and they try to get you to spend your time and energy worrying about what they might do to you. Stay focused. Jesus said, "Do not be afraid of those who can only harm your body."

But we read in Nehemiah 2:20, "Then answered I them, and said unto them, The God of heaven, he will prosper us." Can you say that with me? *The God of heaven will prosper us!* I am not talking about prosperity like some preachers talk about financial prosperity. I am talking about the prosperity that comes when people put their hand to the plow, put their hearts on the altar and wholeheartedly desire the things that God wants most. When that happens, the God of heaven will prosper us.

Nehemiah answered his enemies, saying, "The God of heaven, he will prosper us; Therefore we his servants will arise and build: but ye have no portion, nor right, nor memorial, in Jerusalem." He said, in essence, "You can try to stop me, but you are not going to have any part in this work!" Those who hinder the work of God will have no reward in His kingdom.

We should be more concerned about God and His church than we are about anything the Sanballats and Tobiahs and Geshems of today can do. Remember Nehemiah's concern, his call and his confidence for God's work and God's will to be done. Isn't that what Jesus taught His disciples to pray? "Thy will be done right here on earth. As it is in heaven, make it so on earth." I wonder how many people who pray for "*Thy* will" really only want "*my* will."

When we get to Nehemiah 4, we will find the same kind of opposition again. After they built the wall, it says, "It came to pass, that when Sanballat heard that we builded the wall, he was wroth, and took great indignation, and mocked the Jews." And this opposition will be ongoing throughout the whole book; the same enemies will keep resurfacing. But let me highlight four verses that demonstrate the results of staying faithful. Nehemiah 2:8 says, "According to the good hand of my God upon me," and Nehemiah 2:20 says, "The God of heaven will prosper us." Now jump ahead to Nehemiah 4:14, where we read, "Be not ye afraid of them: remember the Lord." And our fourth verse is Nehemiah 4:20: "Our God shall fight for us." We read earlier, "The God of heaven will prosper us." Now say with me, "*Our God shall fight for us.*" That is our assurance. God enters in to the call for laborers for His work. The Lord hears us when we pray; He hears when we ask Him.

Nehemiah 2 can be succinctly summarized by three statements: God is the God who hears, the God who instructs and the God who sustains. He is the God who hears, because He heard Nehemiah when he prayed and asked the Lord about the things concerning God's work and His people. He is the God who instructs, because when Nehemiah went out by night, he did not consult anyone first and he did not follow an instruction manual. He followed what the Lord had put on his heart, which is also reminiscent of the many psalms in which the Lord teaches and instructs His people. And lastly, God is the God who sustains, because He made a way for all of these things to come to pass.

At some point, we have to move beyond the things that hinder. Christ is the One who breaks the chains and the restraints. He is the Liberator. It is in Him that we have the victory, as long as we stay focused. The people who belong to the Lord sometimes sit back and think, "Well, God will do everything." But if you have a concern like Nehemiah, you will say, "I'm more concerned about God's work than about all those petty things on the outside." People can become preoccupied with too many petty things, and this is exactly why many have fallen away from the church. When people are not concerned for God's word and His will, they begin to ask, "What am *I* getting out of this?" or they begin to complain, "I don't like my circumstances." But we are not in charge of the circumstances; we do not get to "call the shots."

If you are wondering how to apply this teaching to your own life, the first thing to do is to catch the spirit of Nehemiah in these passages. Make God's work your priority. There are no guarantees as to how much time you or I will have. You have to take the time you have been given and, as the Scripture says, "Redeem the time." Redeem every day; make it count. Live your life for Christ every single day. When you wake up in the morning, don't say, "Well, I will get around to it tomorrow." I cannot carry your cross for you, and I am not asking you to carry mine. The Bible says that you are to pick up your own cross; you are to die daily. I am asking you to carry your burden in the Lord for the ministry. Jesus said that if you are not willing to pick up your cross and follow Him, you cannot even be His disciple. I am asking you to take these words to heart and recognize that the same challenges that Nehemiah faced, we face today. When people come alive to the vision, when they claim the promises of God and anticipate things happening, the same God who entered in to the situation in Nehemiah's day will enter in to the situation in His church today.

I know the power of God and what He is able to do when we put our trust in Him. He is a mountain-moving God, He is a people-changing God, and He is a heart-changing God. And when we commit our way to Him, as Nehemiah did, He will go to work. Our God will prosper us, and our God will fight for us. When we begin to really believe that and claim it as an absolute promise, everything around us will begin to change. It starts first with you and me, and then it will spread to the people around us, until we can finally say, "This is the God we serve, the God who will not fail us. His work is too important to fail, because it is all about Him and bringing glory to His name. We have committed our heart and our way, and now God will enter in and get the victory. So let us arise and build, in Jesus' name."

CHAPTER 3

GET UP AND BUILD

All of the Bible was given for our instruction. When we read the Bible, we see that we are no different than the people on its pages. The people who built the wall in Nehemiah's day faced opposition, just as the children of God in any age will face opposition. I am grateful for opposition when it comes, and I praise God for my enemies. The opposition shows me that I have something in common with my Lord and Savior, because He also was despised and rejected of men.

We read in Nehemiah 4, "It came to pass, that when Sanballat heard that we builded the wall, he was wroth, and took great indignation, and mocked the Jews." As Christians, we are often ridiculed for what we believe. I do not necessarily mean that the popular preachers who appear on television are always ridiculed. The world tends to approve of much of that preaching, because there is nothing difficult in their message. There is seldom, if ever, any message of the cross and the shed blood of Christ. The Christian life as depicted on much of religious television is always happy and smooth, and everybody is great. But there is ridicule directed against the ones who stay by the book and preach, because our message is considered to be archaic. Ridicule of God's work is not new, and we see it here in the book of Nehemiah.

Let's look briefly at the kinds of attacks that come from the enemy's camp, and conclude with six strategies that God's people should take when confronted with opposition. We read that Sanballat "spake before his brethren and the army of Samaria, and said, What do these feeble Jews?" First, he called them "feeble." Then, he said, "Will they fortify themselves?" In other words, will they restore their wall? He questioned whether they even had the ability to do the work. Next, he said, "Will they sacrifice?" Will they offer offerings? The enemies treat the worship of God, especially the offerings, as a joke. Then, he said, "Will they finish in a day? Will they revive the stones out of the heaps of the rubbish which are burned?" Will they be able to bring these burnt stones back to life and use them again? Then their ridicule became even more malicious. We read, "Now Tobiah the Ammonite was by him, and he said, Even that which they build, if a fox go up, he shall even break down their stone wall." If you have ever seen a fox, you know that they are very light-footed creatures, so this last attack was a real jab at the quality of their workmanship. The enemy was saying, "All the work you are doing is flimsy. If even this light-footed animal should tread upon the wall, it will fall down." If the devil cannot drive you away from the ministry by personal accusation, shame or ridicule, then he will attack the quality of the work that you are doing.

That is one of the reasons why the book of Nehemiah speaks to me. I understand how Satan uses people. He uses the tongue, and he uses discouragement and disappointment. I listen to God's people who have been laboring in the Lord with me, and I hear them say, "Pastor, I am with you. I have been praying, I have been fasting—but nothing is happening." If all else fails and the devil cannot drive you away by ridicule and all of his other attacks, he will try to make you want to give up. Some of you have been listening to too much poison and negative talk, when you should be declaring, "The Lord is able!" We serve a very able God. What it takes is some willing servants surrendering themselves to His use. When we surrender to God, He is the greatest "Potter" the world has ever seen. He is able to take something that looks like a mess and make it into something beautiful.

When people attack us personally, or when they attack the workmanship of the church, they are not really attacking you or me, they are attacking Christ. We are God's workmanship; we are His work. The enemies are in fact attacking what lies behind the precious activity that God is doing in our souls. When I was out in the world, with all of its worldliness and carnality abounding, I never thought that I was going the wrong way, or that my very being was in the wrong. But then I turned to God and He turned my life around, and my eyes became focused on the things of God. I began to think, "This is the way everything should be." But it was not until I stepped into the pulpit that I began to see that not all people who claim to be a part of the church understand what happens when you encounter the risen Christ. God is able to change people; He does it every day and He does it from the inside. God doesn't change people because they try to keep the law with all of its "do's" and "don'ts." But He does change people, and He changes them for the better. Yet we can see how malicious some people can be, even those who call themselves "brethren" in the church.

The Bible tells us to pray for our enemies. God's wrath will be poured out on His enemies and the enemies of His chosen people who have answered the call, and that wrath will be terrible. Pray for them that God will be merciful on that day when they stand and give account for the things they have done against the body of Christ. Nehemiah prays, in verses 4 and 5, saying, "Hear, O our God; for we are despised. . . ." The Hebrew word for "despised" is the same word that is used in Isaiah 53, where it says, "He was despised and rejected." But Nehemiah says, "Hear, O our God; for we are despised: and turn their reproach upon their own head, and give them for a prey in the land of captivity: and cover not their iniquity, and let not their sin be blotted out from before thee: for they have provoked thee to anger before the builders."

This prayer has much force in the original Hebrew. My translation is similar to what we have read, but it may help us to better see the emotion of Nehemiah's prayer: "for we are despised; turn back their taunt upon their own heads, and give them up to be plundered in a land where they will be captives, and do not cover their guilt and their sin from thy sight; let it not be blotted out, for they have provoked (by implication) Thee, before the builders." That is quite a prayer to pray for your enemies: "Lord, heap it back on them!"

Verse 6 says, "So we built the wall." The translation here is a little misleading, because the wall was not yet finished, for it says, "and all the wall was joined together unto the half thereof." Half the height of the wall had been built at this point. And it says, "For the people had a mind to work," literally in the Hebrew, "the people had a *heart* to work."

I want us to consider the kinds of things that the enemy throws at us. We read in verse 8, "And conspired all of them together to come and to fight against Jerusalem, and to hinder it." When ridicule did not work, they formed a conspiracy. The conspiracy turned into an attempt to hinder, and that turned into anger. Anger was followed by rumor; rumor was followed by threats and peril of life. Then came the fiery darts, bringing the message from the enemy right to their ears. The devil can be very crafty at managing to deliver those fiery darts under the guise of someone who says that they have a message for you. That is why Ephesians 6 says we are to put on the whole armor of God to quench the fiery darts. The devil will use people as his weaponry. They are the missiles; they are the envoys for Satan, sometimes unbeknownst to themselves.

We read in verse 7, "But it came to pass, that when Sanballat, and Tobiah, and the Arabians, and the Ammonites, and the Ashdodites, heard that the walls of Jerusalem were made up, and that the breaches began to be stopped, then they were very wroth." What was it that engendered such opposition? Think of it: the people were participating in God's work. They were not simply building a wall for the sake of doing something, because I am sure that they all had other things they could have done. But they had returned to the city with one heart and one mind, at least initially, to get the walls back up. The book of Ezra records that they rebuilt the altar and the temple, but the walls and the gates also had to be rebuilt so that the city could be fortified and worship could be fully restored.

So the people had a purpose. They were not just randomly busy for the sake of being busy.

We read on from verse 8, "And conspired all of them together to come and to fight against Jerusalem, and to hinder it. Nevertheless we made our prayer unto our God, and set a watch against them day and night, because of them. And Judah said, The strength of the bearers of burdens is decayed, and there is much rubbish; so that we are not able to build the wall. And our adversaries said, They shall not know, neither see, till we come in the midst among them, and slay them, and cause the work to cease." The adversaries must have been rather desperate at this point that they would say, "We are going to eliminate you, so that the work will be eliminated." Then came the fiery darts: "And it came to pass, that when the Jews which dwelt by them came, they said unto us ten times, From all places whence ye shall return unto us they will be upon you." Think of that! "Therefore set I in the lower places behind the wall, and on the higher places, I even set the people after their families with their swords, their spears, and their bows. And I looked, and rose up, and said unto the nobles, and to the rulers, and to the rest of the people, Be not ye afraid of them: remember the Lord."

Let's look more closely at some of the words that are used in verse 10. The King James Version says, "The strength of the bearers of burdens is decayed, and there is much rubbish." The word translated "decayed" in the Hebrew text is *kashal*. It means "to totter" or "to waver," and it is used in a diversity of places. Sometimes it is used of people, as in Hosea 5:5 where it says, "therefore shall Israel and Ephraim *fall* in their iniquity," and in Ezekiel 33:12 where it says, "as for the wickedness of the wicked, he shall not *fall* thereby in the day that he turneth from his wickedness," that is, he shall not waver, fall down or be brought down. The word for "rubbish" is also interesting. The Hebrew word is *aphar*. It is translated "dust" in Genesis 2:7, where it says, "God formed Adam out of the dust of the ground." I could make an application to the meaning of rubbish in the church today: there are many people who bring into the church their own worldly ideas of how to do God's work. That is also a form of rubbish. But if we just take what is said here at face value, it means that they felt that the job was too great. Let's look at the word for "bearers of burdens." If you were to look at a Hebrew translation of the New Testament, you will find this word used in Galatians 6:2, where it says that we are to bear one another's burdens. From an Old Testament perspective, Isaiah 53:4 and 11 say that Christ carried away our sicknesses and He lifted or bore our griefs and sorrows. Christ then is the ultimate Burden Bearer.

Again, the King James Version says, "The strength of the bearers of burdens is decayed, and there is much rubbish." What does it mean to say that our "strength is decayed"? How is our strength decayed, and how is it brought to the point of wavering or tottering? The main cause is discouragement, which is probably our most pernicious enemy, because we think that when we come into God's program, He should start doing things in a certain way. And if God does not do something in that exact way, we get discouraged. We think, "I know this is God's will, so shouldn't He be doing this thing?" But how do you know that God isn't already doing something and hasn't already entered into the situation, and He is simply waiting, as He sometimes does? His timing doesn't always seem ideal to us. But God may be waiting to see what will happen, whether you will have faith and hang in there, or give up.

This passage speaks to me greatly, because I have a burden for the Lord. I am not *the* Burden Bearer, but I am a burden bearer, like many of you are. And that is why I mentioned Galatians 6:2, because there is burden bearing and there is *the* Burden Bearer. The Scripture says, "Cast your cares upon him," because it matters to Him about you; He cares about you. But many times, especially when we are in the work of the ministry, we will come under the attack of the enemy and get discouraged.

It is easy to listen to the voice of ridicule from enemies or people who are angry. Doesn't the Bible say you are to love those people, including the people you don't necessarily think will love you back? Because if you love those who love you back, what is so special about that? All of us have succumbed, at least once in our lifetimes, certainly once in the last month but more probably within the last week, to being discouraged, because what we thought should have happened did not happen.

But God's people stayed by the stuff. Yes, they came under attack and had to endure the vitriol of these adversaries, but they stayed. These verses in Nehemiah are a road map for anyone who has ever desired to put their hand to the plow. The moment you begin to plow, enemies will come along, either visible and audible enemies, or that sneaky, unseen enemy known as discouragement or disappointment.

Paul asks in the book of Romans, "If God be for us, who can be against us? Who shall separate us?" The answer is that sometimes *we* can become the best separators; either we incline our ear to listen to the voice of the enemy, or in ignorance we engage in his tactics ourselves. In a moment of weakness, anybody can get caught up in participating in this type of behavior. And if you start entertaining the words of the enemy, they will begin to provoke you in your spirit. When people want to tell me about "the rubbish," I have learned to say, "I am not going to engage in this discussion. Do you have anything else you'd like to talk about?" That is not because I want to ignore the reality of the situation. But the reality is that the Lord, the God whom I serve, will deal with these problems. That is His business. He is the expert at working things out. I am not saying that the Lord always does special things for me personally, but He knows who are His and He protects His own. He builds a wall of protection around us, even though it doesn't look like it sometimes, but that is what He does.

The Bible says, "Be not weary in well doing." The Bible also warns us about those who plant seeds of contention and strife. Paul says in the book of Romans, "Mark those who cause divisions and avoid them." In the Old Testament, Proverbs 6 says, "There are six things the Lord hates; seven are an abomination unto him," and the last one is "sowing discord among the brethren."

It is so easy for us to allow our strength to fail because of discouragement or disappointment, or because we cannot see what is really going on. So the first thing I want to do is tap into some of the promises of God that you may have heard and read many times, but they are still true. Zechariah says, "Not by might, nor by power, but by my Spirit. . . ." The Scripture tells us that when we are at our weakest, that is when God enters in. That is when God opens the door of strength. Isaiah says that He gives power to the faint. The Hebrew word he uses for "power" is the same word that is translated *strength* in Nehemiah 4. God gives that ability to those who have lost it.

This is something that all of us as Christians will experience, and it does not reflect any kind of weakness in our personalities. It is just a fact of existing as a Christian: You will come under some type of attack, whether it be by seen or unseen forces. Your strength will waver. But instead of saying, "The strength of the bearers of burdens is decayed," let's talk about the Burden Bearer Himself, the One whose strength never fails. He knows our frame. He knows that we will falter and that our strength will ultimately fail; but when we run out of our own strength, that is when He supplies His strength. When we have depleted our own resources, that is when He gives us the ability to go on.

The people were looking at the wall in its state of disrepair, and they were overwhelmed because it seemed like there was too much work to do. Read the latter half of verse 10, and notice the vocabulary that was ushered in: "that we are not able to build the wall." We must be on the alert for that vocabulary. It not only speaks of fear and the fatigue of faith, it also sends a message to others that says, "You can't do it. Just forget about it. *Don't even try.*" When I am faced with a task that appears to be overwhelming, I can look at the mountain and say, "We are not able. It is too big!" Or, I can get to work and start chipping away a little at a time, without looking at the whole mountain. It may take a while to get the job done, but it will eventually get done.

We have looked at the enemy and his methods, and now I want to present the cure. I will give you six key words that will help us to understand what people of God should do when they are facing a great challenge and overwhelming opposition to doing God's work.

The first word is *prepare*. That does not mean you can prepare to never fail or be disappointed, but you can prepare. Nehemiah 4:6 says, "For the people had a heart to work." Their heart was prepared to undertake this task. Not only were they prepared in their hearts, it was God who had prepared their hearts. There will never be a time when we can say on our own, "I want to do God's work." God has to do the preparing first to bring someone to help in the ministry. If you want to build up God's work and build up your life of faith, you must prepare your heart by abiding in His word. There are many verses in the Bible that illustrate this concept. Psalm 31 says, "Be of good courage, and he shall strengthen your heart." It is God who does the strengthening.

It is very easy for people to just talk and say, "I am going to do something," but it takes courage to stand in the face of adversity and stay by the stuff. It matters to God that someone will stand up and not be worried about what the world thinks. It takes courage to stay by the stuff when you are tempted to think, "What does it matter?" The enemy will use those words against you, and discouragement will set in. You must first prepare your heart, and that begins with our second word, *prayer*. Nehemiah 4:9 says, "Nevertheless we made our prayer unto our God."

The work of God, the work of the ministry and the life of faith is a life of prayer. You cannot escape it. I have heard some people say, "But it is difficult for me to pray. I don't really know what I am doing when I pray." Don't make it complicated. You say that you find it difficult to talk to God? Yet you seem to have no difficulty at all talking to your friends and texting people on the phone. Figure out how to sit down and talk to God the same way you talk to other people, and that will do just fine. God does not want you to pray in stained-glass tones; He just wants you to talk to Him!

The Scripture says that we are to pray without ceasing. You keep going back to God and you keep bringing your petitions to Him. But you do not approach God like you are holding a club over His head. You need to spend some good old-fashioned knee time; not *me* time, *knee* time, where it is just you and God working it out.

Sometimes that can be a long time. It can seem like a lifetime; it might be a lifetime, but you are to keep going back to God.

Our next word is *perseverance*. Nehemiah 4:14 says, "Be not ye afraid of them." You must get up. If you cannot stand up, then sit up. If you cannot sit up, then at least nod your head. And if you cannot nod your head, then blink your eyes. Do *something* by faith! Perseverance is not will-worship. It means you keep getting up when you fall down, because you know that God will work it out. You know that you are going to have opposition. Christ even warned His disciples about this, and we are not immune from these things. He said, "In the world ye shall have tribulation." And Peter said, "Think it not strange concerning the fiery trial which is to try you," whatever it may be. So we must prepare our hearts, we must pray and we must persevere.

Our next word is *power.* We must use the power that is available to us. And in this case, I am talking about the power of memory, because Nehemiah 4:14 says, "Be not ye afraid of them: *remember the Lord.*" The Scripture says, "Remember all the ways the Lord hath led thee." That is not just for the children of Israel, it is for any child of the Lord. Remember all the good things that the Lord has done. When you start to get discouraged because you don't see something happening, stop right there in your tracks and start thinking about what the Lord has already done in your life.

There are some people who might say, "Well, I have a very short list." To those people I say that they need to learn how to be more grateful, because everybody has a list. Every child of God should be able to say, "I know what the Lord has done for me, including bringing me out of darkness and into the light, saving me, delivering me and helping me along the way to find and understand His purpose, His will and what His word declares in my life."

When discouragement comes, I will sit down and start to think about all of those things, and along the way, I will remember how the Lord led me to this point. Then I start thinking about all the blessings I have received in my lifetime, and all the ways that the Lord led me then and is still leading me. Then suddenly, I think to myself, "Wait a minute! Why am I feeling disappointed? I know that the Lord is going to come through! What is wrong with me? Okay, I have got to get up again . . . Let's go!" You might say that is insanity, but that is the way you shake off whatever the enemy puts in your pathway in his attempt to take you out of the work, and that is what you see is going on in the book of Nehemiah.

The fifth word is *protection*. Nehemiah 4:9 says they "set a watch" or a guard. I can superimpose Ephesians 6 over that verse, where we are instructed to put on the whole armor of God, and the protection is the armor of God. So the people in that day set a watch, and they worked with a tool in one hand and a sword in the other.

There are too many people who go to work in the ministry and expect that the Lord's work will be easy. In truth, some of the dirtiest jobs are the most gratifying. David said that he would rather be a janitor, a doorkeeper in the Lord's house, than dwell in the tents of wickedness. It all depends on the way you see things. Ephesians 6 warns us to be vigilant. They set a watch. We must be on guard, and the Bible promises that God will garrison and protect our hearts.

Our last key word in this study is *praise*. Praise is important, even though it is not specifically mentioned in this chapter before us. The Scripture says that God inhabits the praises of His people. We know that these people who were called of God actually built the wall. We know that they accomplished the task even while they faced all of this opposition. We can look at this record and say, "Praise God that we serve a faithful God who will enter in and do the same thing for us as we rebuild the house of faith." If you are doing a work for God, praise God that you even want to, that you even have the desire to lift a finger to help.

There are many people who say, "Well, I'd like to go to church, but I don't have the time." Contrast that attitude with the people who put God first and say, "Thank God for the opportunity to let me come to church and participate in whatever the work is, even if it is cleaning the floors! Praise God!" And that is why I added this word *praise* to our list, because it is important in our condition.

I started this message by saying that I praise God for my enemies, because I know that had it not been for all the adversity that has come my way, I probably would not have clung as closely to the cross and to my Savior. That is what adversity, discouragement and disappointment have the capacity to do: they will either drive you away from God, or they will make you run towards God. Praise God, they made me run towards Him, towards His word. And I think that any one of us who has suffered these things along the way has to look back and say, "If I consider all the parts of this whole equation, maybe instead of ending with praise, that is where I should start:

Thank You, Lord, for whatever I am going through. I know that You are going to enter into it, and I know You are going to fix it. And thank You, Lord, for letting me be a part of Your program and letting me build in Your program, a house that is not made with hands."

The Scripture says, "Except the Lord build the house, the builders labor in vain." Today we are not building a physical structure for God; rather, we are being used by God for His purposes. And when you get that clear in your mind, you can also say, "Praise God! He lets me be a part of that," even in the face of adversity, even in the face of people saying, "You can't do it."

We will not be like these people who said, "For we are not able." We will say, "We *are* able." Why? Because our God is more than able! God specializes in things that are thought impossible. He will accomplish His purpose for us too. All we have to do is to keep *faithing* and keep trusting that God's word is settled in heaven, and He will make it come to pass. Look to Nehemiah as our example. Nehemiah was not Moses, Nehemiah was not David, nor was he any of those great people, but he did something. He came back to Jerusalem and instead of lamenting, tearing people down or complaining about the circumstances, he said, "You, get over there and do this; and you, get over there and do that. Come on! Let's arise and let's build!"

Chapter 4

THE FEAR OF GOD

Exposure to the risen Christ as revealed in God's word will change you. You do not have to beg God to change you, but exposure to the evidence, exposure to God's word, and staying and abiding in that word will change you. There will always be people who see you the way they want to see you, but God looks on the heart, and He sees us exactly the way we are in Christ.

The book of Nehemiah teaches us that there is nothing new; there will always be people who will ridicule and attempt to drive you away or even lure you away from your commitment to doing God's work. Once you begin to master this book, you will realize that we are living in exactly the same circumstances today.

I am a person of the Book. I was not always a person of the Book, but I am a person of the Book now. And when you stay in God's Book long enough, you start to realize that there are ways to handle things. This is what separates Christians from "Christians": they are either people of the Book, or they are people who may call themselves Christians, but they know nothing about God.

People may say all kinds of things about you. I have had all kinds of things said about me, but I am not concerned because I know who I am in Christ Jesus. I am a blood-bought child of the King, and He is my King. One of the reasons why the book of Nehemiah ministers to me is that Nehemiah prayed that God would fight for His people, and I know that He will fight for us too. But God is not going to fight against your inactivity or your will. I am not preaching works; I am preaching that we ought to abundantly live the life of faith. Commit your way to God, and if the circumstances end up messed up, let them belong to God, because ultimately, He is in control. He is the Sovereign One who controls everything. It is His responsibility. Once you have committed your way to Him, then you have to say, "By faith, I have left it all with Him." The consequences then belong to Him.

We read in Nehemiah 4, starting at verse 20, "In what place therefore ye hear the sound of the trumpet, resort ye thither unto us: our God shall fight for us. So we laboured in the work: and half of them held the spears from the rising of the morning till the stars appeared. Likewise at the same time said I unto the people, Let every one with his servant lodge within Jerusalem, that in the night they may be a guard to us, and labour on the day. So neither I, nor my brethren, nor my servants, nor the men of the guard which followed me, none of us put off our clothes, saving that every one put them off for washing." We can see that the people were constantly on guard and working.

Nehemiah 4 ends with all the people armed and working, and no one taking a break. Then Nehemiah 5 opens rather strangely, because it seems somewhat disconnected from what came immediately before. We read, "And there was a great cry of the people and of their wives against their brethren the Jews. For there were that said, We, our sons, and our daughters, are many: therefore we take up corn for them, that we may eat, and live." There were too many people and not enough food. There is a second group of people described in verse 3: "Some also there were that said, We have mortgaged our lands, vineyards, and houses, that we might buy corn, because of the dearth" or famine. And there is a third group described in verses 4 and 5: "There were also that said, We have borrowed money for the king's tribute, and that upon our lands and vineyards. Yet now our flesh is as the flesh of our brethren, our children as their children: and, lo, we bring into bondage our sons and our daughters to be servants, and some of our daughters are brought unto bondage already: neither is it in our power to redeem them; for other men have our lands and vineyards."

We have three groups of people here with different issues: The first group had too many children and not enough food. The second group had to mortgage their property in order to buy food because of the famine. And the third group had to sell everything to raise enough money to pay the king's tax. Nehemiah's response is recorded in verses 6–8: "I was very angry when I heard their cry and these words. Then I consulted with myself, and I rebuked the nobles, and the rulers, and said unto them, Ye exact usury, every one of his brother. And I set a great assembly against them. And I said unto them, We after our ability have redeemed our brethren the Jews, which were sold unto the heathen; and will ye even sell your brethren? or shall they be sold unto us? Then held they their peace, and found nothing to answer."

The first thing that Nehemiah did was to find out who the guilty parties were, and they were the nobles and the rulers. Nehemiah's reaction was anger, and his response was to go and confront the offenders. He had no fear of them. I want you to see that he went directly to them and rebuked them face to face, which is what we are taught to do in the New Testament. He did not act like someone who was uncertain about what he should do. To express this in New Testament terms, Nehemiah was speaking the truth in love.

Sometimes speaking the truth in love means to simply say "this is that." He didn't call them names; he just described the situation exactly the way it was. He spoke without hypocrisy. He didn't come to them and say, "Now, listen, my brethren, I know you didn't mean to do these things." He simply said, "It is not good that ye do," that is, what you are doing is wrong, and "ought ye not to walk in the fear of our God because of the reproach of the heathen our enemies?" I pray that people will begin to understand this concept of the fear of God. We are living in a generation, like those recorded in the book of Judges, where people do whatever seems right in their own eyes. People wield their own swords in whatever direction they feel like.

Nehemiah said, essentially, "Shouldn't you fear God?" Then in verse 10, "I likewise, and my brethren, and my servants, might exact of them money and corn: I pray you, let us leave off this usury." So he was making an appeal to these men, saying in essence, "You are taking advantage of your weak brothers. What you are doing is not right. You had better think twice and start walking in the fear of God. How will this look in front of our heathen enemies?"

You might ask how any of this applies to us today. I will tell you how, because this goes on all the time in churches across America: people take advantage of other people because they are weak or because they succumb by ignorance, by not knowing the word of God, or by not understanding. People can easily get drawn into a situation like that. So Nehemiah said, "Restore," using the Hebrew word *shub*. That is also the word for "to turn" or "to repent," and it carries a plethora of meanings. Nehemiah said, "Restore, I pray you, to them, even this day, their lands, their vineyards, their oliveyards, and their houses, also the hundredth part of the money, and of the corn, the wine, and the oil, that ye exact of them."

The leaders and the nobles were making out like bandits. The people were already in a bad situation, but the leaders and the nobles were making it far worse. And this godly leader Nehemiah confronted the wrongdoers face to face without fear of them, without hypocrisy, speaking the truth in love. Their reaction is recorded in verses 12–13: "Then said they, We will restore them, and will require nothing of them; so will we do as thou sayest. Then I called the priests, and took an oath of them, that they should do according to this promise. Also I shook my lap, and said, So God shake out every man from his house, and from his labour, that performeth not this promise, even thus be he shaken out, and emptied. And all the congregation said, Amen, and praised the LORD. And the people did according to this promise."

There is an important piece of information in the next verse. It says, "Moreover from the time that I was appointed to be their governor in the land of Judah, from the twentieth year even unto the two and thirtieth year of Artaxerxes the king, that is, twelve years, I and my brethren have not eaten the bread of the governor." These events occurred during the first of two periods when Nehemiah was in Jerusalem, and from this passage we know that the first period lasted at least twelve years.

Notice the repetition in this chapter of the words *brethren* or *brother*. That means we are talking about people who are close, though not necessarily blood brothers, but "brother" as in "brother in the Lord," or "brother in the family of God." Maybe some of them were indeed real brothers; I do not know. But it is interesting that the words *brethren* or *brother* occur seven times in this chapter. We are talking about brothers abusing other brothers, taking advantage of others, in this case, through greed.

When Nehemiah arrived, there were people who were already installed as authority figures. And you know what happens with power: absolute power corrupts absolutely. It is easy for any person to become corrupted by power unless you are a person of God who is checked by God, and you walk in the fear of God.

The people in that day listened to Nehemiah. Most people in today's church world resent leadership. Someone sent me an article about church leadership which said that churches need to "modernize" the way they are leading people. And I thought, "How would we modernize Moses? How would we 'update' Joshua?" But the reality is that this is God's way. He is God and He doesn't change. So when people tell me, "You need to be more modern," I say, they can do whatever they want, but I am going to follow His word, because I know that the Bible contains the road map for me to understand more about God. My time with Him should focus less on asking, "What about this?" or "What about that?" Rather, my time with God should be spent in understanding His word, because this life is only the beginning. We begin our journey with God down here on earth, in preparation for eternity where we will stand before Him.

God shows us His ways throughout His book. Nehemiah 5 could be superimposed onto Galatians 6:1, where it says, "Brethren, if a man be overtaken in a fault, ye which are spiritual, restore such an one in the spirit of meekness . . . lest thou also be tempted." We could also take this chapter in Nehemiah and superimpose it onto Matthew 18:15, where Jesus says, "If your brother shall trespass against you, go and tell it to him."

In our generation, there are too few people who have the courage to simply say, "Let's sit down and talk." The Bible says you are to first talk one-on-one with the person who has offended you, and you are not to confront them in front of a group of people. In this day, there is no place more public than the internet where cowards anonymously spread their poison. You are to approach the person, and whether that person is a brother or not is for God to decide. You address the issue just as Jesus tells us to do in Matthew 18:15. And if that person will not hear you, it says that you are to take two or three witnesses with you, because out of the mouth of two or three witnesses, a thing is confirmed. And if that person still will not hear you, then you tell it to the church. And if that person will not listen to the church, then that person becomes as a heathen. In fact, the King James Version says you are to treat them as you would a heathen and "a publican," that is, as a tax collector. Do not even be bothered anymore. Turn the matter over to God; you have done your part. I have not met many people who will obey these words of Christ. Yet here in Nehemiah 5, when the people were crying out, you do not see Nehemiah plotting and scheming with all the victims or counseling them. He went straight to the offenders and confronted them face to face. And by speaking the truth, they were boxed in.

It is true that sometimes you may have to confront people who have a bad attitude. You cannot fix a bad attitude, but these people obviously knew that they were doing wrong. That is the beauty of this chapter. We can see that long before the New Testament was penned, God's way of leading was the same. He has not changed. So Nehemiah addressed this group of people and they said, "We will restore and we will do our part."

Let's now read starting from Nehemiah 5:15 to the end of the chapter. "But the former governors that had been before me were chargeable unto the people, and had taken of them bread and wine, beside forty shekels of silver; yea, even their servants bare rule over the people: but so did not I, because of the fear of God." This passage gives us a glimpse of the man's character. When people talk about godly men, Nehemiah has been highly underrated. He said, in essence, "All of those things were going on before I arrived here, but when I was made governor, I did not do those things." What did Nehemiah give as his reason? He said, *"Because I fear God."*

Nehemiah went on to say, "Yea, also I continued in the work of this wall, neither bought we any land: and all my servants were gathered thither unto the work. Moreover there were at my table an hundred and fifty of the Jews and rulers, beside those that came unto us from among the heathen that are about us." We see that he was a very benevolent man. He came to do a work, and he did not come to take advantage of the people, which he easily could have done. He could have said, "Hey everyone, I am your savior! I came to rescue you, and I deserve special attention!" Nehemiah kept things in balance. He let all things be done in moderation. He did not take the things that the former governor demanded of the people. We read about the provision he shared with the people who gathered at his table: "Now that which was prepared for me daily was one ox and six choice sheep; also fowls were prepared for me, and once in ten days store of all sorts of wine: yet for all this required not I the bread of the governor, because the bondage was heavy upon this people."

He described what was prepared for him daily and said it was enough for him and enough to share. You can see the mindset of this godly leader: he had abundant provision, but he didn't just store it all up for himself, he shared with the people around him. The chapter closes with Nehemiah saying, "Think upon me, my God, for good, according to all that I have done for this people." Now some might think that this was a braggadocious statement. But there is a parallel passage in Hebrews 6:10 that speaks of the same idea: those of us who are able to do good must share. There is even a parallel to Galatians 6. The concept is that God remembers. He not only remembers all the idle words that proceed out of our mouth, He also sees our works: the good, the bad and the ugly. So Nehemiah says, "Think upon me. Remember me, God, that I didn't take advantage."

All of this was a backdrop to the core of this message. In Nehemiah 5, we see a problem that happens to many Christians and can happen in any church, which is people taking advantage of other people. And we see the character and behavior of Nehemiah in how he addressed those brethren who took advantage. But there are two key phrases that will help us understand why Nehemiah rebuked these leaders. He said in verse 9, "Ought ye not to walk in the fear of our God?" And he said in verse 15, "I didn't do what the people who were here before me did, because of the fear of God." He did not act greedily because of the fear of God.

Let's look at the word *fear.* There are several different Hebrew words that are translated with the word *fear*. Sometimes the word *fear* translates a Hebrew word that means "terror" and other times it is a word that means "to tremble," but neither of those are being used here in our text. The word here is *yirath*, and it is used twice in this chapter. When you study the use of this word in the Old Testament, you will have a clue as to why Nehemiah would say this to the people who were abusing their power, and why he would say it of himself regarding the reason he did not abuse his power.

We will briefly survey this concept of the fear of the Lord by looking at many different Scriptures, starting in the book of Proverbs. Proverbs 16:6 says, "By the fear of the LORD men depart from evil." Someone asked me, "Why do you think that people, especially under the guise of being Christians, are so evil?" And the first reason that came to my mind is that they do not fear God. I do not mean *fear* in the sense of being afraid that God is some kind of mean judge waiting to zap you off the planet. But when you fear God with awe, reverence, respect and recognition of His presence, if that kind of fear of the Lord is there, then Proverbs 16:6 says, "men depart from evil."

Proverbs 8:13 says, "The fear of the LORD is to hate evil." We cannot know what was planted in the heart and mind of Nehemiah, but these statements out of the book of Proverbs are in perfect harmony with the spirit of Nehemiah when he said, "Don't you fear God?" and "I didn't do these things because I fear God." When men and women have the fear of the Lord, they depart from evil. They begin to hate evil. Proverbs 15:33 says in the ESV, "The fear of the LORD is instruction in wisdom." Again, isn't that what Nehemiah did? Here is the wisdom: he said, "Ought ye not to walk in the fear of our God because of the reproach of the heathen our enemies?"

Too many people just do not care anymore about how things appear. Some thirty, forty or fifty years ago, people were overly consumed with keeping up appearances. Now, the pendulum has swung so far in the other direction that no one is concerned about how things appear, and everything is accepted. The Bible says we are to shun the appearance of evil. We should shun it first for the eyes of those around us, and then for the eyes that are always watching.

Proverbs 9:10 says, "The fear of the LORD is the beginning of wisdom." That does not mean that the fear of the Lord will make you super-wise, but it does mean that the fear of the Lord will make you wise up quickly. I want you to think about these Scriptures first in the context of Nehemiah, and then what they might mean in a personal application. It is too easy to make excuses for ourselves. Sometimes we say, "Well, you don't know what I am dealing with; it was so hard for me to do otherwise." If you are honest, the first thing you know you can do is have a healthy fear of God, who is always watching. I hate to say this, but fifty percent of the problems that we get ourselves into are because we think that absolutely no one, including God, is watching. Nehemiah was always aware of the presence of God.

Dr. Gene Scott often told the story of how he came from agnosticism to the faith through a study of the evidence for the Resurrection of Jesus Christ. When he finally reached the conclusion that Christ did indeed come out of the grave, he set out to practice an awareness of God's presence. So he set an alarm watch to go off every thirty minutes, just to discipline himself to remember the presence of God. Now I am not recommending that you do that, but Nehemiah simply said, "This is that. I will not do these things because I fear the Lord."

I do not fear God in the sense that I am afraid of what He will do to me. I have too much respect for God to think that. In Nehemiah's case, the Lord obviously had given him favor by allowing him to travel to Jerusalem to rebuild, and he knew that. Nehemiah did not think that he came to Jerusalem all on his own. When you understand what God is doing in your life and you stop acting like it is something that you are doing on your own, the fear of the Lord will be ever before your eyes, because you will realize that it is all God's doing. You will begin to realize, "I am not doing this. God is doing this, and glory be to Him!"

Proverbs 1:7 says, "The fear of the LORD is the beginning of knowledge." Turning to the book of Psalms, Psalm 111:10 says (following the literal word order in the Hebrew), "The beginning of wisdom is the fear of the Lord, and all who follow his precepts have a good understanding." It does not say that they have a *perfect* understanding; it just says that they have a *good* understanding. Again, Proverbs 9:10 says, "The fear of the LORD is the beginning of wisdom: and the knowledge of the holy is understanding." So we might say that this wisdom, which is the product of the fear of the Lord, also comes with the knowledge of God; you get to know God. Proverbs 10:27 says, "The fear of the LORD prolongeth days," or "*addeth* days: but the years of the wicked shall be shortened." And Proverbs 14:26 says, "In the fear of the LORD is strong confidence." Nehemiah understood that God would stand by him. Earlier, Nehemiah said, "our God will fight for us." He said, "*our* God," that is, the God who is with us. So Nehemiah expressed his confidence in God.

There are many more examples of the expression "the fear of the Lord" in the Bible, but let me take you out of Proverbs and have you turn to Jeremiah 32:40: "And I will make an everlasting covenant with them, that I will not turn away from them, to do them good; but I will put my fear in their hearts, that they shall not depart from me."

We have looked at what can happen between people in a believing community, and the kinds of abuses that can occur. Nehemiah said to the perpetrators, "Don't you fear the Lord?" And then he said, "I didn't do these things because of the fear of the Lord." Nehemiah tuned in on a principle that runs straight through the Bible. I am not saying that Nehemiah legalistically kept some kind of rule, but rather that he lived and walked with an awareness of this principle.

We have been looking at the Old Testament, but there are also many references to the fear of the Lord in the New Testament. The last reference is in Revelation 14, where it speaks of those who are the "redeemed from among men, being the firstfruits unto God and to the Lamb. And in their mouth was found no guile: for they are without fault before the throne of God. And I saw another angel fly in the midst of heaven, having the everlasting gospel to preach unto them that dwell on the earth, and to every nation, and kindred, and tongue, and people, saying with a loud voice, Fear God, and give glory to him." Think about that: it is a principle that runs from cover to cover in the Bible. That means Nehemiah's message to the people in his day is a message that we should take to ourselves today.

Someone might say, "Okay, I hear you. But how do I put this into practice? What exactly is it that I am supposed to *do?*" The answer is not necessarily something that you *do*, so much as it is something that is placed in a person's heart. Let me say again that the fear of the Lord is not fear in the sense of being afraid. Rather, it is the great recognition of God's presence with us. One of God's names is *Emmanuel*, meaning "God with us." The fear of God is the great recognition of the One who is watching us at all times. Regardless of what you and I may think, there is no time when God is not watching.

Nehemiah could have very easily lined his pockets. He was a cupbearer in a king's palace. Maybe when he was in Babylon he lived in a servant's quarters, we do not know, but he certainly was used to being surrounded by luxury. If he were a carnal man, he might have said upon his arrival in Jerusalem, "Now I can become king here!

Come on, people, give me tribute. Pay up!" But instead, he said, "I did not do that." And God provided abundantly for him to feed one hundred fifty people at his table daily.

Let's return to the first challenge of Proverbs 16:6, because it is the one that stuck with me the most: "By the fear of the LORD men depart from evil." The fear of the Lord brings a man or a woman to hate evil.

These are instructions out of God's book. It is a shame that too many people want to be told something other than God's word. I am not giving you commandments or telling you to live your life in a certain way; rather, I am telling you what God's word says, and you can take His word and apply it today. At the very least you can begin to meditate on it so that it might become engrafted into your heart.

I am talking about people who are in the body of Christ, and I am going to make another application. Think about people who grapple with some issue. That really describes all of us. Each one of us has to deal with some issue that is always there. It is the temptation that is ever before you, whatever that is. I am not saying, "Hey, stop doing that!" I am not pointing a finger or judging someone, because every single human being who is honest before God can say, "I have issues I have to deal with." But the fear of the Lord can help us overcome whatever those issues are, if we would not only recognize God's presence, but also reverence and worship Him. The Psalter talks about those who serve the Lord and worship Him in fear in the sense of reverence.

I want us to see the possibility of turning away from the things that have overtaken us, which is why I mentioned Galatians 6:1. It begins with a thought process that acknowledges, "God, I know You are here and watching me. Now God, I need Your help to not go down that pathway." What does the Scripture say concerning temptations and every diverse kind of evil that can fill our minds? It says that for every single temptation, God makes a way of escape, if we will just trust Him and turn to Him. If we have this fear of God, we will be able to turn away from that temptation. God makes plenty of doorways of escape, if we will take them, but those doorways are always towards Him, and they are never man-made. The man-made ones seldom if ever work, or they might work for a time and then they falter again.

We need to start applying this in our own lives. Walking with the fear of God daily is a healthy way to remind ourselves that the God who called us, who knows how many hairs we have on our heads (or how many hairs we have left on our heads), is the same God who is watching to see if our hearts are ever turned towards Him in all things.

More than a few people have said to me, "But Pastor, I am dealing with a difficult situation, because I cannot overcome this one thing," whether it is a personal temptation, or a situation where someone is taking advantage of another person, as it was in the case of Nehemiah 5. When these kinds of things come upon us, we should be able to look at Nehemiah's words and say, "I have the fear of God too." These Bible lessons are tools to help us as we journey on through all our diverse pressures.

Nehemiah rebuked the leaders, saying, "Don't you have any fear of God?" Then he said of himself, "I did not do these things because of the fear of God." And any one of us today, in any condition, in the grips of something, is able to overcome when we can come to that mindset. You do not overcome by means of sheer willpower, by declaring, "I will not do a certain thing anymore," or "I will keep a checklist of do's and don'ts." Rather, you start with a mindset that says, "I have the fear of God." And you can pray with a mindset that says,

"God, today, if You will hear my prayer for help; God, today, if You will help me to overcome the things that have bound me; God, if You will help me to overcome the people who are oppressive towards me; I recognize You in all of these things, and I turn all this over to You, just like Nehemiah did, recognizing that You see it all. You will ultimately take care of it all, but I know You want me to talk to You and have a healthy reverence towards You, because You do watch over me and it does matter to You what I do while I am here. I am redeeming the time that I have. I am looking to You and trusting You."

The Scripture says, "We are more than conquerors." I think that sometimes our minds can grow a little numb at the repetition of certain promises in God's book, and it is too easy to say, "Oh, I have heard that before." Many times I hear preachers teach on such verses out of their context. So maybe it is time to put something new in our brains, which is not really new. It is an old-time expression right here in the book of Nehemiah that says that God can help you through whatever you are going through, if you will commit it to Him and walk, not in trauma or in terror, but with a heart that says, "God, I am in awe of You that You would even care about me." Sometimes I cannot help but sing the song, *Who Am I?* Who am I, Lord, that You would do these things for me? But yet, You do. I am well aware that the God who has taken me from where I was and put me where I am is the same God who will continue to watch His word and His people prosper, as long as we are looking to Him, trusting Him and *faithing* in Him.

Everywhere you turn in God's book, there is something to meet your needs and feed you spiritually. I want our faith to continue to grow in order that we might better understand that God has a great plan for us, if we would just listen and stop stubbornly thinking that we can solve our own problems. God has the solutions. If you will abide in the word and take His solutions, He will begin changing whatever it is that hinders; and the fear of the Lord will help you remember that God is able to enter in to everything you are dealing with.

Chapter 5

BUILDING FOR GOD IS A BATTLE

Each chapter in the book of Nehemiah provides us with timeless information. I do not want you to get discouraged when you read Nehemiah 6 and see the kinds of things that can happen to God's people. I want you to see some patterns, because they are patterns found throughout the Bible, and you know they are true. If you do not read the Bible and you watch the things that are shown on Christian television, you will find a contradiction between what we are teaching and what the church world at large is saying. First of all, the Bible teaches that no one comes to Christ except that they first be drawn. That is called "prevenient grace." But when you come to God, you do not always jump in right away with both feet. For some, it is a gradual work that God does in their life. I know there are people who like to go around and testify of incredible things that happened to them, as if those things were the focus of their faith. But in reality, the greater miracle is God's patience as He keeps working on these crocks of clay.

The pattern in the Bible is that any time you do something for God, you can be sure that you will come under attack. The attack may come in the form of a bunch of blatant lies or in the form of a little aggravation, just enough to distract you. But I want us to remember that the book of Nehemiah, and specifically Nehemiah 6, shows us that the devil has not changed at all. In fact, the things that happened to Nehemiah can happen to any of us.

Nehemiah wasn't of a special bloodline, he wasn't of a special priesthood; he was just a man. I would like us to look at his character. Here is a good man doing a great work. We can see that he was a man of great faith, of prayer, of perseverance and of focus, because once the burden was put on his heart, he began the task and he did not stop until it was finished. We read in Nehemiah 6:15, "So the wall was finished in fifty-two days." It only took about seven weeks to complete the restoration and rebuilding of the wall.

When you think about it, building a wall is not a very glamorous thing to do. It would have been much more glamorous to build the temple or the altar. Who wants to know about wall-building? But there was in fact something very important about it, which we will begin to understand as we study this book.

We do not know what Nehemiah's personal life was like. We only know certain things we are told at the beginning of the book bearing his name. At that point, we do not know if he was a ruthless person or a good person. We can only know what is given for us to know, and that is what anyone pursuing God should be concerned with. Each and every one of us has a past, and each and every one of us has a future in Christ. You can deceive yourself and say that you are special and different and you do not have anything in your past, but that would be a lie. While we do not know about Nehemiah's past, we know what is recorded in this book, and that is where God wants us to focus our attention. Nehemiah was not seeking fame or notoriety, but he was concerned with the place of worship and with God's people. That is what made him a target.

The devil knows he only has a short time; but sometimes we forget, and some of us take spiritual vacations. Dr. Gene Scott preached many messages on this very subject and the attacks that come against God's people who are rebuilding for Him, and he would often say, "There is an easy way to escape the pressure: just quit." It is easy to quit, and the pressure and the attacks will cease.

The devil will probably give you peace for a time. But if you leave the place of persecution, if you leave the place of affliction, if you leave the place where there is the greatest conflict, then you will also leave the place of blessing, because that is where the blessing occurs. The blessing doesn't occur on the mountaintop; it occurs when you are in God's hands being squeezed just a little bit more every day.

The devil can transform himself into an angel of light, and he or his agents will try to lure you away from your commitment. Think for a moment about things that have happened in your own life. Maybe you came under pressure from people who tried to lure you away under the guise of being your family or your friends. There are some saints who were never bothered by anyone when they were drunkards and getting high and doing whatever else they did. But the moment they turned to God and committed their way, they became a target, both a target of the devil and a target of so-called brothers and sisters in the church who thought, "Here's a new punching bag. Here's some fresh flesh we can verbally beat down."

We know little about Nehemiah's life in Babylon except that he was a cupbearer to the king. If you think that being a cupbearer is a position for people who cannot do much else, you are mistaken. The man who would fill that position must be a servant of the highest rank, because he would serve in close proximity to the king. That means he would have to interface directly with the king and only speak when he was spoken to. Nehemiah must have been greatly trusted to have been allowed to occupy such a position. Imagine the composure of such a man. He would have to follow a protocol. When he would pour the wine for the king, he would have three fingers on the goblet to make it easy for the king to take the cup. Then he would use a ladle to pour some of the wine into his left hand, and he would immediately drink it down. And if he didn't drop dead, the king would know it was safe to drink. Nehemiah's comportment, the way he carried himself, qualified him for this position. And when Nehemiah heard the news of what had happened in Jerusalem, he wept, fasted and prayed. So we can begin to see his character from what little we know about him that is revealed in these few verses.

We know why God's people had been carried away into captivity. God through the prophet Jeremiah had prophesied that the captivity would last for seventy years, and that their punishment was because of the people's chasing after other gods; it was because of their unfaithfulness and their refusal to listen to the prophets. Finally, God said, "That is enough," and in three successive waves, the people were carried away. Jerusalem was destroyed, its walls were broken down and its gates were burned with fire. All of that is known, so at this point in history, we are really not interested in what Nehemiah did prior to the time he heard the report of the conditions in Jerusalem. We are only interested in what he did at the moment that this burden was placed on his heart. And that should be our only concern when it comes to God's leaders.

Any person who has been called of God has lived some kind of life before they came to a point of understanding that there is nothing of greater worth than what is revealed to us about God in the Bible. I would not want to listen to someone teach who has not lived enough of life to know that. While there may be pleasure in sin for a season and pleasure in the world for a time, at some point you must realize that God has something infinitely better for you, and then you begin to steadfastly pursue an understanding of what saith the word of the Lord. This is the quality that matters in any God-ordained leader.

Nehemiah had an excellent rapport with the king, and most likely he was an important person in the king's eyes, because the king granted him letters for safety and for provision. The king also gave him guards and horsemen. There was nothing in Nehemiah's character that we have seen that would have made someone point at him and say, "He shouldn't have gone," or "He wasn't the right one for the assignment." Everything we read about this man shows us his outstanding character.

The most important thing about Nehemiah is that he was a man of faith. We know that he prayed to the God of heaven, and when he arrived at Jerusalem, he wasted no time and went out to assess the damage. Maybe someone else would have gone to

Jerusalem and said, "Hey, while I am here, let's kick back and have a party for a few days. Feed me. Bring on the women and the wine, and after that we'll get to work." But Nehemiah went straight to work. He was all business—that is, he was all about God's business.

There is a reason for our revisiting and reestablishing Nehemiah's character. In previous messages, we looked at the antagonists and their general attack on all the people. Now in Nehemiah 6, the attack will be focused directly on and personally against Nehemiah. What did he do to deserve this treatment? The same question might be asked about a young man named Joseph, who was sold into slavery by his brothers. What did Joseph do to deserve being mistreated, sold into slavery and thrown into prison? But God entered into that cruelty, and Joseph was in prison for a purpose.* Likewise, Nehemiah was in captivity for a reason. He stayed behind in Babylon until the time was right when he would have favor with the king; then and only then would he go to Jerusalem to build. And we know that he accomplished his mission, because Nehemiah 6 says that they finished the wall. So the question again is "Who would have anything against Nehemiah?"

Nehemiah 6 opens with, "Now it came to pass, when Sanballat, and Tobiah, and Geshem the Arabian. . . ." You may have a reference in the margin of your Bible that shows that the name Geshem is a variant of Gashmu, who is referenced in verse 6. After naming these three enemies, Nehemiah says, "and the rest of our enemies." Only three were specifically named, though there were many more. This chapter has a message for every individual: do not be surprised if, as a Christian, you have plenty of enemies.

So "When Sanballat, and Tobiah, and Geshem . . . and the rest of our enemies, heard that I had builded the wall, and that there was no breach left therein; (though at that time I had not set up the doors upon the gates;) that Sanballat and Geshem," or Gashmu, "sent unto me, saying, Come, let us meet together in some one of the villages in the plain of Ono. But they thought to do me mischief."

I want you to write in the margin of your Bible a series of words that all begin with the same letter, which will serve as a

*For additional teaching on this topic, see Pastor Scott's "Joseph Series," message number VF-1810, "In Prison for a Purpose," available on DVD from DoloresPress.com.

memory aid when you are studying this chapter. For verse 2, the first word I am assigning is *emissaries*, that is, "emissaries from hell or close by."

We read, "They sent unto him, saying, Come, let us meet together. . . ." I can imagine what this letter might have sounded like: "Dear Brother Nehemiah, you are a great man doing a great work." The devil always uses the same tactics, and one of them is flattery. "Now, come on down and meet us. Let's have a little compromise. Maybe we can have a little mediation and talk about this." The second thing the devil always manages to do is to get the saints to compromise under pressure. The devil always uses that "Come, let us reason together" method, and some of us succumb to it.

Let's read this passage from a couple of different translations. The Wycliffe Bible says, "Come thou into a field, and smite we [a] bond of peace." When I read that, I thought immediately of Cain and Abel. I am sure there was a "let us reason" moment before one brother killed the other. Nehemiah said, "But they thought to do me mischief." That is from the King James Version. The NLT simply says, "I realized they were plotting to harm me."

It is mind-boggling, but they sent this same message to Nehemiah four times. And four times he gave them the same answer: he "sent messengers unto them, saying, I am doing a great work, so that I cannot come down: why should the work cease, whilst I leave it, and come down to you?" When we read his response in our English version, we might mistakenly believe that Nehemiah had an inflated ego, as though he were saying, "Listen, I am really important. Don't bother me." Let's look at the meaning of some of these words in Hebrew and pay close attention to the kind of language he used. The word "messenger" is *Strong's* number 4397 and it is related to the same Hebrew word that is translated "angel." Ultimately, it can be traced back to a word that means "king." And the word for "work" is *Strong's* number 4399; it is a cognate of the word for messenger.

This Hebrew word for "work" is very important. There are at least nine Hebrew words for the word "work," but this word is first used in Genesis 2:2, when it says that the Lord rested from *His* work.

We find the cognate of the word for "messenger" used in Exodus 35 and 36, where the subject is work associated with the tabernacle. So this word translated "work" is primarily used to describe a work or workmanship *of God.* While the sense is not reflected in the English, Nehemiah was really saying, "I sent messengers to them to say that I am doing something *of ministry.* I am doing a work of God." Nehemiah was not saying, "Hey, I am important." To put his answer in New Testament terms, he was saying in essence, "I have put my hand to the plow and I am not looking back!" That is why Nehemiah said, "so that I cannot come down: why should the work cease, whilst I leave it, and come down to you?" One of the great tricks of the devil is to get the work of God to cease.

Another way to understand this word for "work" is to read from a Hebrew translation of the New Testament. You will find this same Hebrew word for "work" used in John 17:4, where Jesus says, "Father, I have finished *the work* which thou gavest me to do." So when I tell you that the church is doing "a great work," that means that it is a work connected to God. The spirit of Nehemiah's reply was as though he were saying, "I have a responsibility of workmanship that I am doing for the Lord." And the devil will always try to get us to take our hands off of that kind of work.

Now someone might say, "You seem to be focused on the concept of spiritual warfare." That is absolutely right! I often warn people who have recently been baptized: You have stepped out in faith and made a commitment or a rededication. It is a time of new beginnings and spiritual renewal. But the devil at that moment has you in his sights. Someone foolishly wrote, "Nehemiah must have been up on a ladder, so that is why he said, 'Why should I come down?'" He may have been working on the wall in an elevated position, but I want you to understand that the devil will do anything to bring you down, and he doesn't care how he brings you down. The attack can come from anywhere. You could be riding high and suddenly, everything falls in upon you. Then you get discouraged and think, "I am not making any spiritual progress. In fact, I feel like I have taken about twenty steps back." You can get into that state of mind and forget that we are dealing with the crafty methods of the devil. Here is the man who was the leader of the builders, and he was very aware that if he were to step away from the work, the work would cease.

If a pastor steps away from the pulpit, there would be no work going on. I am not saying the church would not continue, but there would be no work to do. In other words, the whole work centers around the person who is leading and saying, "Come on, let's march forward in faith!" That is why a congregation has a duty to be spiritual armor-bearers for their pastor. You should come to church already "prayed up." Pray during the week; pray for people you know who are just hanging on by a thread; because prayer, coupled with your faith in Jesus Christ, changes everything.

Nehemiah replied, "I cannot come down: why should the work cease, whilst I leave it, and come down to you?" Now four times they sent him letters after this sort, and four times he answered in the same way. Then Sanballat must have thought, "Well, that tactic didn't work, so let's try something else." "Then sent Sanballat his servant unto me in like manner the fifth time with an open letter in his hand."

You cannot read the book of Nehemiah without understanding some of the customs of that time. Letters were never sent open unless they were letters of passage, like the letters Nehemiah received from the king to grant him safe passage and supplies. Letters were always sealed, and they were deliberately sealed to ensure their authenticity.

Sanballat sent his servant with "an open letter in his hand; wherein was written, It is reported among the heathen. . . ." The next words I would like you to write in the margin of your Bible are *egregious lies.* An open letter means that every person who handled that letter would read that letter. So there would be lots of gossip, innuendo, rumors and lies being spread around against Nehemiah and his band of workers.

"It is reported among the heathen, and Gashmu saith it. . . ." In other words, if you hear it from Gashmu, it must be true! Just as we have Sanballats and Tobiahs in our lives, there will always be Gashmus. "It is reported among the heathen, and Gashmu saith it," that is, "Geshem saith it, that thou and the Jews think to rebel." In other words, "You are planning a rebellion, and this is why you are building the wall! See, if you fortify the city, then you can start a rebellion and you will be protected. You have all of these evil motives. You are a bunch of crooked builders. You are a bunch of liars! You are not here because you care about the people or the place. Not only that, you want to be their king, according to these words. And thou hast also appointed prophets to preach of thee at Jerusalem, saying, There is a king in Judah."

That is why I started this message by painting the character of Nehemiah. Some of the saints in today's world are looking for the wrong things when they look for a leader. The person who is standing in the pulpit should be taking the Bible and using it as a compass. The word of God must be their focus. It does not matter that we know very little about Nehemiah's personal life. Can you imagine someone saying, "I need a little more personal information about Nehemiah before I can follow his ministry. I need to know where he grew up, where he went to school and what he has for breakfast every day. And only when I know those things will I consider following him and helping him build the wall."

There was a greater work going on than simply building a wall. The wall-building was preparation for the time when Christ would appear, several hundred years later. By analogy, we are building up the walls of the church, if you will, in anticipation of Christ's return. And He asked the question, "When the Son of man cometh, will he find faith?" How does faith come? Faith comes by hearing. That is why I teach, because I believe that the Lord will honor His word. I am not asking you to do anything except open your heart and receive the word by faith.

Some of the people must have said by this point, "Nehemiah must really love God's work and God's people to stay by the stuff in the face of all this opposition." Nehemiah recognized exactly what it was: it was all a bunch of lies. And he was not the only man in the

Bible to have this problem. You will find abundant lament on the part of David in his psalms, such as in Psalm 27:12, where he said, "False witnesses are risen up against me, and such as breathe out cruelty." In David's case, the list of enemies was endless.

The moment you say, "Lord, I desire more of You. Mold me, use me, take me," that is when the devil is going to make a beeline for you. The people who say, "You talk too much about the devil," are likely in churches where they do not talk enough about God, so the devil does not even bother them. Why should the devil bother them? In fact, the devil will make sure that the multitudes go to those churches.

We are just like these people in Nehemiah's day, and unfortunately any one of us can get caught in the crossfire of reading an open letter, figuratively speaking, because it is our nature. It is much easier to believe the bad than it is to believe the good. It is easy to lend an ear to gossip when someone says, "Have you heard this?" or "Did you know that?" It is easy for us to believe an evil report and start to question the motives of others.

We read in verse 7, "Come now therefore, and let us take counsel together." Now why would Nehemiah want to take counsel with a bunch of liars? Do you think you can reason with the devil? But Nehemiah gave them some wonderful answers. First, he said, "I am doing a great work, so I cannot come down." Then he sent another reply, saying, "There are no such things done as thou sayest, but thou feignest them out of thine own heart. For they all made us afraid, saying, Their hands shall be weakened from the work, that it be not done."

These three enemies represent various sources of attack, whether it be from the people in the church, from your friends or family, or from anywhere else. Sanballat represents a political adversary, Tobiah might be a religious figure, and Gashmu was most likely a businessman. He might have been a person who did not like religion or any kind of religious enthusiasm. Maybe he did not like people of faith. I have met many people like that. They make a target of anyone who has stepped out in faith.

The enemy's intention was to bring fear, to weaken the hands of the people so that they would stop doing God's work. That is one reason why I continue to preach that we must keep on trusting God, no matter what the circumstances. Remember that God is not the author of fear. We are supposed to be a *faithing* people who trust God and His promises. When God has said something, we are supposed to take Him at His word.

Whenever you are building up the church, you will have a battle. Jesus said, "I will build my church, and the gates of hell shall not prevail against it," which means there will be a battle. After a time, you will begin to see the devil's patterns. The devil does not tend to use many new tactics because he knows that the old ones work so well. He looks for people who, in their heart of hearts, desire to press close to God, but become weak in the flesh. And like an arm-wrestling match, the flesh wins over and brings down the spirit-man. Then people begin to question their walk and ask "Is this worth it?" and "Why am I here?" when in fact, God has given us His Spirit to give us wisdom, comfort and strength.

The devil and his emissaries think that if they can create enough fear and panic, they can get you to leave the church. Or if they can spread enough negative things about you and your past, then they can convince people to avoid you. Thank God that the Jesus Christ we serve does not avoid us and welcomes us with open arms. The body of Christ is a body being built up, and anyone who comes to try and tear it down is not from God. There are only two camps: those who are building with God in the unity of faith, for Christ's sake, and those who are tearing down and tearing apart. That is why Christ said, "If you are not gathering with Me, you are scattering."

Nehemiah said, "You are making all this up to make us afraid, saying, Their hands shall be weakened from the work, that it be not done. Now therefore, O God, strengthen my hands." The words "O God" are in italics, indicating that they were added by the translators, but we can see their reason for the addition. They added those words because Nehemiah's declaration was in the form of a bold and quick utterance that was definitely aimed at God, because we know that Nehemiah received his strength from God.

"Afterward I came unto the house of Shemaiah the son of Delaiah the son of Mehetabeel, who was shut up." Our next word to write in the margin is *entrapment.* "And he said, Let us meet together in the house of God, within the temple, and let us shut the doors of the temple: for they will come to slay thee; yea, in the night will they come to slay thee." In other words, "Nehemiah, they are coming for you! Quick! Hide! Let's turn God's house into the house of cowards. You can find safety there, you can find refuge there." There was a serious problem with this advice, which is not as clear in the King James Version as it is in the Hebrew.

Shemaiah wanted Nehemiah to go into an area of the temple where he was not allowed to go in order to take refuge. Remember that Shemaiah was not an enemy from the outside; he was one of Nehemiah's people. This shows us that people who are near to you can turn against you. Shemaiah said, "Let's go inside and shut the doors." You can see how crafty this is if you read Numbers 18.

Numbers 18:7 says, "Therefore thou and thy sons with thee shall keep your priest's office for every thing of the altar, and within the veil; and ye shall serve: I have given your priest's office unto you as a service of gift: and the stranger that cometh nigh shall be put to death." Nehemiah was not of the priesthood, so he would qualify as a "stranger that cometh nigh." Therefore, if he had entered in, he would have to be put to death.

The devil changed his tactics, as though he thought, "If intimidation does not work, we will try entrapment." It might possibly have worked, if they had succeeded in causing Nehemiah to fear. We are not talking about the fear of God; we are talking about the fear of man. What did Christ say? "Don't fear what they can do to the body. Fear the one who can destroy the soul." But Nehemiah was very wise. He said, "Should such a man as I flee? and who is there, that, being as I am, would go into the temple to save his life? I will not go in." The Amplified Bible gives us a clue to the meaning that we just looked at in Numbers 18. It says, "Should such a man as I flee? And what man such as I could go into the temple [where only the priests are allowed to go] and yet live? I will not go in."

Nehemiah said, "And, lo, I perceived that God had not sent him; but that he pronounced this prophecy against me: for Tobiah and Sanballat had hired him. Therefore was he hired, that I should be afraid, and do so, and sin, and that they might have matter for an evil report, that they might reproach me." Think about how staggering that is. And Nehemiah concluded with a petition, saying, "My God, think thou upon Tobiah and Sanballat according to these their works, and on the prophetess Noadiah, and the rest of the prophets, that would have put me in fear."

One of the things I love about Nehemiah is that he was not a coward. If God called you to do something, then do it. And yes, you will have opposition. Let me go back to something that was said earlier about a great work. How did we define a great work? It is a work that pertains to something of God, and with a great work of God there will always be opposition and difficulty, and with a great work of God there will also be a reward for the people who are faithful. When we put that in perspective, we can see that Nehemiah understood his responsibility and opportunity.

And I love what it says in Nehemiah 6:15: "So the wall was finished in the twenty and fifth day of the month Elul, in fifty and two days." For those of you who want to follow God and press in close, but you have let every obstacle get in your way, make this passage in Nehemiah a prototype in your mind. And for the next fifty-two weeks, or maybe only for the next fifty-two days, put God first. Give God preeminence in your life. When you wake up in the morning and begin your day, instead of first reaching for the coffee cup, start out by thanking God for waking you up. Thank Him for all things, including the opportunity to participate in His work, which some people mistakenly think will just function all by itself.

Nehemiah started something, and he finished it. Our work will not be finished until God says, "Time's up." That should be an encouragement. We have an opportunity of faith that lets us say, "I am going to get up again. I am going to recommit and rededicate myself, because I know the tactics that the devil has used in the past and is still using."

Let me ask you a question: during this last year, has there been any time when the devil managed to drive a wedge between you and God? There came a moment of time when you thought, "Today will be the day when I am really going to follow God," and then all of a sudden you were knocked sideways. The devil likes nothing better than to put a wedge between you and God, and he makes sure that he creates the most stinking mess so that you will want to stay away.

There is a battle for your soul. Do not be afraid of that, be encouraged. If you have gone through tribulation, affliction or any of these things, take another look at these passages in the book of Nehemiah. He was assailed both by people from the outside and by those who were close to him. Jesus said that your foes will be those of your own household. I am not preaching a divisive message; I just want you to understand that where Christ comes, there will always be division. While there is no specific revelation of Christ in these passages, we have a prototype of a man of faith. And we see again the pattern that when anyone comes along and says, "I have a true burden and care for God's people and God's house," there will always be division. Read John 7, 9 and 10, and look at what happened when Christ came. You will find that it says three times, "And there was division amongst them." Some said, "He is a good man," but others said, "He deceiveth the people." You can listen to anyone you want to listen to, but at some point, you must start listening to God's word and "try the spirits," as the word of God tells us to do. And when the truth is preached, you will know it.

The wall was finished, and verse 16 says, "And it came to pass, that when all our enemies heard thereof, and all the heathen that were about us saw these things, they were much cast down in their own eyes: for they perceived that this work was wrought of our God." At least the enemies could recognize that God did it; and God is still doing His work today. Don't think for a minute that God has stopped doing, that He has stopped healing, that He has stopped making a way, or that His word is void, because the reality is that our God is still the same God. The God of Nehemiah was also the God of the intertestamental period, and the same God who walked on the face of the earth while tented in human flesh: Jesus Christ.

The enemies saw that this was the work of God, yet they did not give up. We read starting from verse 17, "Moreover in those days the nobles of Judah sent many letters unto Tobiah, and the letters of Tobiah came unto them. For there were many in Judah sworn unto him, because he was the son in law of Shechaniah the son of Arah; and his son Johanan had taken the daughter of Meshullam the son of Berechiah." There was no better way to infiltrate someone's camp than to intermarry. I want you to label these last two verses in Nehemiah 6, *emotional sabotage.* And that is because it clearly says, "Also they reported his good deeds before me, and uttered my words to him. And Tobiah sent letters to put me in fear." It never ended. Nehemiah said that they reported Tobiah's "good deeds" to him. I must ask the question, "What good deeds?" Can anybody tell me anything that Tobiah did that was good? You cannot, because he did not do anything good.

We have been looking at this chapter verse by verse to comprehend the nature of the constant attacks on Nehemiah. We should not make the mistake of thinking that he is the only one to have faced this kind of opposition, because there have been many "Nehemiahs" throughout the history of the church and up to the present day. The beauty of this chapter is that God is still doing the same thing. Like Paul said in 1 Corinthians, God uses the foolish and weak things to confound the wise.

God is still doing the same thing when He calls leaders. He is still calling people today, like He called Moses and Joshua. God is still calling people and giving them a burden and an aim, and when He calls you, it will be with one aim. You will not be called to take on the vast universe. When you are called to the ministry, you are called to minister the word of God. In the book of Ephesians, where Paul speaks of the gifts that God has given to the church, they all point back to one place: the word of God. Whether you are a prophet, an evangelist, or a pastoring-teacher, they all bring you back to the word of God. When you are abiding in the word of God, you can take on the world, the flesh and the devil, because you will know how to fight. And while you engage in that battle, God will take care of you.

God will even take care of your reputation. If you really believe in eternity, quit worrying about your reputation here on earth. Let God, the one who hands out the crowns and the glory, let Him decide what that reputation will be, because only you know what you have committed to Him. No one else knows your heart.

How did all of these attacks affect Nehemiah? After all these brutal personal attacks, he did not say, "It is getting a little too tough for me to stay here in Jerusalem. I don't like it. I thought I was going to receive a big fanfare, but nobody here seems to like me that much. So I think I will get out of here." As we continue reading, we will see that Nehemiah will appoint certain people for specific tasks. Ezra the scribe will read the law in front of the people, and there will be an incredible revival. It will all start when the people will be gathered together as one man. There would be no Sanballats, Tobiahs or Gashmus in the crowd when they come together for the purpose of God.

The devil is still a liar. The devil is still deceiving people and trying to lure them away from their commitment to the Lord. The devil's goal is to keep you from God, to keep you from the fullness that God has promised to each believer. You do not need talent to be part of the great work of God. You do not need great eloquence. What you need is faith in the promise that God will fight for us. We are not building a physical wall like these people in Nehemiah's day. Unbeknownst to them, they were preparing for the coming of Christ. We are building another kind of wall, which is in preparation for the Lord's second coming. I know my responsibility: I will keep on preaching the words that bring forth the hearing of faith and the obedience of faith, until your heart can rise to the level of saying "*amen*" to God's word of promise, and you can say, "I am not taking my hand from the plow. The devil cannot pry my fingers off, and I am still the apple of God's eye, no matter what happens. The Lord will take care of the rest." You keep on *faithing*, and let's all keep on building!

Chapter 6

YOU COUNT FOR GOD

It is the pastor's responsibility to equip the saints with the word of God. The world is changing and things are happening that are outside the realm of our control, but we can always cling to God's word, which never changes. Psalm 119:89 says, "For ever, O LORD, thy word is settled in heaven." When you come to know that, you will see the insanity around you for what it is: it is the world, the flesh and the devil, which you can do nothing about. And you will be able to hold on to what is good, which is the word of God, not only on a Sunday morning, but throughout the whole week. Abide in the word. You can look for help in other places, but there is only one who will always be your help, and that is Jesus Christ our Lord and Savior.

We read in 2 Timothy 3:16 that all Scripture is profitable for doctrine, reproof, correction and instruction in righteousness. In the King James Version, the next verse says, "that the man of God may be perfect." But in the original Greek, it does not say that a man or woman of God has to be perfect; rather, it uses a word that means "not needing anything more." In other words, if you go to the Scriptures, you will find all the instruction you need. I am thankful that we do not have to look to the world for the solutions to our problems.

God gave us His word for more than just reading or entertainment. We are supposed to look into the Bible and see ourselves, our problems and our nature, and be confronted with the reality that God already knows where we are. And when we read God's word, we see that He has a purpose and a plan. One of the first lessons to learn is that God does the drawing. He draws people into the church; you cannot make someone become a Christian by getting them to recite a prayer. But once people have been in the church for a time, the novelty can wear off and you will hear people say, "What's the point? What is the point of my being here?" If you will stay in the word long enough, you will discover that God has already revealed the point. The book of Hebrews says, "Today, if you will hear His voice, harden not your hearts." Today may be the day when you say, "I get it now!" There is a reason for your being in the church. You count for God.

God takes note of even the smallest things done in His name. Now, I am not speaking of doing "good works." I do not teach people to do "works," because works will not get you into heaven. I teach people that faith comes by hearing. And when faith does come, the expression of that faith will be an out-raying of God's nature, which will indeed produce good works. But you do not do good works in the sense of performing a checklist to get God's approval. That was the great dilemma of the Reformation, when many people did not understand what counted for God and what did not. The work of God's Spirit in a person is all His work, but salvation is all by faith. We start by faith, we stay in by faith and we make it to heaven by faith. We become the habitation of God, and what is expressed through this habitation of God will be things that are Godlike. Although the Spirit abides in us, we are still just crocks of clay, and from time to time that ugly old nature in us will rear its head. It is easy to fall into the trap of saying "What's the point?" when you forget that God called you out of the darkness and into His glorious light. You can forget that God does have a purpose and a plan for you.

God is keeping a record. In our society, there is hardly anything you can do that isn't being recorded. There are cameras on the streets recording where you are going. When you get into your car, if you have a GPS, you can be tracked. When you use your phone, your credit card or the internet, your whole history is being recorded. These are concepts that we can tangibly understand. But God keeps a record too. That does not mean that God is keeping a record of our sins. The Bible clearly says that when we come to the Lord and understand His forgiveness, as the prophet Micah said, our sins are plunged into the darkest depths of the sea, never to be retrieved. Isaiah 53 says that Christ bore them all. Yet God sees everything. His word says that He spoke your name before the foundation of the earth. Some people are more concerned about how they are perceived by worldly eyes than about how they are seen in God's eyes.

Romans 8 teaches that there is now no more *ultimate* condemnation for those who are in Christ Jesus. But we will all stand before the judgment seat of Christ and give account. That is not said to make us fear, rather it is something that should resonate in everything we do, in every word and every thought. It is all important to God. You need not go around terrified that God will punish you for looking to the left or looking to the right. Jesus paid it all for the believer who looks unto Him and trusts Him from start to finish for his or her salvation. But God does keep records and the records are kept for a reason.

Hebrews 11, for example, gives a list of the heroes of faith, who are Old Testament saints who died without having received the promise that we have in Christ. In Romans 16, the apostle Paul gives a list of greetings, salutations and thanks to many men and women whom he calls his *sunergous*, which means "fellow workers." We read about a "book of remembrance" in Malachi 3:16: "Then they that feared the Lord spake often one to another: and the Lord hearkened, and heard it, and a book of remembrance was written before him for them that feared the Lord, and that thought upon his name. And they shall be mine, saith the Lord of hosts, in that day when I make up my jewels; and I will spare them, as a man spareth his own son that serveth him. Then shall ye return, and discern between the righteous and the wicked, between him that serveth God and him that serveth him not." And the book of Revelation says of the one who overcomes, his name will remain in the book of life.

There is another list in Nehemiah 7. It memorializes the names of those who returned to Jerusalem after the seventy years of captivity were fulfilled. With the exception of possibly a few omissions and spelling errors, this list is comprised of essentially the same names that are recorded in Ezra 2, though the list in Nehemiah 7 is recorded for a different reason. It is recorded to teach us that even the smallest things in God's eyes can be precious and valuable. The things you do for God can make a contribution to a larger picture that you cannot see, but God sees.

In Nehemiah 6:15, we saw that the wall was finished. Then we read in Nehemiah 7, "Now it came to pass, when the wall was built, and I had set up the doors, and the porters," or gatekeepers, "and the singers and the Levites were appointed, that I gave my brother Hanani, and Hananiah the ruler of the palace, charge over Jerusalem: for he was a faithful man, and feared God above many. And I said unto them, Let not the gates of Jerusalem be opened until the sun be hot; and while they stand by, let them shut the doors, and bar them: and appoint watches of the inhabitants of Jerusalem, every one in his watch, and every one to be over against his house. Now the city was large and great: but the people were few therein, and the houses were not builded."

The first thing that Nehemiah did after the wall was completed was appoint porters, or gatekeepers. First there was a need for physical protection. In Nehemiah 6, we read about many enemies, including Sanballat, Tobiah, Gashmu, "and the rest of our enemies," which included a prophet and a prophetess. There were also marauding bands of people who might attack at any time. All of the work that they had put into restoring and rebuilding could suddenly be undone, so the order was given for gatekeepers to fulfill the need for protection.

The Scripture warns us to be sober, to be vigilant, to be on guard and to be watchful. Complacency is the greatest danger to the Christian. You cannot rest on yesterday's faith, yesterday's accomplishments and yesterday's sacrifices; they do not count for anything today. Spiritual complacency can happen at any time without warning. It could come in a form as subtle as waking up on a Sunday morning and telling yourself, "I'm too tired to go to church." God might have had something specific to say to you through His word on that day, but you would never know. People can also become complacent in their giving, and say, "I will get around to it later." It is so easy to become complacent, and I do not condemn you for it, for we are all guilty of it in some form or another. In the book of Revelation, the church of Laodicea was faulted for saying, "I am rich and have need of nothing." When we start to depend upon ourselves and our own resources, we cease to depend upon God for all our provision, and our spiritual lives start to degrade quickly.

We are warned to guard our heart, because out of the heart flow the issues of life. We must stay in the word of God in order to be gatekeepers of our hearts and minds. Ephesians 6 says to put on the whole armor of God, so that we might take our stand against the methods of the devil. Satan does not care how he eliminates you. That is his whole purpose, and until you come to that knowledge, you will be helpless against the enemy's methods.

The next thing that Nehemiah did was establish the singers, which put a priority on praise and worship. Psalm 147 says, "Praise ye the LORD: for it is good to sing praises unto our God. . . . The LORD doth build up Jerusalem: he gathereth together the outcasts of Israel." The singers were to minister to the Lord in praise. We know we have a God who provides and we praise Him for that, but there is a duty of praise for each believer. In the midst of a crisis, in the midst of needing God to fix something that is broken, we need to consider the greatness of our God and stand amazed that He would condescend to relate to even the smallest and basest of His creatures. In Ezekiel 44, we read about a ministry to the Lord in the inner court of the sanctuary, which typifies drawing near to God in praise and worship. Praise was an important part of the life of faith for these people, and the singers were responsible for the spiritual vitality of the community.

Then Nehemiah appointed the Levites. The Levites' role in the history of God's people was very important, and it is clear that their role had to change in the postexilic period. It is a common misunderstanding to think that the Levites had the same responsibility as the priests; in fact, they had very specific tasks assigned to them. Now that there was no longer a tabernacle, the Levites' chief assignment would be to give thanks and to praise. But when the tabernacle was moved in the wilderness, it was the Levites who were responsible for taking it down and setting it up, and they were responsible for moving all of the articles of the tabernacle.

The sons of Levi were Gershon, Kohath and Merari. One of the three groups of Levites was given two carts with oxen to move the elements of the tabernacle. Another group was instructed to use poles instead of carts. And the third group moved everything with their hands. Perhaps one person had the job of moving only one seemingly inconsequential utensil. But it mattered to God that that one person was responsible for that one thing. Remember the parable of the talents in the New Testament. That same concept of being faithful with whatever God has given and entrusted to us is found here in Nehemiah with the Levites. When God calls people to do even the smallest thing, it is not small in God's eyes. No task in the kingdom of God is small. It matters to Him and it counts for something. In 1 Corinthians 12, the apostle Paul teaches that there are diversities of gifts, but the same Spirit. God has not changed at all. He gives to each person "severally as He will," as He sees fit to give. He may give the gift of diligence and responsibility, the ability for you to make a commitment and to keep it.

Some people think that in order to count for God, you must go out and preach from either a pulpit or a street corner somewhere in the public view. But what about the small things that cannot be seen by other people? I am talking about the prayers that are prayed for others, for people who are sick and for families that are broken. These unseen, quiet things, as they ascend Godward, are not seen as small at all. Again, no task in the kingdom of God is small.

We have seen Nehemiah's character and we have seen his priorities. Now let's look at the quality of the people whom he chose as overseers. We read in Nehemiah 7:2, "I gave my brother Hanani, and Hananiah the ruler of the palace, charge over Jerusalem: for he was a faithful man, and feared God above many." The Hebrew for "faithful man" is *ish amet.* Our English word "Amen" is a cognate of the Hebrew word *amet.* We can translate *amet* as "faithful, stable, firm, truthful, or reliable." It doesn't say that this man was perfect. These people were no different than us. They were the descendants of a people who were carried away into bondage because of their fathers' or their fathers' fathers' disobedience. They were a people who were not completely committed to God, which makes them less than perfect and rather on a par with you and me.

What were the criteria for putting this man in charge? First, it says that "he was a faithful man." Recognize that when God calls you to any task, you should be faithful in that task. Second, it says that "he feared God above many." We read of no criteria other than being faithful and God-fearing. God gave gift ministers to the church to equip the saints, and the pastor must be faithful in that commission and must fear God.

Then Nehemiah said, "Let not the gates of Jerusalem be opened until the sun be hot; and while they stand by, let them shut the doors, and bar them: and appoint watches of the inhabitants of Jerusalem." The people of that community would be on duty. Likewise, we are part of a community, and there is something for everyone to do in the church. At the very least, you can pray and be faithful. Everything we do down here is training; we are in spiritual "boot camp" in preparation for eternity.

Nehemiah appointed watches of the inhabitants of Jerusalem, "every one in his watch, and every one to be over against his house." For "the city was large and great: but the people were few therein, and the houses were not builded." What does that mean for us? These people were preparing for the coming of the Righteous Branch. Although they did not know it, they were preparing for the time when Christ would enter into the city. They just did the work. In our day, we are preparing for Christ's return. It is the pastor's responsibility to teach the people to have faith and trust in God's word and to recognize God's fidelity to His word and to His people, so that when the Son of man comes, He will find faith. Remember the parable of the wise and the foolish virgins. We have a responsibility to be diligent right now. Nehemiah's words, "Now the city was large and great: but the people were few therein," also echo into the New Testament, where Jesus said, "Strait is the gate, and narrow is the way, which leadeth unto life, and few there be that find it."

We read in Nehemiah 7:5, "And my God put into mine heart to gather together the nobles, and the rulers, and the people, that they might be reckoned by genealogy. And I found a register of the genealogy of them which came up at the first. . . ." And here begins the memorial of the people who returned from captivity in the first wave under the leadership of Zerubbabel.

Nehemiah believed in the future of Jerusalem, and therefore he would not permit the city to remain in a ruined state. He was not of a mind that would say, "Okay, now the walls are up, so we have nothing more to do." He recognized that the backbreaking and at times spirit-crushing work of rebuilding the walls would have been absolutely meaningless if there were no people in the city to protect. So God put it into his heart to gather the people together and recount their genealogy before them. He read the names of all the families that first returned to take part in the rebuilding of the temple and the city. It was as though God was saying to the people, "I want to remind you of your rich heritage; but more importantly, I want you to know that you have a future ahead of you."

The people who are chronicled in this record were not randomly included. They all counted for something as a part of God's plan to repopulate the city and to continue the line all the way to the time of Christ. Anyone who knows that they have been bought by the blood of Christ also has a genealogy. Your genealogy is not written on the pages of the Bible; rather you are recorded as a child of God in the Lamb's book of life.

Praise God that He called us! There may be multitudes going in the wrong direction, but God has called us out of the darkness and said, "This is the way, walk ye in it." That is the only way that anyone comes in to the kingdom. Jesus said, "No man comes to the Father save through the Son," and "I will raise him up in the last day."

The people hearing the genealogy read by Nehemiah would have had a reaction to hearing the names of their families being read. They would have felt, "That's me! That's my family! That's where I belong!" We should have that same reaction today in the church, not necessarily because our parents grew up in the church, but because we were once aliens, outsiders and foreigners to the church. And then suddenly one day, God opened our hearts.

Now I know who I am. Just like Paul, I bear in my body the marks of a bondslave of Christ, and this crock of clay is inhabited by His Spirit. I belong because the Lord Jesus has bought me. I am His. When He went to Calvary, He bought the whole field to get the treasure out of the field. His blood covered everything; and though our sins be like scarlet, He made them white as snow.

Any of the children of God in exile could have returned, but many of the people had settled down in Babylon and established their lives there. Some may have even questioned why they should be bothered to uproot themselves to return to Jerusalem and rebuild. Over 600,000 people in captivity in Babylon had an opportunity to return to Jerusalem to help rebuild it, but relatively few returned. Those who returned did so because it mattered to them, and they are the ones whose names are recorded in Nehemiah 7.

God's word is still speaking to the hearts of those who have gone their own way, and His word is calling them to return and rebuild. People all over the face of this planet have the opportunity to stop dead in their tracks, turn from their way to God's way and begin following after Him.

I do not perform "altar calls." I believe that the response to God's word happens in the heart as the word goes forth. Understand that you matter to God. When you think that *you* matter, that is, that *you* are important, that is when you cease to matter. But if you are one of those who understand that you don't deserve the mercy you have received, you matter to God.

The people in Nehemiah's day had to repopulate the city. The church of Jesus Christ is the city of God today, until the new city descends: a new heaven and a new earth. We have a responsibility. Your place in God's history matters. It is possible to rebuild a wall and a building, but a building is just a building; it has no meaning without the people.

If you think that someone else will do what you have been called to do, you are mistaken. There will never be another you in the kingdom. Commit yourself first to do the things that matter the most to God. Matthew 6:33 says, "Seek ye first the kingdom of God and his righteousness, and all these other things will be added to you." When the church finally learns this lesson, it will move forward and make great progress.

You count for God. And if you think that whatever you have been called to do is not important enough to count for something, you are mistaken. I would ask you to read about the sons of Levi in Numbers 3 and 4, and the responsibilities that they were given by God, which included the minutest details such as spreading cloth and setting up poles. There is no job that is menial when it touches the things of God. And these are chronicled and embedded in the word as a memorial for us. How much more should the things of God matter to us today? We have the knowledge of the revelation of Jesus Christ, which should make us want to say, "Let me carry something. Let me participate. Let me put my hand to the plow."

Everything we do, from the smallest to the greatest, from the seen to the unseen, is seen by God and He is memorializing it all. He cares about you. Begin to order your life in that knowledge, as a child of a heavenly kingdom. God knows our frame, He knows our frailty and He knows all our ways. He knows how easily we can be persuaded and tossed and drawn away. You who have made commitments and have fallen away need to remember that even the greatest of saints in God's book made mistakes and went in the wrong direction. The apostle Peter is just one example. By God's grace, you can get up again and He will give you another chance to start over afresh. Some of you may have said, "Well, I'm trying to count for something, but it seems as though everything I have done has ended in failure." Then get up again knowing that even those failures are behind you, and go forward from this day. Start looking unto Him, and He will take care of the rest. Reach out to Jesus, because He is able to take away those things of the past and let you get up and start over today.

Chapter 7

GOD HAS A PLAN AND YOU ARE IN IT

God is not only faithful to His word and to His people, He is faithful to fulfill all of His prophecies concerning the things yet to come. And as there are certain things in the Bible that are not always clear, likewise we will encounter situations in our own lives that do not always make sense at the time we are going through them. It is not always perfectly clear why certain things happen. I have heard many people say, "I just happened to be in this situation" or "I was born into this." Some say, "I was born into a Christian home" or "I was born into poverty." We may be born into something that is outside of our control, and yet God is still in control.

There are people in the Bible who are just like that. The person of whom I am speaking today is Zerubbabel. His very name bears the idea of being born into something: his name means "born in Babylon" or "sown or begotten in Babylon." He is mentioned in the book of Nehemiah in chapters 7 and 12, and he plays a key role in the book of Ezra as well as in the prophecies of Haggai and Zechariah. And we will see that his name is also included in several different genealogies in God's book.

We are going to look at God's fidelity, His faithfulness to perform the things that He said He would do. At the same time, I want you to think of yourself as someone like Zerubbabel, someone who was born into something. When we think of Zerubbabel, we think of a man who was born in a land of darkness. If you had been born in that land, you would only be familiar with the things that were around you, a land full of people who had been carried away into captivity. God had foretold of this captivity. Back in Leviticus, God gave an outline of what He wanted from His people. Later, He sent prophets like Jeremiah to warn the people of what would happen to them for refusing to listen to God's word. Failure to abide by what God wanted resulted in His saying, "I am going to get what I want, no matter what My children do. I am going to accomplish My purpose."

After seventy years of bondage in Babylon, the people were allowed to return to Jerusalem. There were several waves of people who returned, and Zerubbabel was either a part of the first group or possibly a second group that returned to rebuild, as recorded in Ezra. The events recorded in the book of Nehemiah happened shortly after that. When I say "shortly," it was still a number of years, because the events recorded in Ezra and Nehemiah did not occur back-to-back. Ezra records that Zerubbabel the son of Shealtiel built the altar and the temple, and he encountered the same kind of opposition as Nehemiah faced. People came against him, but the work continued.

Let's start with the first two verses in Ezra 3 to give us a frame of reference. "And when the seventh month was come, and the children of Israel were in the cities, the people gathered themselves together as one man to Jerusalem. Then stood up Jeshua the son of Jozadak, and his brethren the priests, and Zerubbabel the son of Shealtiel, and his brethren, and builded the altar of the God of Israel, to offer burnt offerings. . . ." I want you to notice that almost all of the references to Zerubbabel the son of Shealtiel are found in close proximity to Joshua (sometimes spelled Jeshua) the son of Jozadak (sometimes spelled Josedech). Usually, Zerubbabel and Joshua are named in the same verse.

In Ezra 5, we encounter the prophets Haggai and Zechariah. We know that God stirred up their spirits and raised them up to preach and to encourage the people who were rebuilding. We read, "Then the prophets, Haggai the prophet, and Zechariah the son of Iddo, prophesied unto the Jews that were in Judah and Jerusalem in the name of the God of Israel, even unto them. Then rose up Zerubbabel the son of Shealtiel, and Jeshua," that is, Joshua, "the son of Jozadak, and began to build the house of God which is at Jerusalem." Once again, we see the two men being referenced together, and there is a reason for this.

Haggai is a short book. It only has two chapters, which contain four prophetic messages that were preached sometime between August and December of the year 520 B.C. The first prophecies were given to encourage the people to keep on rebuilding. When you read through the book of Haggai, pay attention to how many times it specifically addresses Zerubbabel the son of Shealtiel along with Joshua, the high priest. Haggai 1:1 says, "The word of the Lord came to Haggai unto Zerubbabel the son of Shealtiel, governor of Judah, and to Joshua the son of Josedech, the high priest." Then we read in Haggai 1:12, "Then Zerubbabel the son of Shealtiel, and Joshua the son of Josedech, the high priest, with all the remnant of the people, obeyed the voice of the LORD their God, and the words of Haggai the prophet." We read again in verse 14, "The LORD stirred up the spirit of Zerubbabel the son of Shealtiel, governor of Judah, and the spirit of Joshua the son of Josedech, the high priest." And we read again in Haggai 2:2, "Speak now to Zerubbabel the son of Shealtiel, governor of Judah, and to Joshua the son of Josedech, the high priest."

Then something unusual happens in Haggai's fourth prophecy. We read in Haggai 2:21, "Speak to Zerubbabel, governor of Judah, saying. . . ." Notice that this prophecy is addressed *only* to Zerubbabel, and not to Joshua the high priest. Also notice that it names "Zerubbabel," but it does not at first say "the son of Shealtiel." It is in fact the same Zerubbabel, and we will see the significance of this prophecy later in this message.

Let's read the fourth prophecy in its entirety, starting at verse 20: "And again the word of the LORD came unto Haggai in the four and twentieth day of the month, saying, Speak to Zerubbabel, governor of Judah, saying, I will shake the heavens and the earth; and I will overthrow the throne of kingdoms, and I will destroy the strength of the kingdoms of the heathen; and I will overthrow the chariots, and those that ride in them; and the horses and their riders shall come down, every one by the sword of his brother. In that day, saith the LORD of hosts, will I take thee, O Zerubbabel, my servant, the son of Shealtiel, saith the LORD, and will make thee as a signet: for I have chosen thee, saith the LORD of hosts."

Now, why are we discussing Zerubbabel? And what does this have to do with you and me today? Zerubbabel is an important figure, not just in the rebuilding, but also in the fulfillment of prophecies concerning the redemption of mankind. God through Haggai said, "In that day," whatever that day will be, "In that day, saith the LORD of hosts, will I take thee, O Zerubbabel, my servant, the son of Shealtiel, saith the LORD, and will make thee as a signet," as the ring of a king, the ring of authority, "for I have chosen thee, saith the LORD of hosts."

In order to understand why this is so significant, I need to take you way back to the beginning. This same Zerubbabel is named in the genealogies of Christ in Matthew 1:12–13 and in Luke 3:27. Zerubbabel provides a major lesson for us about the way that God sometimes does things. If you are ever tempted to think that God's plan must work out in a certain way, or that God's people must be a certain way, I want you to remember Zerubbabel, who was born in Babylon and would come out of Babylon for a purpose. And that purpose was much more profound than just to appear in a couple of genealogies.

When we compare the two genealogies in the Gospels, we notice that there are some similarities and some differences. However, both of them trace the line of Christ back to King David. David had an affair with Bathsheba and ended up murdering Bathsheba's husband, Uriah. In 1 Chronicles 3:5, we are told that Bathsheba had four sons including Solomon and Nathan. Solomon's and Nathan's respective descendants are listed in the two genealogies. Many people have stumbled over this, so our intention is to help clarify the apparent discrepancies between the two genealogies, and to help us see why this is such an amazing revelation. When we see God's control of the smallest details, it lets us know that no matter where we are, God has a plan for us. You may have been born in a "Babylon" place, but if you are one of those whom God has called and chosen, He has a plan for you. And when God has a plan, it may look kind of crazy at first, until He makes it come to pass; and then you have to just step back and say, "Wow! God really is in control!"

The first thing we notice about the genealogy of Christ in Matthew 1 is that it starts with Abraham and his descendants and it ends with Christ. The genealogy in Luke 3 is in the opposite order, starting with Christ and tracing His lineage all the way back up to Adam.

In Matthew 1:6–7, David's son Solomon is named. After Solomon died, the kingdom was divided into the northern and southern kingdoms of Judah and Israel. The kingdom was divided because of Solomon's disobedience. He had 1,000 women, counting concubines and wives, who turned his heart from God. When we read down through verse 12, we come to Jechonias. The name Jechonias is the New Testament spelling of Jeconiah, who is also known as Coniah and Jehoiachin. After Jechonias is Salathiel, which is the New Testament spelling of the name Shealtiel. Then it says that Salathiel begat Zorobabel, who is Zerubbabel.

Both Matthew and Luke say that Zerubbabel was the son of Shealtiel. But in Luke's Gospel, we see a different sequence of names. And when you get to Shealtiel, it says that he was a son of Neri, not Jechonias. That has caused many people to say that you cannot reconcile these two genealogies, but you can, and I will show you how.

After Zerubbabel, there is another bifurcation in the genealogy and again there are differences between the two Gospel records. These differences are accounted for because Matthew's Gospel traces Jesus' lineage through his legal father, Joseph, while Luke's Gospel traces Jesus' lineage through Mary.

In Matthew 1:11, we read, "Josias begat Jechonias and his brethren, about the time they were carried away to Babylon: and after they were brought to Babylon, Jechonias begat Salathiel; and Salathiel begat Zorobabel," that is, Zerubbabel. Josias (or Josiah) was the last goodly and godly king of Judah, the last good king in a line of many bad kings. He was a reformer. Jehoahaz was king after him, followed by Jehoahaz's brother Jehoiakim. Then Jehoiakim's son Jeconiah (that is, Jehoiachin or Coniah) became king. One of the things to keep in mind about this genealogy in Matthew's Gospel is that it deliberately omits certain names. You will not see Jehoahaz or Jehoiakim named; it jumps from Josiah straight to Jeconiah. Jeconiah was the second to the last king of Judah before the people were carried away into captivity. It is a very strange record. Zedekiah was the last king of Judah, and he was actually an uncle of Jeconiah, not a son.

About thirteen years into Josiah's reign, the prophet Jeremiah warned the people that they would be carried away into bondage for a period of seventy years. That prophecy is recorded in other places, including in Ezekiel, though without the specific mention of the seventy-year period. The reason for the specific duration of the captivity can be understood from Leviticus 25. God had commanded the people to let the land rest every seventh year. They were not to till the land, but they were to let it lie fallow and trust that God would provide enough food in the sixth year that they could let the land rest in the seventh year. But the people ignored that command for 490 years. They continued to till the land throughout that time, so they failed to let the land rest for a total of seventy years.

Ultimately, the people were carried away into captivity, and the land would rest for seventy years. It is as though God was saying, "I will have My way." But before the people were carried away into captivity, Jeremiah came on the scene and he warned the people. When you read the record you might ask, "Was anybody listening?" We tend to think that if Jeremiah were to speak to us today, we would listen. But that is not true, because human nature has not changed. I have heard people say, "Why should I listen to a preacher?" The preacher may not be a Jeremiah, but they are proclaiming God's word and that is all the reason you need. But in every age, people are hardheaded.

When the period of seventy years was coming to an end, it says in Daniel 9 that Daniel was reading and he "understood by books the number of the years" that had been foretold by Jeremiah. Isaiah prophesies of a heathen king who was not yet born, and in Isaiah 44 and 45 he names him as Cyrus. God said, in essence, "Cyrus will be the one to issue the edict that allows My people to return to Jerusalem and rebuild." We read the record of those who returned to rebuild in Ezra and Nehemiah, and we know it was a very small number in comparison to the number of those who were carried away into bondage.

Zerubbabel is considered to be one of those who returned to Jerusalem, but he didn't really "return" since he had never been there before. God took a man who had no training in altar-building or temple-building, yet Zerubbabel was a man led by God to supervise such a work. Whatever God does, He does it perfectly; and sometimes He uses the strangest vessels to get the job done.

In order to understand the genealogies of Christ in the Gospels, we must go to 1 Chronicles 3, which is the record of the sons of David. We read beginning at verse 15, "And the sons of Josiah," the last godly king, were "the firstborn Johanan, the second Jehoiakim, the third Zedekiah, the fourth Shallum. And the sons of Jehoiakim: Jeconiah his son," sometimes known as Coniah or Jehoiachin, and "Zedekiah his son." It says, "Zedekiah his son," but it should say, "Zedekiah his uncle." "And the sons of Jeconiah; Assir, Salathiel his son," that is Shealtiel; he is supposedly the father of Zerubbabel. "Malchiram also, and Pedaiah. . . . And the sons of Pedaiah were, Zerubbabel. . . ." This introduces another puzzle, because here Zerubbabel is called a son of Pedaiah, yet Zerubbabel is called the son of Shealtiel in so many other places in the Bible.

Shealtiel and Pedaiah were both sons of Jeconiah. It is a little difficult to see this because of the verse division and punctuation in the King James Version. Let's read it without the punctuation, which was added by the translators and not in the original text: "The sons of Jeconiah Assir Salathiel his son Malchiram also and Pedaiah and Shenazar Jecamiah Hoshama and Nedabiah." You can see that these are all one family.

Now Shealtiel would have been married, but he died not having children. Under the Levitical law, Shealtiel's widow would have married his brother Pedaiah to raise up children in the name of the deceased. It was that union which produced Zerubbabel. That explains how Zerubbabel can be called a son of Shealtiel and also be called a son of Pedaiah.

Another complexity is the presence of Neri in the lineage recorded in Luke's Gospel. Who is Neri? Jeconiah must have married a daughter of Neri, which is why Shealtiel is said to be a descendant of *both* Jeconiah and Neri. So the various genealogies can in fact be reconciled.

Zerubbabel had sons and one daughter, Shelomith. Shelomith married Rhesa, and that produced the line descending to Joanna, Juda and so forth, and on to Christ as recorded in Luke's Gospel. But in both genealogies in the Gospels and in prophecy, Zerubbabel is referred to as "Zerubbabel the son of Shealtiel." There is a reason for that. Many have looked at these genealogies and said, "Well, this can't be true, and so it proves that the Bible is not true." No, what it proves is that someone was recording the lineage and thought that all of these details were important.

I have read many commentaries that say, "If Ezra, Nehemiah and Haggai thought that Zerubbabel was that important, don't you think they would have mentioned the fact that Zerubbabel would be a part of the lineage to the Messiah? It is not mentioned anywhere." So, some have concluded that there must be two different Zerubbabels, and that the two are not related. This is unlikely. Besides, Zerubbabel is not that common a name. He was from the line of Judah, which was supposed to rule and sit on the throne. Yet when we get to Jeconiah, something truly terrible happens.

Now turn to Jeremiah 22. The whole chapter is comprised of prophecies against the kings of Judah. Jeremiah starts to prophesy some thirteen years into Josiah's reign and he continues to prophesy through Zedekiah's reign. Zedekiah was the last king, whose eyes were plucked out before he was led away into captivity. We read in verse 24, "As I live, saith the LORD, though Coniah the son of

Jehoiakim king of Judah were the signet upon my right hand. . . ." Does that sound familiar? We just read in Haggai 2 that God would make Zerubbabel as a signet, and the Lord said through the prophet, "for I have chosen thee."

But God said "though Coniah," that is, Jeconiah, "the son of Jehoiakim king of Judah were the signet upon my right hand, yet would I pluck thee thence." The "right hand" in the Bible is a symbol of power. God was saying that if Coniah were the signet ring on His right hand, He would pull him off. "And I will give thee into the hand of them that seek thy life, and into the hand of them whose face thou fearest, even into the hand of Nebuchadnezzar king of Babylon, and into the hand of the Chaldeans. And I will cast thee out, and thy mother that bare thee, into another country, where ye were not born; and there shall ye die. But to the land whereunto they desire to return, thither shall they not return. Is this man Coniah a despised broken idol? is he a vessel wherein is no pleasure? wherefore are they cast out, he and his seed, and are cast into a land which they know not? O earth, earth, earth, hear the word of the LORD. Thus saith the LORD, Write ye this man childless," that is, record him as if he were childless, as if he had never had a child. Jeconiah was cursed by the word of the Lord through the prophet Jeremiah: "For no man of his seed shall prosper, sitting upon the throne of David, and ruling any more in Judah." After Jeconiah was led away into captivity, Zedekiah was temporarily made a king. Jeremiah would then come to warn Zedekiah and tell him, "Look, this is what is going to happen," but Zedekiah did not want to hear about it.

Note that in some of the earlier records, there is some confusion regarding Jeconiah's age. One record says that he was only eight years old, and another says that he was eighteen. The record that says he was eighteen is correct, because we know that he was carried away with his wives and his mother. His uncle Mattaniah's name would be changed to Zedekiah, and Zedekiah would rule for eleven years before being led away, blind and fettered into Babylon. The whole family line will seem to disappear. If we ended the genealogy of the kings with Jeconiah and we did not have the record in

Matthew's Gospel, we might simply say, "Well, that is a sad story and the end of the line." But that is why Chronicles includes the name of Shealtiel's brother, Pedaiah, to let us know that the line continued. And Zerubbabel could still be called a son of Shealtiel in both of the Gospel records and in prophecy.

In Luke's Gospel, Zerubbabel is in the line of Neri, a descendant of David's son Nathan; whereas in Matthew's Gospel, Zerubbabel is said to be in the line of Jechonias, a descendant of David's son Solomon. Zerubbabel would be born in Babylon, and he would not come into the land of Judah as a king. He would be the governor and would be called a prince, but he would not be a king.

God is faithful to do what He said He would do. Jeconiah was not only cursed, he was carried away and lived out the rest of his days in Babylon. We know that this child Zerubbabel will come to Jerusalem and become one of its more prominent figures. And he will receive a prophecy from Haggai that points to a future time and the ultimate fulfillment of God's purposes in bringing forth the Messiah. Now with that background, let's return to the book of Haggai and the significance of its final prophecy.

Haggai's first three prophecies were given to both Zerubbabel and Joshua, to encourage the people to keep on building. Haggai's message was, in essence, "Keep on building, for the Lord will enable you to do it." But Haggai's fourth prophecy was addressed only to Zerubbabel, and not to both Zerubbabel and Joshua. God through the prophet said to him, "I will shake the heavens and the earth; and I will overthrow the throne of kingdoms, and I will destroy the strength of the kingdoms of the heathen; and I will overthrow the chariots, and those that ride in them; and the horses and their riders shall come down, every one by the sword of his brother."

It seems like an obvious question, but does this seem like a prophecy concerning events that would happen within Zerubbabel's lifetime? And has the Lord shaken the heavens and the earth yet? We know that there was a great earthquake in the days of Uzziah, but beyond that, we know that the heavens and the earth have not been shaken yet as described in this prophecy. And the words, "I will destroy the strength of the kingdoms of the heathen; and I will overthrow the chariots," speak of a time when Gentile power will come to an end, and the instruments of war will be destroyed. Again, has this happened yet? It is self-evident that this is a prophecy of events that will occur in the distant future.

"In that day," meaning a future time, "saith the LORD of hosts, will I take thee, O Zerubbabel, my servant, the son of Shealtiel, saith the LORD, and will make thee as a signet." To Jeconiah, the Lord had said: "If you were a signet on my right hand, I would pluck you off. You are being discarded. None of your children will ever sit on the throne." But to Zerubbabel, the one born in Babylon, God said, "I will make thee as a signet: for I have chosen thee, saith the LORD of hosts." Imagine God speaking this prophecy like launching an arrow through time, pointing to Zerubbabel and penetrating through Zerubbabel straight to the Messiah, Jesus Christ!

It is easy for us to read the books of Ezra, Nehemiah, Zechariah and Haggai as history or prophecy, but I want us to put flesh and blood on Zerubbabel. Think of this man who came from a line that otherwise would have been discontinued, based on Jeconiah's record and the curse that God had pronounced on him in Jeremiah 22. And yet, somehow, God preserved his line. The study of these genealogies in the Gospels shows us that God was busy weaving a great fabric to ensure the preservation of the seed of David and to fulfill all of the prophecies concerning the Messiah.

Now we can see the significance of the manner in which Haggai addresses his prophecies. His first prophecies were addressed to *both* Zerubbabel and to Joshua the high priest. But Haggai's last prophecy, speaking of a day far into the future, was addressed only to Zerubbabel. Why? Because Zerubbabel represents the royal line, and Joshua represents the priestly line. But suddenly the two offices will be merged together in Christ, when He comes as our King and High Priest!

The study of God's word lets us see His control of history and of prophecy, including all of the things yet to be fulfilled. Many of you say, "I am worried about what will happen tomorrow." Friend, do not worry about what will happen tomorrow. Recognize that if God's hand could be in so many details—the foretelling of the people being carried away, the naming in advance of a man, Cyrus, who would allow the people to return, and the preservation of the Davidic line until the coming of Christ—how much more will He enter into all the details of our lives?

When we see that God used Pedaiah to preserve the line that produced the two genealogies of Christ, we can recognize that God had a great plan, even for someone who was born in Babylon, born into a place of confusion, darkness and impossibility. God had a plan and preserved the seed, even though Jeconiah was cursed and we see none of his children sitting on a throne. But to Zerubbabel, God said, "I have chosen you, and I will make you as a signet," which is the symbol of authority, the symbol of the right to rule and reign.

God was going to have His way. He managed to preserve a child in the line descending from King David. That is one of the reasons why both Nehemiah and Ezra were furious when the people were intermarrying with the surrounding heathen nations. It wasn't because they were opposed to interracial relationships; they wanted the people to stay faithful to preserve the seed that would ultimately bring us to Christ.

Many of us read the Bible and tend to think that some of these passages are merely great history lessons. They are more than that; they are lessons on how God deals with His people. Too many people say, "Well, I just don't see how God is going to do this thing." Do you really believe that Zerubbabel could have had any comprehension of how the Lord was going to do this thing? But his was the seed that would be preserved to bring us to the line of Christ.

We can take this history lesson of God's faithfulness and say, "God made good on His promises." There was no shadow of turning from what He had said; when He declared seventy years, it was seventy years. There are some who call themselves Bible scholars who will argue that the seventy years were not completed, but they reckon from the wrong date. If you read Daniel 9 very carefully, you find out that Daniel "understood by the books," and he saw the exact numbers. God did not randomly pick "seventy years" because He thought that the number seventy sounded good. Seventy was the number of years that God had decreed the captivity would last.

So again I ask the question, which I think is greatly important: If God was this careful to fulfill His promises and ensure that His promised seed would come, can you not trust Him, both in the affairs of His church and in your personal life? Can we not declare with confidence, "God is in control"? Maybe all of us live in Babylon, figuratively speaking; this world is a place of darkness and confusion. We are all born into that confusion; Romans 3:23 says that all have sinned. Yet in the book of Ephesians, God talks about those whom He has chosen out from this world. The word for "chosen" in the Greek is *exelexato*, which literally means that He has chosen us out *for Himself*.

If you have any concern for the things of God, if you have any desire to hear the word of God, that means God is speaking to you today. Whatever your troubles, whatever your burdens, God has a plan for you. I am not saying, "This is an easy message. Now, click your heels three times and all your problems will be gone." It doesn't happen that way. Look at the record of God's people in captivity in Babylon. Seventy years is a long time to be in darkness. For seventy years, most of them did not have access to the word of God. Even before the captivity, in the days of King Josiah, it says that he found the book of the law, but they did not have a complete written record as we do today. When I see all that God has accomplished, I have to ask myself, "When will I learn the lesson that God has a great plan?" Now, at times it does not look so great. But I want you to remember this message when the circumstances do not look right, when you are fighting health issues, or when you have contention with your loved ones who come against your faith and your commitment to Christ. It is very easy to slip into a state of darkness, confusion or fear, because you can't see anything happening. We know that God is not the author of fear, and we can have the certainty that God has this great plan.

Jeremiah 29:11 speaks of the people who would return from captivity, though at the time he prophesied, they had not yet returned. And God through the prophet said, "My thoughts of you are thoughts of peace." He had a plan for His people, His disobedient people who were carried away into captivity. He had a plan that they would come back. And He had thoughts of peace for them, thoughts of *shalom*, meaning "wholeness" for His people. How much more do we have that promise in Christ?

So let me ask it again: If we can see God's hand unfolding His redemptive plan in history, can we not trust God with all of our issues today? Read His word and recognize that these words that God gave are true words. They are not merely words in a book; they are not words written for occasional entertainment. Any serious scholar who will take the time to research the genealogies will be driven to say, "It is pretty awesome that God would care enough to do all of this." Well then, how much more will God enter in and care for you as a son or a daughter covered and bought by the blood of Christ?

The promise to Zerubbabel at the close of Haggai was a prophecy of future events, pointing to Christ. The prophet Malachi, who was the last prophet of the Old Testament, also spoke about the coming of Christ, and he said, "Who will be able to stand in the day of his coming?" When Jesus came in the flesh the first time, the Bible says, "He came to his own, and his own received him not." And when He returns, He will be looking for *faithers*, people who will take Him at His word.

No matter what your circumstances are, even if you were born in Babylon, God has a plan and you are in it. I have only one goal in preaching, and that is to increase your faith. How does faith come, if not by hearing the word of God? God is so faithful in fulfilling even the smallest details of the words in His book. His word says that He sees the sparrow fall and the hairs of your head are numbered, and there are many more declarations of His care. That means you should take your problems, every single issue, and commit them to the Lord and trust Him. Do not lean on the flesh. It doesn't matter if you are looking at what appears to be a terrible darkness. That is why I said you should remember Zerubbabel. God is faithful. God will enter in.

God said through the prophet Jeremiah that He will perform His word. I cannot think of any greater depiction of that faithfulness than His promise to send His Son. No matter what you are facing, think on this and remember something: you could not be in a darker place than these people were during their seventy years in captivity, not even understanding God's plan. We at least have the whole book to read. They didn't have that book to help them to understand that God had provided a pathway to lead us to the way, the truth and the life. We can study the book that they did not have.

God gave His word through the prophet Haggai to encourage the people. I want you to be encouraged today. I have no desire to listen to people who say, "You can't. They can't." *God can!* It has been a long and tough trip. It will continue to be a tough trip, and people will get discouraged and fall off the wagon. Why does this happen? Because they refuse to look at God's word and say, "God's word declares something to be true, and I will stand on that word and I will keep standing on it until He performs it! And if I die not having obtained His promise, I know that when I am in His presence I will hear Him say, 'Well done, good and faithful servant; enter in.'"

Some people only walk by sight; everything for them depends on what they can see. If I lived that way, I would have given up a long time ago. I walk by faith. I am Zerubbabel. You are Zerubbabel. We walk by faith in God's word. This is something for you to wrap your mind around: the faithfulness of God, in all the big things and the small, to work His will for you, and to accomplish His good for you.

Chapter 8

GOD IS IN CONTROL

C. S. Lewis said in *The Great Divorce*, "There are only two kinds of people in the end: those who say to God, 'Thy will be done,' and those to whom God says, in the end, '*Thy* will be done.'" You can either yield to God and hear His voice speak to you through His word, or you can choose to go your own way.

God's book is a record for us of people who many times did not listen. That does not mean we should foolishly think that we can do better than they did, because even though we have the lessons in front of us, we are constantly guilty of treading on God's word, sometimes blatantly, ignorantly or foolishly ignoring what saith the Scriptures.

Today we will start in the book of Ezra, which is a precursor to the book of Nehemiah. We read in Ezra 1, "Now in the first year of Cyrus king of Persia, that the word of the Lord by the mouth of Jeremiah might be fulfilled, the Lord stirred up the spirit of Cyrus king of Persia, that he made a proclamation throughout all his kingdom, and put it also in writing, saying, Thus saith Cyrus king of Persia, The Lord God of heaven hath given me all the kingdoms of the earth; and he hath charged me to build him an house at Jerusalem, which is in Judah." Then came the call for the people to legally return to Jerusalem and rebuild.

That may not sound like a very inspiring beginning to a message, until you begin to study the history of this heathen king and see God's precise control of history. An incredible amount of detail was woven into the prophecies concerning Cyrus, including where he would come from, what he would do and all that he would accomplish. Cyrus' edict marked the beginning of the people's returning to Jerusalem and the end of their seventy years of captivity in Babylon.

The last two verses of 2 Chronicles 36 are essentially the same as the opening of Ezra 1. We read, "Now in the first year of Cyrus king of Persia, that the word of the LORD spoken by the mouth of Jeremiah might be accomplished, the LORD stirred up the spirit of Cyrus king of Persia, that he made a proclamation throughout all his kingdom, and put it also in writing, saying. . . . Who is there among you of all his people? The LORD his God be with him, and let him go up." In essence, Cyrus decreed, "Anyone who wants to go, let him return."

We know that relatively very few of the people who had been in bondage chose to return, but here is what I want us to ponder. Many times we think that God cannot possibly be in control, even though we say that we know He is in control. God *is* in control, but at times it sure does not look like it. If I did not know what was revealed in the word of God, I might just spin out of orbit, because there are times when the circumstances look impossible. We think that God could not possibly fix something or maybe that God is not even watching and does not know what is going on.

At least 120 to 150 years before these events recorded in both 2 Chronicles and Ezra, the prophet Isaiah foretold of Cyrus and the returning of the people. That is one of the reasons why I hold on to God's word when everything looks like it is going to hell in a handbasket. If God is faithful to fulfill all of these incredible details in history exactly the way He said things would happen, then I know He will fulfill His word in my life, as long as I keep on trusting Him. And I pray that you come to realize that God is faithful to fulfill His word of promise for you today wherever you are, whatever your circumstances.

Turn now to Isaiah 41, because I want to show you God's control of history and His faithfulness in even the smallest details. Students of prophecy will see the need to distinguish between the references in the Bible to the city of Babylon that existed during the period from Nebuchadnezzar's reign through Cyrus' reign, and a Babylon of a future time, a future judgment foretold in the book of Revelation. In the book of Isaiah, the references to Babylon seem to be interwoven. Prophecy can be viewed as a series of mountain ranges: when seen from a distance, you cannot tell if there are valleys or chasms between the ranges. A few short prophetic verses can often leap over long spans of time. That happens sometimes in Isaiah, so we have to be careful when interpreting these passages and looking at the things that were foretold of Cyrus. But the background to this message is that God is in control.

Isaiah prophesied throughout the reigns of several kings. His prophetic ministry began sometime during the reign of King Uzziah and ended in the reign of King Hezekiah. We can safely say that Isaiah's ministry lasted at least sixty-four years. During his ministry he foretold many things that would happen during his lifetime, many things that would occur 120 to 150 years later, and many things that would occur in the distant future. So the prophetic parts of his book can be complicated to interpret at times.

In Isaiah 41, God suddenly says through the prophet, "Keep silence before me, O islands; and let the people renew their strength: let them come near; then let them speak: let us come near together to judgment. Who raised up the righteous man from the east, called him to his foot, gave the nations before him, and made him rule over kings?" The "righteous man from the east" is a reference to Cyrus. The word for *east* is used because Cyrus was born in Persia, which is east of Babylon.

Later in this same chapter, it says, "I have raised up one from the north." It would be easy to misunderstand this passage and think that the Scripture is describing two different people, but it is describing the same person. "I have raised up one from the north, and he shall come: from the rising of the sun shall he call upon my name:

and he shall come upon princes as upon morter, and as the potter treadeth clay." At a young age, Cyrus was removed from Media, north of Babylon. He returned and settled there in Media, and it was from Media that he came down to attack Babylon. So both of these references in Isaiah 41 pertain to Cyrus.

If you want to learn more specific details about Cyrus' background, you can go to *The Histories* written by the secular historian Herodotus. When evaluating the accuracy of the writings of Herodotus, we should remember that he wrote only about a hundred years after Cyrus died, therefore Herodotus' *Histories* are likely to contain good information. In the writings of Herodotus there are even greater details concerning Cyrus' life that show us that God had to be in control.

Herodotus describes prophecies that were given about Cyrus' mother. There was a vision that told that the child she would bear would essentially usurp his father's throne. So when Cyrus was born, his father gave an order for the child to be murdered. The baby was put into the hands of a faithful servant, but the servant could not bring himself to do such a deed, so he delivered the child to someone else. That happened to be a man whose wife was about to give birth, and when she gave birth, the child was stillborn. So the two children were swapped. The dead child was taken to the woods, and it was reported that this was the royal child who was put to death. But this couple kept Cyrus and raised him. It was discovered later as he grew older that he was indeed the heir to the throne, and the rest is history. Cyrus almost did not survive his childhood, but as was foretold, he ended up taking the throne. When you look at the history of Cyrus along with its foretelling in the book of Isaiah, you cannot help but say, "God was there all along." He was working all this out.

Cyrus established a vast kingdom that would ultimately be taken over by Alexander the Great. All of this was foretold in the book of Daniel when Daniel interpreted Nebuchadnezzar's dream of a great statue. The head of the statue represented the Babylonian kingdom, followed by Cyrus' kingdom, followed by Alexander the

Great and then the Roman Empire, and then another kingdom that would arise in the last days.

In Isaiah 44, we have the beginning of prophecies specifically mentioning Cyrus, and they are quite staggering. We read in verse 28, "That saith of Cyrus, He is my shepherd, and shall perform all my pleasure." Remember this was all written more than one hundred years before Cyrus was born. Imagine for a moment if you had discovered that your grandparents were told in advance your name, your career, how many children you would have, and what year you would die. The details here are so crystal clear that many have tried to argue that this could not have been written before the events that were foretold, and that it must have been written much later. If you do not believe in God's control then I suppose that might seem to be true. I unequivocally believe that Isaiah was given many prophecies about many different kingdoms, and God was using him as His mouthpiece to declare His purposes. You either believe that, or you do not. If you do not, I cannot help you. If you do, it is staggering to discover that God said of Cyrus, "He is my shepherd, and shall perform all my pleasure: even saying to Jerusalem, Thou shalt be built; and to the temple, Thy foundation shall be laid."

What is even more remarkable is that Jerusalem was still standing at the time that this was written. Here is a prophecy regarding Jerusalem that the temple would be built and the foundation would be laid, but the city and the temple were still there! The city had not yet been sacked. And we read in Isaiah 45, "Thus saith the LORD to his anointed, to Cyrus, whose right hand I have holden. . . ." The right hand in Scripture symbolizes power, in this case the power "to subdue nations before him," which he did. This man had not yet been born, and we are told he would subdue nations. God would give him the right hand of power.

Babylon was the most glorious, impenetrable kingdom. And Cyrus would come along and conquer that kingdom and conquer that fortress, which everyone said could not be penetrated. He would liberate the people and issue an edict for them to return to Jerusalem. And that would all take place 120 to 150 years after the prophecy was written.

"I will loose the loins of kings, to open before him the two leaved gates; and the gates shall not be shut." Though that city lies in ruins today, there has been much archaeological research done. There is a museum in Germany that has a beautiful reconstruction of the gates. Babylon was a fortified city and its gates always stayed shut, but somehow they were left open one night for Cyrus and his army to take the city.

The Lord says of this heathen king, "I will go before thee, and make the crooked places straight: I will break in pieces the gates of brass, and cut in sunder the bars of iron," referring to the gates of the city of Babylon, and an event still in the distant future. Babylon in that day could be called the "Fort Knox" of civilization, yet we read, "I will give thee the treasures of darkness, and hidden riches of secret places, that thou mayest know that I, the LORD, which call thee by thy name, am the God of Israel. For Jacob my servant's sake, and Israel mine elect, I have even called thee by thy name: I have surnamed thee, though thou hast not known me."

There are some who say that Cyrus was a believer in the Lord. Though he was used by God to give the decree that allowed the people to return to Jerusalem, that does not mean that he exclusively worshiped the Lord, for he also did obeisance to many other gods. The Scripture says, "Though thou hast not known me." How could Cyrus have known the Lord when he hadn't been born yet? But even during his lifetime, he still would not recognize the Lord as his God. Anyone who reads these prophecies and knows of their fulfillment in history can only say, "Wow!"

Here we have this incredible picture of Cyrus being foretold in prophecy. "I am the LORD, and there is none else, there is no God beside me: I girded thee," I gave you strength, "though thou hast not known me: that they may know from the rising of the sun, and from the west, that there is none beside me. I am the LORD, and there is none else. I form the light, and create darkness: I make peace, and create evil: I the LORD do all these things. Drop down, ye heavens, from above, and let the skies pour down righteousness: let the earth open, and let them bring forth salvation, and let righteousness spring up together; I the LORD have created it."

Turn now to Isaiah 13, where there are even more staggering prophecies. Remember that Cyrus was of the Medo-Persian Empire, and that he conquered Nebuchadnezzar's Babylon. Isaiah 13 begins, "The burden of Babylon, which Isaiah the son of Amoz did see." The first sixteen verses refer to a future judgment. The passage we are concerned with begins in verse 17: "Behold, I will stir up the Medes against them, which shall not regard silver; and as for gold, they shall not delight in it." And here is a picture of what will happen: "Their bows also shall dash the young men to pieces; and they shall have no pity on the fruit of the womb; their eye shall not spare children. And Babylon, the glory of kingdoms, the beauty of the Chaldees' excellency, shall be as when God overthrew Sodom and Gomorrah."

God has woven in some very interesting things. Again in Isaiah 14, there are prophecies concerning the king of Babylon, but again God says in essence, "I will use the Babylonians to accomplish My purpose for the seventy years. And when the seventy years are accomplished, I will take vengeance on the ones who carried away My people, punishing the king of Babylon, and Cyrus will be the vessel to do it." God says the same thing through the prophets Jeremiah and Ezekiel.

It is more amazing when you consider what Cyrus had to overcome to get into Babylon. Remember that Isaiah had not only said where Cyrus would come from, but also that he would be God's vessel, His shepherd to accomplish His good pleasure. There are passages in *The Histories* of Herodotus that describe how Babylon was conquered, and if his account is correct, Cyrus and his army first had to penetrate a city that was called impenetrable. The city walls were perhaps 300 feet tall, and they were said to be so wide that two chariots could pass each other on the walls. There was a moat surrounding the city that was fed by the Euphrates River. And the people on the inside were thoroughly prepared for any siege; varying accounts say they had one to five years' supply of food on hand.

So Cyrus and his army dug a canal to divert the Euphrates River. Herodotus said that when the men crossed over the river, it was no higher than mid-thigh. This may explain passages in Isaiah that refer to Babylon's "marshlands." Cyrus and his army crossed over with all of their horses and equipment, and they penetrated the city's defenses and took the city in one night. In the account in the book of Daniel, there was a grand party going on and everyone had had much to drink, when suddenly the enemy came upon them. Cyrus took the city and overthrew the kingdom; and we see that God carried out His purpose through Cyrus, a heathen king.

If God could precisely maneuver this man who did not even recognize Him, could stay in complete control and cause him to issue the decree to let the people go back after the seventy years were accomplished, can He not be in control of our lives? If you really believe God's word, if God has that much control over the details, how much more does He have control of your life? Now if you are like me, you have probably said many times, "God did it for those people in the Bible, but He certainly cannot be in control of my mess!" But He is in control.

Isaiah 45:15 says, "Verily thou art a God that hidest thyself." Have you ever felt that way? I want you to imagine the people who were in Babylon for seventy years, not those who were born in Babylon, but those who remembered the former glory of the temple in Jerusalem. They might have been saying, "Where are You, God? You are a God that hides Yourself!" When we look at history, we can say with assurance that if God can do all of this, then He can certainly be in control of our lives. These passages in Isaiah resonate with the sovereignty of God. And as we read on in Isaiah 45 and see the precision of prophecy and its fulfillment, we can do nothing other than declare, "The Lord is the Lord of history!"

God's control of history becomes even more astonishing as we study the prophecies concerning Cyrus given in the books of Jeremiah, Ezekiel and Daniel. I am sure that there were some who read these passages and argued with God, saying, "There is no way that God could use someone unclean, someone who was unprepared," in their view, "and someone who didn't belong to His people to accomplish His purpose."

Isaiah 45:9 says, "Woe unto him that striveth with his Maker!" The Hebrew word translated "Maker" is a form of the word translated "potter" in Jeremiah 18. Genesis 2 says, "the LORD God *formed* man of the dust of the ground," using a form of the same word. "Woe unto him that striveth with his Maker! Let the potsherd strive with the potsherds of the earth. Shall the clay say to him that fashioneth it, What makest thou? or thy work, He hath no hands?" Literally, it says, "your work has no handles," that is, there is nothing to grab on to. "Woe unto him that saith unto his father, What begettest thou? or to the woman, What hast thou brought forth?" The passage gives a picture of someone who is quibbling with the Potter or the Parent.

God frequently uses an illustration from the potter's house to make an analogy to His relationship with His people. God also sent Jeremiah to the potter's house and His lament was, "Can God not do with Israel what a potter does with the clay? Is God not able to reshape and reform?" The message is the same here in Isaiah, in a prophecy given to a people who were about to be carried away into captivity: is God not able to do with His people what He chooses? In the New Testament, Paul also uses the analogy of the clay and the potter, quoting from Isaiah. Remember, Paul was writing to the Gentiles in the book of Romans, in a particular passage regarding Israel. The lesson is that God is in control of history. And His sovereignty over history is clearly shown in the fulfillment of the prophecies concerning Cyrus.

We looked at the passage in Isaiah about striving with one's Maker, striving with God. That is the concept of *The Great Divorce;* the choice is heaven or hell. Some people may think that they don't really have a choice in the matter. If God has opened your ears to hear, you have a choice either to hear or not to hear.

It is staggering to think that God would speak with precision of a future time and a king who would ultimately rise up to conquer a nation and then be conquered himself, who would liberate a people and fulfill the seventy years of captivity. Now if God, our Maker who is in control of everything, can do all of that, my question today is this: are we striving with God and talking back to Him about even the smallest details in our life? The lesson concerning Cyrus in history, in prophecy and for us today, is also a warning against rejecting God's way.

We know God's way with man; we know that He gave His word, and that He is not a man to lie. He declared, "This is My way, walk ye in it." In the New Testament, the message is the same. We can choose whether or not we will follow God. I do not believe that everything is wound up like a clock and that we have no say in the matter, because God gave us free will. God gave us the ability to decide whether or not we will desire Him, and whether or not we will follow His word and His way.

I suppose that if we were living before these events unfolded, we might have a discussion as to whether or not God could use or would use a heathen king, but our opinion would not matter, because that is exactly what God did. God had given His word and said, "This is how I am going to accomplish My purpose." I often have to remind myself that this is the way God is accomplishing His purpose through us. The "container" does not have to appear religious. The container just has to be willing. We are vessels that are supposed to desire to know God's way and His word.

Someone once said to me, "I am trying to follow after God and be committed to the best of my ability. What should I do?" And I thought to myself, "the best of my ability" will not accomplish anything for God. You must abide in His word and listen to what His word is saying to you today. And you must never get to the place where you think you have heard enough of God's word and you no longer need it.

That is the lesson of the potter's house. God is going to accomplish what He designed you to do. He is not going to fight you for it, but if you are yielded and surrendered and listening to His word, He will accomplish His purposes with you.

The people who were in captivity were probably saying, "God cannot be in all of this." They didn't know the word like we know the word, even though the prophet came to warn them. They didn't know what we know today. So then that brings me to the question of rebellion. How many people hear the word of God and still decide that they don't have to yield to it?

There are far too many people on the face of this planet who think they are following after God's way and His word, but when you talk to them, you discover that they really know nothing about God's way and His word. We know about God's way because the history reveals it. To know about God's word, you must abide in the word. That is the message of John 15.

There are some people who will at least say, "God is going to accomplish His purpose," but they have not spent any time in the word. And even that becomes a form of rebellion. People who are out in the world and do not know the Lord might plead ignorance for a time. But it is different for someone who has come to know what God has clearly laid out in His word. Sometimes we have to "put the brakes on," and stop and ask ourselves, "Am I fighting God? Am I striving against His purposes? Am I asking *why?*" Now it is not inherently evil to ask *why*, but it becomes evil when it becomes rebellion and you say, "I know what God's word says, but I will not respond. I refuse." And if people persist in that rebellion, after a time God turns them over; He turns them away. God is not saying, "I want everybody. The whole world will be saved." There was a preacher who used to say, "Even the devil will be saved." I do not believe that for a moment, especially when I study the book of Revelation.

The rebellious nature is part of man's estate; it is written into the blueprint of mankind. Our natural man constantly says, "God cannot." I want you to look at these prophecies about Cyrus and make an application to yourself: ask yourself if God could possibly use you to accomplish His purpose for you to grow in God's grace and grow in His word. At some point you will recognize that God is doing something in your life. I have heard people say, "What could *I* possibly do?" You might be surprised. God has a great plan, if you would just shut up and quit complaining. You might say, "Well, it does not look like it right now." It may not look like it, but what you are going through is just the normal manifestation of striving with God.

We may never in our lifetimes get to the point where we say, without any complaints, "Okay, God, I am surrendering to this. I am going to yield and You are going to work it out." If we are honest, we will acknowledge that we still complain about what God is doing because we don't think that He is doing anything. The manifestation of striving with God is innate to the natural man or woman, which is why we are told in the New Testament in Galatians to walk in the Spirit, to come under the control of the Spirit.

Isaiah 45 speaks to me about God's sovereignty, specifically His sovereignty in accomplishing what He set out to do. It may be an old-timey message, but we need to hear it again. Never think that you have arrived at the point where you don't need to hear something over and over again. God says in verse 12, "I have made the earth, and created man upon it: I, even my hands, have stretched out the heavens, and all their host have I commanded." God is saying, "I have done all of this." It is almost as though God were saying to us, "Do you really believe that I would do all of these things and then leave you alone and not be in control of your life too?" God wants you to see Him as the Maker, the Potter, and the Parent.

God used Cyrus to crush the Babylonian Empire and to liberate the captives. The people were then allowed to return to Jerusalem to rebuild the temple and repopulate the city. That reestablished worship in preparation for the coming of Christ. Can you not see God's hand in all of that?

The New Testament says that God enters in to all things to work His good. So I ask you, can God fix the problems in the church today? The answer is yes. Many times it seems we are at a standstill and that God is not doing anything. Striving against God's purpose and His plan will not help you, but it does reveal something about you spiritually, which is your refusal to acknowledge God's sovereignty in all things.

God is in control. We know from the book of Nehemiah that the walls were rebuilt. The book of the law was brought out, Ezra read the law and all the people wept. It was a great revival. But it did not take very long after that great revival for the people to revert to their old ways. The prophet Malachi closes the Old Testament with an indictment against God's people, who had essentially backslidden and fallen into another terrible state.

So we must not deceive ourselves and simply say, "Okay, God, I am going to cooperate now, and I am not going to strive against You anymore," because there will be a perpetual battle during your lifetime. Your whole Christian life will consist of ebbs and flows; you will be committed and love the Lord and abide in His word, and then you will fall back a little. You will take ten steps forward and five steps back. And depending on where you are in life, you may need to adjust the number of steps to make this description apply to you. For some people it is so many steps forward and twice as many back.

Again I ask you, if God is in control of history and can precisely fulfill all the details given in prophecy, can He not be in control of your life today? As we continue reading history, we learn that Cyrus' kingdom will come to an end with the rise of Alexander the Great. In fact, the extent of the territory conquered by Cyrus essentially set the stage for Alexander's domain. And after Alexander's death, his domain will be split up among his four generals. This will bring us up to the rise of the Roman Empire and the time of Christ, and all of these events were clearly foretold in God's book. That is one of the reasons why I love the Scriptures so much. Many people wonder, "How could Alexander the Great possibly have conquered so much territory?" The stage was being set for the time of Christ and for the events that will take place in the last days.

That is why it is important to look at the genealogies recorded in Scripture, to see God's control in bringing forth the promised Seed. God does not make mistakes when He carries out His word, and He does not make mistakes in our lives, either. He said, "I will do this thing." Jeremiah said He will accomplish His word. Some of you are starting to recognize God's sovereignty and His control. You are still striving with God, but not as much as you used to.

Isaiah 45 describes the clay talking back to the potter, which is something that we all have done. We have all said, "God, what are You doing?" We translated the latter part of verse 9, "He hath no handles." The clay was saying to God, "Your work has no handles; there is nothing to grab on to." And if we use the imagery of a potter's house where we are the clay and the potter's wheel represents our circumstances, sometimes it seems like there is nothing to hold on to, but we know that is a lie. You know that when things are out of control, you must grab on to God's word. You must turn to God's word and talk to God and say, "This is my handle." There are faith handles in God's book; they are places you can reach into when everything around you is spinning out of control. There was a time when I didn't want His hands on me; I just wanted to do my own thing. But God said, "Well, we will see about that." I know that is true for many of you also.

Now you may be saying to God, "What are You doing with me?" Imagine the clay saying to the Potter, "Your work has no handles!" Or imagine children talking back to their parents, as Isaiah said, "Woe unto him that saith unto his father, What begettest thou? or to the woman, What hast thou brought forth? Thus saith the LORD, the Holy One of Israel, and his Maker, Ask me of things to come concerning my sons, and concerning the work of my hands command ye me."

God does have a plan. That is why I have centered my ministry on the word of God. I only want people to come to know God's word and for their faith to increase. The moment we start conforming to the world's idea of what the church should be, we have succumbed to the temptation to please people in the ways of the flesh, as opposed to growing in the Spirit. How do you grow in the Spirit? Faith comes by hearing God's word. Listen to a pastor whose focus is on the word of God, and study in order to grow in your understanding of God's way, God's word, God's will and God's work in your life.

There are few churches remaining in this country that do not engage in worldly methods of attracting people to come and listen.

There are few churches that do not use worldly methods to bring in money. It is rare to find a church that simply declares God's word, which is the only thing that will bring forth faith; and faith is the only way to make it in to the kingdom.

You can keep striving with God and saying, "I will not," and at some point that spirit of rebellion may cause God to say, "I have had enough." You can know that Christ died for you, and that the thirty pieces of silver for which Judas betrayed the Lord were used to purchase a potter's field, in type to teach the lesson that the price of our Lord's death was paid to purchase the whole field and buy up all the rejected, broken vessels. The Bible says that Christ paid the price to buy up the whole field, so that He might get the treasure in the field. You can know that you are children of a heavenly God, yet you can continue to say, "But I still want to act like a child of the world, and I will do what I want to do the way I want to do it." And that is what the Bible defines as sin.

You can read these passages concerning Cyrus and say that if God used a heathen king to carry out His plan, how much more will He use you and me to carry out His plan? How much more is He in control of the details? When you superimpose your life onto the pages of the Bible, you will recognize that God is still doing the same thing now that He did back then. Now there are no kingdoms to conquer except the kingdom of darkness. In the minds of some, that kingdom does not even exist. But to those who know that it does, the Bible speaks much about the necessity of obedience. We read in 1 Samuel 15:22–23 that obedience is better than sacrifice; and rebellion is as the sin of witchcraft.

There are many people who say that this way is too difficult. They say, "But I only want to go to church to be comforted." To those I would say, "Then you do not want God as your Maker. You do not want God to have His hands on you like the Potter. You do not really want God's word, His will, His way or His work in your life. You only want what you want." God calls that sin, and at some point He will say, "Okay, have what you want," and He will be done with you.

I am asking people today, those who are not completely seared over, those who have not ultimately said, "No, I cannot," to consider their ways and to consider God's ways. Those in Isaiah's day said, "Truly thou art a God who hidest thyself," but God may be in the smallest voice, like that still small voice that came to the prophet Elijah. God may be in everything around you, but if you are not paying attention, you will be like Jacob, waking up one day and saying, "Truly the LORD was in this place, and I knew it not."

You do not come to church because the Lord is physically present in the building. The church is a people who belong to the Lord. You should come to church to hear. You should come to church to grow. You should come to church to get connected to the rest of the body. And when it comes down to making a hard choice, you come to a point where you say, "I would rather be someone whom God is still pressing into an uncomfortable situation." Look at how God has placed you in the body of Christ. Maybe He has taken everything away from you. Maybe He has given you things that you did not think you should have or things that you did not want. It does not matter. In the big picture, God is saying, "I am God. I am the Lord of creation. I created man, I created Cyrus, and I created you. Now, if you will quit fighting with Me, I will accomplish My purpose." It is a wonderfully good purpose, but it takes a mindset that says, "This is uncomfortable, but I am going to yield."

In the New Testament, Romans 6 talks about yielding your members. Many people treat that passage as just something to consider. It is not just something to consider, it is a way of life. "To whom ye yield yourselves servants to obey," that is whom you will serve. Essentially, it means that if you decide to yield yourself to yourself, you will serve yourself. But when you yield yourself to God, you become a tool of the righteousness of God.

So I return to C. S. Lewis and say there are really only two types of people in the end: those who say, "Lord, Thy will be done," and those to whom God will say, "*Your* will be done." It is a tough thing to open your mouth and say, "Lord, Thy will be done," because you know what will happen. It means that God may take you just like He took the apostle Paul and lead you down a path. For the apostle Paul, it was a pathway unto death. Maybe it will mean that many people you were leaning on and depending on will flee from you. They may leave you alone and leave you feeling like you are friendless and hopeless, and that your circumstances are impossible to resolve. Maybe uttering the words "Lord, Thy will be done on earth in me" means I will lose everything that I have been holding on to. Maybe it means I will gain some things that I didn't think I should have or that I could have.

There were many living in Cyrus' day whose names are not chronicled in God's book. They were the ones who decided that they ought not to return to rebuild. Those are the ones who essentially said, "My will, my way. I will remain here in Babylon." But those who answered the call from this heathen king to go back and prepare the way for the Lord were the ones who said, "Lord, Thy will be done," although they may not have even known it at the time.

You do have a choice about something. You can keep striving against God and say, "My way," or you can say, "Lord, Your way: shape me and mold me. If You can control history and accomplish Your purpose with Cyrus, a heathen king, You can certainly do it with me, in me and through me in my life."

Chapter 9

THE UNDERSTANDING THAT COMES FROM GOD

If you have ever attended the reading of a last will and testament, you were probably listening very carefully as someone, usually a lawyer, read the exact contents of the will. You might not remember the lawyer's tone, whether he sounded gloomy or happy, but you remember the reading, because you were named as part of a group of people or family members who were included in the will. You will remember if something was bequeathed to you by virtue of that will. It does not matter whether the lawyer sounded good or was entertaining; what matters is that the lawyer presented the facts so you could know what you inherited. Now hearing the word of God should be just like that: you should be concerned with the contents of what has been bequeathed to you, not with the sound of the preacher's voice or how entertaining or dull the sermon was. The effectiveness of the gospel message is not based on someone's presentation skills or their lack thereof; rather it is based on the content presented. You should be concerned with the content of this last will and testament left to us by God the Father, and you should want to hear about what He has left to those whom He calls His children.

We are in Nehemiah 8 today. The book of Nehemiah can generally be divided into two parts. The first six chapters are about the reconstruction of the walls of Jerusalem, and the last seven chapters are about the restoration and reinstruction of God's people. We read from the beginning of Nehemiah 8, "And all the people gathered themselves together as one man into the street that was before the water gate." The people who had gathered there were the descendants of those who originally returned under Zerubbabel, who are listed in Nehemiah 7, and may have also included those who returned with Ezra.

If we pay close attention, we will see that this gathering occurred on the first day of the seventh month, and that is really quite important. The wall had only recently been completed, as recorded in Nehemiah 6:15, which says, "So the wall was finished in the twenty-fifth day of the month Elul, in fifty-two days." Elul is the sixth month, and the wall was completed towards the end of the month. The events recorded in Nehemiah 8 took place on the first day of the seventh month. That means only four or five days had passed between the events recorded in Nehemiah 6 and the gathering recorded in Nehemiah 8. It seems like it should be a longer period of time, but it was only a few days. So we can imagine that when the people all came out and gathered together, there was still a lot of excitement in the air after the completion of the wall, but there was something else going on as well.

We know from Leviticus 23:24 that the first day of the seventh month was the Feast of the Trumpets. As you continue on in the seventh month you will find a series of feast days. The tenth day was the Day of Atonement, Yom Kippur, and then the fifteenth day of that month was the Feast of Booths, or Tabernacles, which is what these people would celebrate here in Nehemiah 8.

What is unusual is that the people do not appear to be following the sequence of feast days as they were given in the book of Leviticus. I do not think that we can blame them for this, for they had been away for over seventy years and some of them had never celebrated any feast days before or even heard the word of God. I believe that this is recorded for us intentionally and is an example of what I call progressive revelation. Sometimes we start out thinking that we are doing a certain thing the right way, and then we realize that we missed a couple of details here and there, and that is how we grow in God's word. These people were in many ways like us.

"All the people gathered themselves together as one man into the street that was before the water gate; and they spake unto Ezra the scribe to bring the book of the law of Moses, which the LORD had commanded to Israel." It is no accident that they gathered together "as one man" demanding, "Bring the book," and they were gathered in front of the water gate. In the Bible, water usually represents the word or the Spirit.

The people were ready, they were receptive, and they were reverent. These were the people who had returned and rebuilt, and they were standing together saying, "Bring us the book, Ezra. Read on, for we want to hear!" So "Ezra the priest brought the law before the congregation both of men and women, and all that could hear with understanding, upon the first day of the seventh month." There is the date that proves that this happened just a few days after they finished the wall. "And he read therein before the street that was before the water gate from the morning until midday." From sunup to midday he read, for about six hours. Do you know of any congregation today that would listen to a preacher preach or read from the Bible for six hours? Today if you go longer than thirty minutes you will hear people start to grumble and say, "Wow, this is getting long. When is this going to be over?" I am sure that some people will be asking that question in eternity, but it really depends on where you will be when you ask that question. That is why I say we can learn much from this passage: perhaps it will highlight our lack, or it will highlight the gift we have been given.

For six hours Ezra read "before the men and the women, and those that could understand; and the ears of all the people were attentive unto the book of the law. And Ezra the scribe stood upon a pulpit of wood, which they had made for the purpose; and beside him stood Mattithiah, and Shema, and Anaiah, and Urijah, and Hilkiah, and Maaseiah, on his right hand; and on his left hand, Pedaiah, and Mishael, and Malchiah, and Hashum, and Hashbadana, Zechariah, and Meshullam. And Ezra opened the book in the sight of all the people; (for he was above all the people;) and when he opened it, all the people stood up."

Something very profound was happening here. Many of these people had never heard the word of God before, but in hearing they were attentive, they were reverent, they were ready and they were receptive. They were listening and taking it in. So Ezra began to read, and "all the people stood up: and Ezra blessed the LORD, the great God. And all the people answered, Amen, Amen, with lifting up their hands: and they bowed their heads, and worshipped the LORD with their faces to the ground. Also Jeshua, and Bani, and Sherebiah, Jamin, Akkub, Shabbethai, Hodijah, Maaseiah, Kelita, Azariah, Jozabad, Hanan, Pelaiah, and the Levites, caused the people to understand the law: and the people stood in their place. So they read in the book in the law of God distinctly, and gave the sense, and caused them to understand the reading. And Nehemiah, which is the Tirshatha," or governor, "and Ezra the priest the scribe, and the Levites that taught the people, said unto all the people, This day is holy unto the LORD your God; mourn not, nor weep. For all the people wept, when they heard the words of the law."

When we study the law as Christians, it means something different to us, because the law was fulfilled in Christ. But it is still needful for us to see all the things that were fulfilled; it is needful for us to understand what the law represents. Paul said that the law is not a bad thing, but the only problem is that no man can keep it. No one can attain and keep the level of perfection that is required by the law; only Christ could fulfill it.

These people were presented with the word of God, and we see that a concept is repeated again and again in these verses. We read first in verse 2, "hear with *understanding,*" and in verse 3, "that could *understand,*" and in verse 7, "caused the people *to understand,*" and again in verse 8, "caused them *to understand* the reading." In verse 9, it says, "And the Levites that *taught* the people." The word translated "taught" is another form of this same Hebrew word that is translated "to understand." The people not only heard, they heard with understanding.

In the English language, we have a number of words with related meanings like understand, comprehend, know and perceive. In the Hebrew language, there are a few words that are used somewhat ambiguously, because of the nature of Hebrew. But this specific Hebrew word translated "understand" in Nehemiah 8 has special connotations that we need to grasp when we discuss our own ability to understand.

We read in verses 10 through 12, "Then he said unto them, Go your way, eat the fat, and drink the sweet, and send portions unto them for whom nothing is prepared: for this day is holy unto our Lord: neither be ye sorry; for the joy of the LORD is your strength. So the Levites stilled all the people, saying, Hold your peace, for the day is holy; neither be ye grieved. And all the people went their way to eat, and to drink, and to send portions, and to make great mirth, because they had understood. . . ." There is that same word again, "because they had *understood* the words that were declared unto them."

There is a concept being laid out here that is abundantly clear in its application to the church. The people were gathered as one man in the street. This is reminiscent of the Day of Pentecost in the book of Acts, when the people were gathered with one accord in one place, and the Spirit was poured out. Then the apostle Peter preached the sermon and those who could hear, the King James Version says, were "pricked in their heart" and they asked what they should do at the hearing of those words.

The word of God should be penetrating. Hebrews 4 talks about the word of God being alive and able to penetrate into and divide a whole person's being. The Bible says that the same words bring life to some and death to others. My prayer is that this study will enable us to be a little bit more grateful for the capacity to receive and understand. The people in Nehemiah's day had a reaction to the word. Remember they were hearing the law; they were not hearing about grace; they were not hearing about Jesus Christ. They heard the law that says, "Thou shalt, and thou shalt not," and they wept.

This is what is lacking in the body of Christ in general. People love to talk about how great a certain minister is and what he or she does or does not do. That should not be the focus. You need to listen to someone who will open up God's word. But it is God who must first open your ears and eyes to give you the understanding. And that understanding normally doesn't happen all at once. I have encountered many people who listen to Bible teaching and say, "I just don't understand." I tell them to keep listening. At some point a light is going to turn on, and they will say, "Oh my God, why didn't I see that sooner? I get it now!" Some evangelists give you the impression that all you have to do is come to an altar and at that moment, everything will change and will make sense to you. That is not how it happens. Stepping down to an altar may be a turning point for some people, a turning of the mind or the emotions, but that does not mean all the lights will turn on automatically. Not everything will necessarily make sense to you right away when you become a Christian; it takes time. But the first thing that has to happen is that God must turn the soil of the soul to make it ready to receive the seed, the word of God. And in the parable of the sower in the New Testament, only one of the four kinds of soil is able to actually receive the seed and bring forth fruit.

The people were "gathered together as one man." Ephesians 4 talks about one Spirit, one Lord, one faith, one baptism, and one God and Father of all. God was preparing these people. Remember that not everybody responded to the call to return to Jerusalem. Cyrus issued the decree, but only a small percentage of people returned to Jerusalem. Why didn't everybody go? Because not everybody had the capacity. They may have all had the capacity to uproot themselves and travel for four months across the desert, but not everybody had the capacity given by God to respond. This is not a lesson in election and predestination. Rather, I am telling you how God works His way with people. We know that "whosoever will" may come, and anybody could have returned, but in fact very few did. Less than 50,000 people out of about 650,000 in captivity returned. I would make an analogy to church attendance in our day. There are some people who would drive for an hour or more to hear solid Bible teaching, but that means God must have opened their hearts to enable them to receive the word. There are others who would say, "That is just too far to drive."

In John 6, Jesus said that no one can come to the Father except they be drawn. I have heard people say, "I chose to follow the Lord." But Jesus said to His disciples, "You have not chosen Me; I have chosen you." The same principle applies to us. You may think that you chose God, but God chose you. That is the lesson of Ephesians 1:4: God chose you, and literally it says that He chose you *for Himself.* Imagine what a radical concept that is: God actually called you out of a whole body of people whom He did not call. Someone might object and say, "That's not fair!" But that is what God's word says, and God doesn't have to be "fair." God is God, He is sovereign. He is the Boss and He says how it is going to be. There are many in this current generation who are under the illusion that they can stand before God with their sass and their back talk. They do not have any respect for God or the things of God. They have no fear of God, and therefore they can have no respect for anyone else around them.

These people were gathered as one, and they were gathered for a purpose. They didn't gather for a potluck dinner or to hear a speech about how they could have a wonderful day. They gathered for one purpose, which was to hear the word of God. The disciples said to Jesus in John 6, "Lord, to whom will we go? Thou hast the words of life eternal." At least they knew that.

Too many people waste their time gathering to listen to self-help messages that are devoid of chapter and verse. They think they are going to church, but they are not presented with any opportunity for learning God's will by hearing God's word opened up. So of course they have no light, because Jesus said that you cannot know God apart from getting into this word. And if you are not in this word, you will not know about God. The word of God will not be given to you in a special revelation. There have been certain religious leaders who claimed that they received a special revelation, but we know that the last revelation given to us came in a tent of human flesh, shed His blood and died on a cross. John 3:16 tells us this is the method that God used and there isn't going to be another revelation. That is it. If you want to know about your life, death, life eternal and all things in-between, then you must read about God and His Son Jesus Christ. And you become a habitation of God by faith, with the Spirit living in you.

These people in Nehemiah 8 are a beautiful depiction in the Old Testament of what God is still doing today. The people were willing; they were not coerced. They said, "Bring the book." That suggests to me that they were hungry to know what saith the Scriptures. Not many people today want to hear what the Scriptures say. Peter said we are to desire the sincere milk of the word, and the book of Hebrews says we need to move from milk to meat. The meat of the word enables a person who is being brought to maturity to be able to discern between good and evil.

So far we have looked at these people, how long they stayed to listen, their submissiveness, their ability to be taught and their ability to respond. Now let's look at the person in the pulpit. We know from Ezra 7 that Ezra had a great lineage that could be traced back to Aaron the high priest. And we know that he prepared his heart before the Lord to go and teach the statutes, to instruct the people in the law in Israel, and he did just that. We know about his journey to Jerusalem from Ezra 7 and 8. Then suddenly he appears here in the book of Nehemiah to read the law, and the people responded.

From a New Testament perspective, we read in Ephesians 4 about how God gave gifts to the church. The apostle Paul wrote that God "gave some, apostles; and some, prophets; and some, evangelists; and some, pastoring-teachers; for the perfecting of the saints," for a specific purpose. But all of these gift ministries are tied to the word of God; they have no function apart from the word of God. They are not tied to entertainment nor to fun social activities. The purpose of the pulpit is to bring forth the word of God, to open it up and make it clear. John said that no man has seen God, but

Christ has *declared* Him, and John used a Greek word from which we get our English word *exegesis*. The purpose of these gift ministries is to help the people understand. But before someone can understand, something has to happen first. To help us understand why this concept is so important, I want us to pause and focus on the Hebrew word translated "understand" in Nehemiah 8. The Hebrew word sounds like our English word *been* with a long *e* sound. It is *Strong's* number 995.* We find this word or one of its related forms in Nehemiah 8 in verses 2, 3, 7, 8, 9 and 12.

There are several Hebrew words for the concept of understanding. One of the most common Hebrew words is *yada*, which means "to know." It is *Strong's* number 3045. While it sounds similar to a Hebrew word meaning "to praise," it is a different word, having a different final consonant. There is another word, *shama*, which means "to hear." It is *Strong's* number 8085. It is used in the Hebrew prayer known as the Shema, which begins, "Hear, O Israel." There are other words that express a similar concept such as *kul*, *anah* and *sakhal*, which means "to consider." The Hebrew language has a relatively small vocabulary and can be ambiguous in its translation. But this one Hebrew word, *been*, is used six times in Nehemiah 8.

Another important note is that this word occurs in what is called the "Hiphil stem." The Hiphil stem is translated in this passage as *causative*, that is, the form of the word indicates that someone is *causing* someone else to do something. The King James Version translators therefore translated these verses very accurately when it says they "*caused* them to understand the reading."

Why is this important? This word *been* does not mean "to understand" in the ordinary sense, like when someone says, "Do you understand what I am saying?" In the Old Testament, understanding, spiritual insight, is not a faculty native to man as such; it is a gift of God. In the Psalter, especially in Psalm 119, one prays for understanding, and again the word used is *been*. From the Hebrew perspective, the organ of insight is usually the heart. And it is Yahweh's work to give comprehension pertaining to the things of God.

*A more detailed study of this Hebrew word בִּין, translated "understanding," and a survey of its usage in the Bible, is found in Appendix III.

Let's look at how this word *been* is used in another passage. In Isaiah 6, Isaiah saw the Lord in a vision, and the Lord actually spoke to him. We read starting from verse 8, "I heard the voice of the Lord, saying, Whom shall I send, and who will go for us? Then said I, Here am I; send me. And he said, Go, and tell this people, Hear," the word is *shemu*, "Hear ye indeed, but understand not." Again the word for understand is *been*. "See ye indeed, but perceive not." The word for "perceive" is *yada*. "Make the heart of this people fat, and make their ears heavy, and shut their eyes; lest they see with their eyes, and hear with their ears, and understand," again, the word is *been*, "with their heart, and convert, and be healed." Now you might ask, "What kind of message is that?" It is a message to a people who were so rebellious that they would not hear or understand. They would not see with their eyes and their ears would be sealed.

Now Jesus lifts this passage from Isaiah into the New Testament to explain why He spoke in parables. In the parable of the sower in Matthew 13, Jesus speaks about the soil and the seed, and how some seed falls on good ground, bringing forth fruit, and other seed does not. But He concludes with, "Who hath ears to hear, let him hear." You might assume that everybody who has ears can hear. But if you keep reading, Jesus gives the reason why He taught using parables. In verse 11, "He answered and said unto them, Because it is given unto you to know the mysteries of the kingdom of heaven, but to them it is not given. For whosoever hath, to him shall be given, and he shall have more abundance: but whosoever hath not, from him shall be taken away even that he hath. Therefore speak I to them in parables: because they seeing see not; and hearing they hear not, neither do they understand."

Now let's make some connections between these New Testament illustrations and our text in Nehemiah 8. The people were gathered together as one man to listen to Ezra read the law. They said, "Bring the book, we want to hear," and it was given to them to understand. That is why they could react to the word and weep, and at least for a time they desired to keep that word of God. They desired to know more. But if you read on in the book, you will see that their state of mind did not last very long; and by Nehemiah 13, many of the people will have fallen away again.

In the Septuagint Greek translation of the Hebrew Bible, the word *been* is translated by a form of the Greek word *sunesis*. The word *sunesis* primarily means "to bring together" or "union." In the "profane" Greek, the word might be used to describe the union of two bodies of water. When Jesus said, "neither do they understand," He was using a form of this same Greek word, *sunesis*. And He goes on to quote from Isaiah, saying, "And in them is fulfilled the prophecy of Esaias, which saith, By hearing ye shall hear, and shall not understand. . . ." Again He uses a form of the same word, *sunesis*. "And seeing ye shall see, and shall not perceive: for this people's heart is waxed gross, and their ears are dull of hearing, and their eyes they have closed; lest at any time they should see with their eyes, and hear with their ears, and should understand with their heart," again it is a form of *sunesis*, or *been*, "and should be converted, and I should heal them. But blessed are your eyes, for they see: and your ears, for they hear. For verily I say unto you, That many prophets and righteous men have desired to see those things which ye see, and have not seen them; and to hear those things which ye hear, and have not heard them."

This Hebrew word *been* ties together everything I am saying, because it ties in to Nehemiah, it ties in to Christ's day and it ties in to today. God is saying that there are some people who cannot hear. Have you ever heard someone say, "Why do you bother listening to a church service? Who can sit through such a thing?" The reason why they say such things is that they don't have ears to hear.

Speaking of those who have ears to hear, the book of Revelation says, "Let him hear what the Spirit says to the churches." Jesus goes on to elaborate on the parable of the sower in Matthew 13, saying, "Hear ye therefore the parable of the sower. When any one heareth the word of the kingdom, and understandeth it not," *sunesis*, the same Greek word, "then cometh the wicked one, and catcheth away that which was sown in his heart." How many people come through the door of the church, hear a message and yet do not understand it? And then the devil comes, the wicked one, who catches away what "was sown in his heart." The little bit that was sown is gone. Jesus said, "This is he which received seed by the way side. But he that received the seed into stony places, the same is he that heareth the word, and anon with joy receiveth it; yet hath he not root in himself, but dureth for a while: for when tribulation or persecution ariseth because of the word, by and by he is offended." Note that this persecution and trouble come, not because you are you or because I am me, but *because of the word* and for the word's sake.

"He also that received seed among the thorns is he that heareth the word; and the care of this world, and the deceitfulness of riches, choke the word, and he becometh unfruitful. But he that received seed into the good ground is he that heareth the word, and understandeth it," *sunesis*, or *been*, "which also beareth fruit, and bringeth forth" to some varying degree. These are the fruit-bearing ones.

In Nehemiah 8, God placed a response mechanism into the hearts of those who gathered. It is reminiscent of Ecclesiastes 3:11, which says that God has placed eternity in their hearts. God placed in their hearts the ability to receive and a hunger for the word. They heard the law; they did not hear the gospel message of grace. They did not get to hear all the things we hear, and yet they wept. God also brought a teacher and preachers. It says that there were thirteen men with Ezra. Ezra may have read and expounded, but those thirteen men helped to expand the meaning of the word, to open it up and do what we call scriptural exegesis, to bring it to life, so the people were pricked in their hearts and they wept.

God does not give every person the capacity to hear. Out of Christ's mouth, quoting from Isaiah, He very plainly says that not everybody can hear. He says that whoever comes to Him, He will in no wise cast out. But it is not given for everyone to hear and to understand. You might say, "Well, that is elitist." No, that is what Scripture says.

I cannot speak for you, but I speak for myself first and I speak personally. Sometimes I am almost overcome with wonder to think that God gave me the ability to hear, to respond, to desire, and to have a hunger and a thirst for His word. When we consider the miracle that God should give us this capacity to understand through His Spirit, it should result in a different attitude towards God, God's word and the things of God. Wonder of wonders, that God would condescend to pull me from the gutter of life into His kingdom, wash me in His blood, give me the desire, the hunger and the ability to hear, and then place me where I could share this very same love that He has placed in me with others! How could I treat the word of God and His calling on my life as something to put on the back burner? How could I become complacent like it is no big deal?

This knowledge should create a wave of enthusiasm in someone's heart. There is a difference between a response like, "Oh well, okay. I hear you," and a response that says, "You are right! I hear what you are saying!" Even though you may have been sitting in a church for more than thirty years, you will know the difference by the end of this message. You may start to think about all of the people who may not have received the same gift that you have received. It is a gift to have the desire and ability to hear and be taught by someone who loves God's word and respects and honors Him enough to give an *exegesis* every week for one purpose and one purpose alone. And that purpose is to grow the body to a stronger faith, so that God's presence is a greater reality in your life.

Let's not talk about the church corporately, let's talk about individuals. These people in Ezra's day were the relatively few who returned from their captivity in Babylon. About 50,000 had returned in the first wave under Zerubbabel, followed years later by a smaller band that returned under Ezra. The people who chose to remain in Babylon are not even memorialized here in this book. We don't know anything about their whereabouts. But the ones who returned are memorialized right here. God said, "These are the people who would hear." And whatever else they may have heard, it says very clearly that they read in the book about the Feast of Tabernacles or Booths, and in their enthusiasm they immediately went out to gather the materials. Although they didn't have exactly the same materials, they still collected materials to celebrate the Feast of Tabernacles for seven days.

These must have been a people touched by God, that after living for seventy years in captivity and finally having settled in the place where they were supposed to be, they would celebrate the Feast of Tabernacles, which required that they move out of their homes for seven days to live in temporary shelters made of twigs and sticks, and celebrate God's provision, His grace and His love. That is a life touched by God. By analogy, there is a big difference between merely attending church, and giving attention to God and His purpose through His word.

God opened up the ears for these people. They are the last people to have their ears opened up in the Old Testament, and then the prophet Malachi will rebuke the priests and the people once again. Then there will be about 400 years until the coming of Christ. All this was preparation for the coming of Christ. And Christ will say to those very same people who were still in the synagogue and were still reading the law, "Your actions are one thing, but your heart is far from Me." It was only lip service.

Now if God can discern all of these things, then He certainly can discern your state as well. And He can change that state today. I cannot. People say, "You have got to lead people to the Lord," but what did Ezra do? He brought out the book and he read. I do not know if that would be enough for some people in today's generation. But if you are hungering for God's word, or are interested in hearing more, then you are one of those to whom God has given understanding. It may not be perfect understanding, because no human being can ever have perfect understanding of eternal things and the things of God. But God can give us a heart that is open to receive.

In John 3, Nicodemus came to Jesus by night. Here was a man who had heard the law and knew the law, yet he asked what he must do to gain eternal life. And Jesus said to him, "You must be born again from above." The message is still the same: you must be born again from above. It is not the result of a preacher saying, "Walk with me." You must walk with the Lord, and I cannot make you desire to make that journey. If God has placed that *sunesis* or *been* into your being, you will desire to listen and to follow. But remember that it is God who puts the "*been*" into your being!

Some of you will say, "Thank God for putting His Spirit in me to enable me not only to hear with my ears, but also to receive into my heart and understand." And all of us can pray, "God, have patience with me. God, have patience with me in my hardheadedness, because at some point I will get it." Anyone who is able to hear, who desires the word of God, is a part of a special group of people.

There are vast multitudes in mega-churches who do not desire the word; they just want to be a part of something. Maybe God has not placed the desire in their hearts, or maybe it just isn't their time yet; I do not know. But I do know that when God places that desire in your heart, you will begin a quest to be fed, and you will desire this word and this word alone. Nothing else will do. And those are the people who have the capacity to respond.

It is too easy to put all of the pressure onto the preacher and say, "Okay, preacher, you must have some kind of amazing skill and paint beautiful word pictures to grab people." But the reality is that God does not need a painter or a wordsmith. If someone does have that gift, it will only be icing on the cake. But the one thing that is needed is for God to put His Spirit of *sunesis* in you to receive. And then, whether you are receiving simple bread or something fancier, it will still be Bread for your soul. And that Bread is the Bread of life.

These verses in Nehemiah unfold what the word of God should bring into a believer's life. We are not clinging to the law; we have Christ. But it is a profound picture of the response that should happen when God's word is front and center. It may not be tears, but you should go out contemplating, meditating and praying about what you have heard in church. And maybe you will comb the Scriptures and find how often this concept appears, especially in Psalm 119. The writer of this grand old psalm, the largest in the Psalter, used the word *been* over and over again, as he asked for understanding. He said, in essence, "Lord, give me understanding that I may walk in Thy precepts." In other words, "Lord, give me that ability. Lord, help me to *been*, to understand." It was his earnest prayer, and I ask that you make it yours too. That is what enables us to grow together and become a fortified body. When we abide in God's word, He abides in us. That is all the power you need.

As a pastor, my primary care is that you hear and receive God's word. I cannot make that happen, but God can and God will. If you want to listen to and receive God's word, it is because God wants you to hear, even you hardheaded ones; He is still speaking to you through His word. He uses vessels made of clay, but He is still doing the speaking through His word, through His Spirit. Praise God for being able to hear! I pray that you will consider these words and understand how fortunate, how blessed you are to be one of those to whom God has given the power to understand, the *sunesis*, the *been* placed inside of you to enable you to hear and receive. Praise God for that!

CHAPTER 10

THE JOY OF THE LORD IS YOUR STRENGTH

We are taught in this country, or at least we used to be taught in this country, how to read and write, and how to speak; but we are not taught how to listen. Dr. Ralph Nichols pioneered the field of listening at the University of Minnesota, and he developed a department dedicated to helping people understand that there is a need to learn how to listen.

From his pioneering work a group was formed called the International Listening Association or ILA, which still produces many great studies. A recent study pinpointed the physiological effects on someone who is genuinely listening: the body temperature goes up, the heartbeat may increase a little and blood circulation increases. The study's author categorized listening into three levels: hearing, listening and *auding*, which comes from the same Latin root as our English word "auditorium." "Hearing" simply means you are perceiving a sound, but it could be tantamount to just hearing noise; you are not actually listening and therefore you might not react to what you have heard. "Listening" means you are receiving and are able to react to what you are listening to. And "auding" means you are processing, indexing and making mental notes. You are not being distracted and you are fully focused on the speaker. "Auding" results in meaningful impressions being made on the brain.

Ultimately we all know that paying attention to a speaker is more than just being respectful and kind; rather, there are different levels of listening. And it does not require divine intervention to improve our listening skills in this sense. We have all met people who, after you have talked to them for a while, you can tell that they haven't listened to a thing you have said. I have also met people who could repeat back everything that I said to them verbatim. We spend almost half of our time listening, though for the most part we are really only hearing because not all of what we take in is processed. It is like listening to the evening news: not everything you hear will stick in your brain, and some of it you don't want to stick at all. Again, you do not need divine help for that kind of listening.

The average American speaker can speak 120 to 150 words per minute, while our brains can potentially receive and process about 500 words per minute. That means there is an "attention gap" between what you hear and what is going on in your brain at the same time. We all know that we are guilty of this: we hear something that is so riveting or fascinating that our minds grab hold of that one word or concept, and suddenly we are really not listening to the speaker anymore because we are busy thinking about that one word. That is what an "overstimulated listener" does. There is nothing wrong with that, except if you are trying to learn something, you will probably miss the thing you really needed to hear, because your mind has wandered off to explore some idea.

There are methods to improve your ability to listen, but we are usually not taught them in school. We are slipping into what I call a "sound-bite society," where we only want to hear a little bit because our attention gets so easily distracted. Too many people say, "I only need this one bit of information; don't give me all that other stuff." But when it comes to truly understanding the word of God, I believe it is the pastor's responsibility to use his or her God-given gifts to open up the word and make it clear in its context as well as make an application to your life, so that you are not merely "hearing" when you come into the sanctuary. If you are simply hearing, you may not actually be listening and processing and taking in. The

Scripture does say, "Faith comes by hearing," but there must be something that happens on a deeper level; there must be more that goes on as God turns over the soil of the soul to make it ready to be able to receive God's word.

We studied a Hebrew word out of Nehemiah that is translated in the King James Version "understanding." It refers to God's way of opening up the ears and eyes of people to whom He would speak. This is why you will often read in the New Testament, "To him that has an ear, let him hear what the Spirit is saying."

We have funny listening devices; sometimes we interpret things the way we think they ought to be interpreted. But when the truth is presented, it is God who does the opening up of the heart and the mind to enable us to receive the teaching, and at that moment, clarity comes. Otherwise, listening to preaching is simply a waste of time. In true auding, you are focused on what is being said, though sometimes you have to work through moments of your mind drifting. You must hold on to your brain, especially when you come to listen to the word of God being taught. But it is God who enables us to understand His word, and we see that in the book of Nehemiah.

Nehemiah 8 opens with Ezra the scribe, who had prepared his heart to go and deliver the word to the people who had returned from captivity. It begins, "And all the people gathered themselves together as one man into the street that was before the water gate; and they spake unto Ezra the scribe to bring the book. . . ." Here the people were gathered together with one mind, and they wanted the word of God. It is very rare to find people in church today who want the word; it seems they want everything else but the word. Ezra stood up and he began to read to the people. There were other men along with Ezra, including Nehemiah and the Levites, who also taught the people. They would repeat the word so that the people could hear it with understanding. The Bible says that they "caused them to understand the reading." So we know this was beyond just hearing or listening. God must have "primed the pump" of their minds and hearts to enable them to receive. And we know from studying this word that this is what happened. It all revolved around the word of God. And they told the people, "This day is holy unto the LORD your God; mourn not, nor weep. For all the people wept, when they heard the words of the law."

The people were weeping, and they were not simply shedding a few tears of sadness. What were they weeping and mourning about? Was it because they heard the word of God for the first time? Was it in part because some were linguistically challenged? We know that when they went away into captivity and came back, the language had changed. There may have been a number of reasons, but the original Hebrew and the Aramaic make it clear that these people were very sorrowful. In the New Testament frame, we would say it was "godly sorrow that worketh repentance." Whether it was because they were listening to the blessings and the cursings out of Deuteronomy or they were listening to the chronicle of God's great deliverance of His people out of Egypt's bondage, it made these people weep and mourn.

There are several Hebrew words used for mourning and grief. For example, in Genesis 6:6, after God saw man's sinful condition, it says that it grieved the Lord that He had made man. We read in the King James Version, "it grieved him at his heart." We are not talking about grieving in the sense of mourning over someone's death; we are talking about mourning because of sin.

In Nehemiah 8:10, the people were told, "Go your way, eat the fat, and drink the sweet, and send portions unto them for whom nothing is prepared," that is, be charitable to those who do not have anything, "for this day is holy unto our Lord: neither be ye *sorry,*" again using the same Hebrew word for "grief" that was used in Genesis 6. The King James Version translators didn't like to repeat words, so they changed them every now and then, which can cause some confusion. And it is the last part of this verse that we will focus on today: *"for the joy of the LORD is your strength."* I want us to see how we can best understand this text.

Let's talk about the word "joy." Most people say they know what joy is. Well, I know what joy is too: when I am happy, I am happy; and when I am sad, I am sad. But that is not the kind of joy being described in our text. There are different words in the Hebrew language that represent joy, praise and thanksgiving. The word used in this verse describes a type of joy that does not change with our circumstances, because of its divine authorship or source. It is not a joy that is generated by human strength. It is a joy that comes from the Lord.

This word for "joy" presents some translation difficulties because it is not used very often in the Hebrew, and we have to go to other Semitic languages, the Syriac and the Aramaic, to find the essence of its meaning. Sometimes when we use a lexicon it is helpful to look at the words that come before or after the word we are looking up, to help us gain the sense of its meaning. When we use this approach, we find words meaning such things as "one" or "together." If you keep reading in the Syriac lexicon, you will find the word for "bride," and even the cognate root of the word for "breast."

The concept of this word in a pictorial sense represents "unity" or "oneness." It is not simply joy in the sense of happiness; it is a joy that comes from the Lord: He is the Divine Author of this joy. There is also a quality of this word that represents unity. And this unity, the Bible says, "is your strength."

Now let's turn our attention to the last word, which the King James Version translates as "strength." And indeed, it is strength, but it is a special kind of strength. A derivative of this word is defined as a "mountain stronghold" or a "place of refuge." Again Hebrew is a pictorial language and in this case the imagery is of a place of refuge. We could call it a fortress, we could call it a defense or we could simply call it protection. This word occurs in a number of the psalms, which we will look at to help us put some color on the word. But the basic idea of the expression "the joy of the LORD is your strength" is that this joy, this sense of unity that comes from the Lord, is your strength, and with that unity comes a place of refuge or safety. That means in Him I am secure, and in Him I have refuge.

This unity does not come about when people decide they are going to "pray down" a revival in their church. It does not happen that way. It happens when people genuinely face themselves. These concepts are not commonly preached, but they are in the Bible and they are age-old. There must first come a recognition of our condition. Romans 3:23 declares, "All have sinned and fallen short of the glory of God." No one is without sin. Only when we understand our fallen state and our sinning condition can we then begin to turn from our way to God's way. And in the process of turning, God divinely opens up some mechanism that produces a feeling of sorrow, true sorrow that does not make us want to excuse our nature or our behavior. Once we have turned from our way to following Him, this grief and sorrow is immediately turned into joy. It is a paradoxical happening. How does this happen? Because in Him, we have refuge.

Think about these people in the Old Testament frame who were hearing the thunderings of the law, the judgment of the law, and trembling and fear came upon them. Of course they would be gripped with fear and would mourn and weep, because essentially the law rumbled out a sentence of death. We in the New Testament frame know that the law was nailed to a tree in Christ Jesus, who has given us our liberty and the grace of forgiveness.

Let's look at several examples of how this word that means "a place of refuge" is used in Scripture, starting with Psalm 27:1: "The LORD is my light and my salvation; whom shall I fear? the LORD is the *strength of my life;* of whom shall I be afraid?" The word for "strength" is from the same root word we saw in Nehemiah 8:10. Again it has a pictorial sense, and from the Hebrew Masoretic text means "the LORD is my *stronghold.*" We could also translate it as "refuge," "defender" or "fortress." When the Psalmist was surrounded by fear, he used this word.

Now turn to Psalm 31, where you will find two examples. Psalm 31:2 says, "Bow down thine ear to me; deliver me speedily: be thou my *strong rock*, for an house of defense to save me." Here it says "strong rock" and that is another translation of the same word we are looking at. I would translate it "a rock of refuge," a place to run to when danger looms. And Psalm 31:4 says, "Pull me out of the net that they have laid privily for me: for thou art *my strength.*" Here the word carries the concept of strength, but again it is a place to run for refuge.

If you are in communion with God, that unity with God brings a sense of safety. The people in Nehemiah's day were receiving this word "as one man." It was not some ordinary gathering. They were ready to receive, they were attentive and they were able to respond reverently. We have a picture of repentance.

I have heard people ask, "Why are there no great revivals in our day?" For starters, most people in the church today do not even understand the concept of sin. "Sin" is not a mere collection of bad behavior, like "I drink, I smoke, I cuss, I do bad things, I think bad thoughts, etc." The prophet Isaiah defines sin like this: "All we like sheep have gone astray; we have turned every one to his own way." Sin is doing what is right in our own eyes and trying to justify it before God. It is like saying, "Here, God, accept this."

That is the nature of our generation. I hate to say this, but our generation and culture want God to accept everything and even put a halo on it. Therefore, there can be no revival if people do not understand what is actually wrong with them. I am not saying this from the frame of reference of a fundamentalist Bible-thumper. Rather, I am telling you that there is a condition common to all humanity, and failure to recognize that condition is failure to recognize there is a Creator who had a perfect design that became flawed in the garden. It is a simple message.

These people who returned to Jerusalem gathered together and heard the thunderings of the law, which decreed, "You must perform!" There were blessings and cursings, and of course it caused them to weep and to mourn. And this is what is so wonderful: we have a picture of the New Testament right here in the Old Testament. That is why I teach both the Old and New Testaments. When the people recognized their condition before God, they were told, "Go your way, eat the fat, and drink the sweet, and send portions unto them for whom nothing is prepared: for this day is holy unto our Lord: neither be ye sorry. . . ." Do not mourn nor grieve, "for the joy of the LORD is your strength." All the people were stilled, and they went their way to send portions and make a great celebration, "because they had understood the words that were declared unto them."

How terrible would it be if a person lacked understanding? That is why I mentioned Ralph Nichols, because he pointed out that the greatest need of society, in his view, was the need to understand and the need to be understood. Now I want you to take that application from the secular and the fleshly and apply it spiritually. Failure to understand God's purpose, failure to understand what it is to face oneself is failure, essentially, to connect with God's divine plan and manifestation in a person's life.

When we talk about repentance, our language betrays us. Because English is such a young language, we have many words that have been grafted into our tongue. One of them is the word "repent," which comes out of the Latin, and it is a word that connotes self-flagellation and self-abasing. But the word in the original Greek simply means "to turn." The Greek word is *metanoia,* meaning "to turn with the mind." It means to turn from your way to God's way.

So it may seem a strange thing to say "the joy of the LORD" to these people who were mourning and weeping. But they remembered the Divine Author of this joy, this type of unity, because they had turned from their way to His way. The people were now listening and hearing, and they were seeking refuge. In the New Testament, Christ is our refuge. Romans 8:1 says that there is therefore now no ultimate condemnation to them which are in Christ Jesus.

Now we can see why the words "the joy of the LORD is your strength" must not be lifted out of their context and turned into some kind of generic promise of joy available to anyone at any time. We can also see why the concept of Christianity in America is failing hard, while other religions or different interests are rising: it is because we have become part of a culture that believes it is not necessary to teach people about their true nature. By analogy, suppose your name is "Richard" but I only called you "Bob," and I never called you by your true name; I never addressed you as who you truly are. Likewise, we have to come to a place with God where we truly identify who we are before God.

In the book of Genesis, Jacob wrestled with the angel, though actually the angel wrestled with him, and the angel asked him, "What is your name?" And he replied, "Jacob," which means heel-catcher, deceiver or conniver. Only then, when Jacob acknowledged his name and his nature, was his name changed to "Israel." That is exactly the point that each and every individual needs to come to, in order to be able to have a concept of what this joy truly means. Again, the joy of the Lord is not just happiness; it is something that connotes unity. And what stems from the unity with God is a place of safety, a place of defense. There is great celebration when people are able to turn from themselves and face God. And there is great celebrating on God's part as well when you turn to seek refuge in Him.

Run to that shelter. You ought to be running toward it, not running away from it. God is not like an earthly judge waiting to "throw the book" at you, but He wants you to worship Him in truth and sincerity. Sometimes people fail to see the connection between the Old Testament and the New Testament, so I am going to show what this concept looks like in the New Testament, and then we will bring it all together to make an application for us today.

We will see what this looks like from Luke's perspective, starting in Luke 19 with the conversion of Zacchaeus. We read, "There was a man named Zacchaeus, which was the chief among the publicans, and he was rich. And he sought to see Jesus," but he could not because he was small in stature, so he ran and climbed up a tree to get a better view. "And when Jesus came to the place, he looked up, and saw him, and said unto him, Zacchaeus. . . ." Now imagine that! He didn't say, "Hey you, short man; come down!" Jesus called him by name, saying, "Zacchaeus, make haste, and come down; for to day I must abide at thy house."

If you get to know certain Greek words, you will find out that God is a very repetitive preacher; in this case, the word to notice is *abide*. Jesus doesn't barge His way in. But He knew that Zacchaeus had climbed up into the tree in order that he might see Him come by. So there was already something turning the soil of his soul. Verse 6 says, "And he made haste, and came down, and received him joyfully. And when they saw it, they all murmured, saying, That he was gone to be guest with a man that is a sinner!" Isn't that remarkable?

"And Zacchaeus stood, and said unto the Lord; Behold, Lord, the half of my goods I give to the poor; and if I have taken any thing from any man by false accusation, I restore him fourfold." Here is a man who was probably skimming the basket daily. And he said, "If I have taken anything, I restore him fourfold. And Jesus said unto him, This day is salvation come to this house, forsomuch as he also is a son of Abraham." Then Jesus concludes with a statement that crystallizes this concept: "For the Son of man is come to seek and to save that which was lost."

This is still dependent on "that which was lost" to turn, listen to Jesus and receive His words. Jesus is not going to force Himself on the heart of anyone, contrary to the popular misinterpretation of the picture in the book of Revelation where Jesus is standing and knocking at the door. Jesus is not standing and knocking at your heart's door; He is standing outside the church, which has locked Him out. Everything *but* Jesus is being peddled in the church today.

Let's look at another example from Luke's Gospel, the parable of the lost sheep. We read in Luke 15, starting at verse 4, "What man of you, having an hundred sheep, if he lose one of them, doth not leave the ninety and nine in the wilderness, and go after that which is lost, until he find it? And when he hath found it, he layeth it on his shoulders, rejoicing."

We are looking at the concept of unity and communion; and where there is unity, there is joy. "And when he cometh home, he calleth together his friends and neighbours, saying unto them, Rejoice with me; for I have found my sheep which was lost. I say unto you, that likewise joy shall be in heaven over one sinner that repenteth, more than over ninety and nine just persons, which need no repentance." Jesus then goes on to teach the parable of the lost coin and then of the lost son, which is commonly called the parable of the prodigal son, though it is really a parable of the Father.

Keep in mind that we are making an application to Nehemiah 8:10. The people in Nehemiah's day had been carried away into captivity and some were born in captivity. So when they heard and understood that there was a God in heaven who actually cared for them, who was concerned enough for them to bring them back and cause them to hear His word, there was a reaction. That is the significance of the verse "the joy of the Lord is your strength." Don't ever look at this verse in the same way, because you will find that in those words, God is saying, "If you will really turn to Me, I will take care of you. No matter what your circumstances, there will be an unwavering refuge and protection surrounding you." That does not mean you will be shielded from all of the adverse circumstances of life, but it means that in Him there is no condemnation; in Him there is safety.

We read in Luke 15, starting at verse 11, "A certain man had two sons: and the younger of them said to his father, Father, give me the portion of goods that falleth to me. And he divided unto them his living. And not many days after the younger son gathered all together, and took his journey into a far country, and there wasted his substance with riotous living." You do not have to waste your substance on riotous living to make an application of this parable to your own life. You only need to see that God sees all of our insignificant squabblings of life, the time we waste and the things that consume our thoughts. And although He cares for us, in the big picture those things are not as relevant or as important as turning to Him and recognizing our actual state of being.

This is not a message of gloom and doom. There is cause for rejoicing when you really understand the message. Many of us have read about the prodigal son and said, "I identify with that." God gave me many years before the lights were turned on, and I have said in great lament that youth is wasted on youth. And when you finally turn around and you are old enough to understand and know better, you might say, "Well, I could have started serving God a long time ago." But it was not time yet. Thank God for God's timing. It has been said, "God is always on time." Yes, but it is *His* time, though. It seems that He is never on time according to my time, but He is always on time according to His time.

"And when he had spent all, there arose a mighty famine in that land; and he began to be in want. And he went and joined himself to a citizen of that country; and he sent him into his fields to feed swine." A child of God is now reduced down to feeding pigs, "And when he came to himself. . . ." Dr. Gene Scott would translate this verse, "When he came to his sanity," that is, when the son came to his senses, "he said, How many hired servants of my father's have bread enough and to spare, and I perish with hunger! I will arise and go to my father, and will say unto him, Father, I have sinned against heaven, and before thee."

He started thinking about turning from where he was and heading back to his father with the right attitude. And this is how he sees himself in verse 19: "I am no more worthy to be called thy son: make me as one of thy hired servants." At that point he would have done anything to be allowed to come back. So "he arose, and came to his father. But when he was yet a great way off, his father saw him, and had compassion, and ran, and fell on his neck, and kissed him." And that is how our heavenly Father receives us when we return from going our own way and turn toward Him. "And the son said unto him, Father, I have sinned against heaven, and in thy sight, and am no more worthy to be called thy son. But the father said to his servants, Bring forth the best robe, and put it on him; and put a ring on his hand, and shoes on his feet: and bring hither the fatted calf, and kill it; and let us eat, and be merry."

The Greek word translated "merry" appears many times in this passage. You will find that this word is used in the Septuagint Greek translation of the Old Testament; and in Ezra 6:16, it is used to translate the same Hebrew word for joy that is found in Nehemiah 8:10. There is much rejoicing in this parable. The son is taken back and is accepted as part of the family. The father says, "Let us eat, and be merry: for this my son was dead, and is alive again; he was lost, and is found. And they began to be merry. Now his elder son was in the field: and as he came and drew nigh to the house, he heard musick and dancing. And he called one of the servants, and asked what these things meant. And he said unto him, Thy brother is come; and thy father hath killed the fatted calf, because he hath received him safe and sound." Again, the concept is unity: rejoicing and unity, rejoicing and communion, rejoicing and togetherness, rejoicing and oneness. You find it all right here.

And the older brother "was angry, and would not go in: therefore came his father out, and entreated him." Now the older brother says, "You didn't do any of these things for me, but I have been here all the time. You never gave me a kid, that I might make merry with my friends: but as soon as this thy son was come, which hath devoured thy living with harlots, thou hast killed for him the fatted calf. And he said unto him, Son, thou art ever with me, and all that I have is thine. It was meet that we should make merry, and be glad: for this thy brother was dead, and is alive again; and was lost, and is found."

The people in Nehemiah's day received a measure of grace without knowing it. When we read our English translation, it does not carry the same essence of meaning. But the joy that comes from God provides safety, protection and refuge. It makes us not be afraid anymore; it makes us not worry. I am sure that these people knew from their Old Testament frame of reference that the wages of sin is death. But in the New Testament, One died who was worth enough to stand in my place and yours, who paid the full price to redeem us.

We have looked at the Old Testament and we have looked at the New. I want us to learn something from God's word that should make this concept a little clearer to those who are burdened down with a sense of sin and guilt. Some people feel as though they can barely move under the burden of their grief-stricken souls. I have heard people say, "I cannot get rid of this nagging in my spirit that somehow whatever I have done, whatever I have been through, whatever I have experienced or whatever junk is in my mind, is still with me." If that describes you to any degree, then take comfort today in the knowledge that Jesus paid it all. The New Testament says that He paid the full price to buy the whole field, and that truly the unity we come to in the faith of Jesus Christ brings us to a safe place, a place of refuge.

I do not have to wonder anymore if I am forgiven. There are some people who ask, "How will I know when I have truly let it be with the Lord and that He has truly forgiven me?" You do not need to frustrate God's grace. In the Old Testament, the people in Nehemiah's day heard the thunderings of the law; they heard that for obedience, there was the promise of life, and for disobedience, the promise of death. They heard the promises of cursing and of blessing respectively in both areas. We read the New Testament and we know that we could never be worth enough, we could never be worthy, but God sent His only begotten Son to do what only He could do.

To the guilt-ridden, sin-stained souls that have no hope, look to this verse in Nehemiah and understand that repentance means that you turn from your way to God's way. Read 2 Corinthians 7. Repentance starts with changing your mind, but it produces something. There is an emotional response, which is described by the Greek word *metamelomai*. It is a godly sorrow which one should not have any regrets about. But it starts with a state of mind that says, "I know I need God. I have been running from God and have been trying to ignore Him."

There are people who will hear this message but they will not be able to receive it. They have no interest in it; it is boring to them. But there does come a time for every person, even atheists. They still have a nagging question in their minds. I do not try to proselytize people; I can only point them to the word of God. I know my own grief, which cannot be exactly the same as what you have experienced. But each person does experience some form of this feeling, no matter how good you have been or how bad you have been. And suddenly these words, though they be from the Old Testament, can resonate in your soul. As long as you are having communion with God, having unity of the faith with Him, conversing with Him, hearing, listening, auding, and with His divine help letting the word sink into your soul, He gives the gift of being able to receive; and you are changed. You are being transformed, and you do not have to be fearful anymore.

The world and maybe the rest of the church world may talk about God as an unjust judge, but I know I serve a loving, kind and caring Savior who cared enough to rescue you and me from absolute destruction. I am reminded of lyrics to the song *Sinner Saved by Grace:* "When I stood condemned to death, He took my place." When you can sing that from your heart, you can have a sense of the reality of what you deserved, and a sense of the reality of what He did for you.

The next time you read the words in Nehemiah 8, "The joy of the LORD is your strength," I want you to remember that God is the Divine Author of joy. He lets us partake in something that becomes the unity of the faith, which Ephesians 4 talks about. And for that unity of the faith, we have a safe haven to run to when all of the storms are rumbling around us. We have that solid Rock and we can take refuge there. I know that in that Rock, safety is provided for me and for you. "The joy of the LORD is your strength" is not just a quaint little saying. It is a powerful punch to those people who understand where they were, who they are in the Lord, and what they have. So we can pray, "Precious Savior, hold my hand and keep me in the safe place, the place that is higher, the place that is above it all."

I know I cannot stay in that state of awareness all the time, and I am not going to be sheltered from everything that is going on around me. But I know in that moment, I am safely in Him, and He cares for me and He cares for you. For those of you who have a heavy burden today, let the joy of the Lord be the delight of your soul, the gladdening of your heart that lifts you up to the place where you can say, "I am safe with Him." I pray for those of you who came to church with a heavy heart, that you do not leave full of grief and sadness, but that you leave knowing that the Lord loves you and cares enough for you to have you hear this message and to have it sink down into your soul. You are a loved and treasured people.

Chapter 11

ABRAHAM: A HEART FAITHFUL TOWARDS GOD

No matter what, God will see you through. God will lead you if you will turn to Him, if you will hear His voice today. The state of affairs today is lamentable, first in the church and then in our society at large. There are very few people who have respect for God's word or even acknowledge that He is indeed the Maker and Creator of all things. The Bible says that He will reward those who seek Him, but it also says that some vessels are created to honor and others to dishonor or destruction. Failure to latch on to God's book basically makes everything else spin out of orbit. But when we turn to Him, He turns to us and takes care of us. Now we cannot fix the world, but we can take a stand for Christ and declare that God is in control even if it doesn't look like it.

We looked at how God not only preveniently draws people, but He also opens up their hearts and minds to enable them to receive. Nehemiah 8:8 says, "So they read in the book in the law of God distinctly, and gave the sense, and caused them to understand the reading." The people began to weep and mourn, but they were told, "Do not weep or mourn, for the joy of the Lord is your strength." The sentence of death that was upon all mankind because of our sins no longer has the sting attached to it for those who look to Jesus Christ and are saved by faith in Him.

We no longer have that looming shadow of death, but the people in Nehemiah's day did not have that promise. Their spiritual life was illuminated by hearing the law, and they recognized that they were far from God and His will. We might take this into the New Testament and listen to Jesus' words: "Blessed are the poor in spirit: for theirs is the kingdom of heaven. Blessed are those who mourn: for they shall be comforted." God makes a way when He opens up our hearts to understand that we are far from what we ought to be or need to be. And just when we think that we have smoked out the last detail that we should put before God, He says, "Here, I will show you some more issues in your life that need to be worked out." That is because we are in a fallen condition.

What is beautiful about this depiction in Nehemiah 8 is that the people were told, "Do not weep and mourn. Rather, go have a feast and celebrate." This happened on the first day of the seventh month. And on the second day of the month, the people were gathered together and they read in the book of the law about the Feast of Tabernacles or the Feast of Booths. So the people went out to gather the materials needed to build those temporary booths, and it says that they celebrated "day by day," and "they kept the feast seven days; and on the eighth day was a solemn assembly, according unto the manner."

Remarkably, this does not follow the pattern of the feast days that was given by God in the book of Leviticus. We do not know what book they were reading from when the law was being read, but in Leviticus, the Feast of Trumpets begins on the first day of the seventh month. The great Day of Atonement, Yom Kippur, is kept on the tenth day, and the Feast of Tabernacles falls on the fifteenth day. The Feast of Tabernacles lasts for seven days and on the eighth day there is a solemn assembly. Many have wondered over the fact that the people in Nehemiah did not celebrate Yom Kippur. But I want us to notice that in Nehemiah 9, the people were fasting "with sackclothes, and earth upon them." So even though Yom Kippur is not specifically named, it is evident that these people were afflicting their souls in confession and in great lament before God.

The fact that they celebrated the Feast of Tabernacles is extremely important for a number of reasons. First, we need to remember that many of these people had only recently made the long journey across the desert from Babylon to return to Jerusalem. Imagine what life must have been like for them; they had a tumultuous time of rebuilding, they finished the wall and they were just settling in to their homes, when suddenly they decided to celebrate the Feast of Tabernacles. Imagine by analogy that you had just moved in to a new home, after much boxing up and a long journey. Then there comes a time of seemingly endless unpacking. Now imagine that you have just finished unpacking your last box when your landlord says, "We are giving you a month to move out!" These people had just barely settled in to their new homes in a new land, but when they heard about the Feast of Tabernacles, they went out and gathered the materials and built temporary dwellings, and they went to live in them, forsaking the comfort of their own homes. It is staggering that they did this willingly and joyfully.

Second, we know that one of the reasons for their returning to rebuild Jerusalem was in preparation for the coming of Christ. Zechariah 14 depicts a final scene on earth when Christ will reign and people will be forced to celebrate the Feast of Tabernacles, or a curse will be put upon them. The Feast of Tabernacles will be celebrated in its fullness to mark the end of the wandering of God's people, and their ultimately coming to worship Him in the place that He designated.

Nehemiah 9 opens on the twenty-fourth day of the seventh month, and the children of Israel were assembled with fasting and with sackcloth and earth upon them as the sign of deep mourning. That kind of spirit is almost universally missing from the body of Christ today. I do not mean that people should be going about in sackcloth and in ashes. Jesus said to repent, which means to change your mind, to cease from following your own way and turn to Him and follow after Him. These people had spent many hours listening to God's word and then praying. We read that a fourth part of the day was spent listening and a fourth part was spent confessing and worshiping. When you spend that much time in the word, there should be a genuine turning and a real stirring of the soul. The tragedy is that so many people only want to hear about delightful things; theirs is a cotton-candy Christianity. I am not saying that Christianity is not sweet. Sometimes our relationship with God enables us to extract the sweet from the bitter. It can be like wine that comes from crushing grapes, or like oil that is pressed from olives. There is a press for the Christian, and that press comes in a diversity of ways. But without that press, no change occurs. And the most important thing is the ability to listen to God's word and let it penetrate as God opens up your heart to receive. Then something remarkable happens: the self becomes no longer that important.

One of the problems with today's society is that the self has been deified. Young people in our colleges and universities are more concerned about someone looking at them in the wrong way than they are about excelling in their studies and becoming leaders in a field. We worship the self, and now everything is about the self. Yet when you begin to read the Bible with a sincere heart, you start to realize how small and almost irrelevant you are with respect to God. When one looks to God and finally turns from being self-absorbed and narcissistic, one can begin to see things differently. You realize that but for God's grace, you would have nothing but a sentence of death. And that is why Nehemiah 8 and 9 speak volumes to me, because without hearing the word of God, Bible reading, Bible teaching and prayer, you will never grow spiritually. If all you say is "Just give me the least amount I need to have," then you will never become what God intended you to be.

Maybe you do not want to hear a message like this, or maybe it will make you miserable enough inside that you will take to heart what I am saying, for I care about people's souls. And those who have actually turned from their own way realize that this problem is a part of the moral decay of our society. God is no longer the center of the universe for most people, but the self is; therefore there can be no repentance, there can be no true grief or sorrow. People today just want to brand everything as being socially acceptable. And if you don't think that someone or something is socially acceptable, then they will make you think that there is something wrong with you.

That is how society brands people who are still rooted and grounded in God's word.

Do you realize what has happened in this country within the last one hundred years? When I look back at the recent history of our country, there are certain things that resonate in my mind. The years 1963 and 1964 were pivotal years for America. Martin Luther King Jr. gave his "I have a dream" speech and in 1964, the Civil Rights Act was passed. Now a whole generation has forgotten that "I have a dream" was rooted and grounded in the word of God, for it spoke of equality as God sees it for all mankind. Today there is a sense of entitlement, but again, it comes back to the exaltation of the self. In today's world, it is frowned upon to even tell people about God in a public forum. Everything comes back to a loss of mooring.

The revelation of God's word should dwarf all other things that we might think are important. That is why I am so grateful that God touched my life and gave me the ability to hear and to proclaim this word of truth to you; and I am praying for people to respond. When the people in Nehemiah's day heard God's word, they were powerfully affected by it. They knew that they had been carried away into captivity because of their fathers' disobedience to God's word. They were obedient when the call came and the edict was issued by Cyrus that they could return. Technically speaking, especially for those born in Babylon, they weren't guilty of the sins that led to the fall of Jerusalem, and yet they responded as if they had been guilty of it all. Isn't that a little reminiscent of Daniel's prayer? He said, "We have sinned," yet he had the most righteous behavior of any man you might encounter in Scripture. Now this is why we are in a bad state today, and why I said you cannot discuss society's problems without looking here first and seeing that the people, at least for a time, were greatly impacted by God's word.

We read in Nehemiah 9:2, "And the seed of Israel separated themselves from all strangers," literally, *strange children*, "and stood and confessed their sins, and the iniquities of their fathers. And they stood up in their place, and read in the book of the law of the LORD their God one fourth part of the day." Imagine this people gathered together to hear the law being read for six hours, and there is no record of anybody complaining about the length of the sermon! One fourth part of the day was spent listening to the reading of the law, and one "fourth part they confessed, and worshipped the LORD their God. Then stood up upon the stairs, of the Levites, Jeshua, and Bani, Kadmiel, Shebaniah, Bunni, Sherebiah, Bani, and Chenani, and cried with a loud voice unto the LORD their God." They were crying out to God, "Then the Levites, Jeshua, and Kadmiel, Bani, Hashabniah, Sherebiah, Hodijah, Shebaniah, and Pethahiah, said, Stand up and bless the LORD your God for ever and ever: and blessed be thy glorious name, which is exalted above all blessing and praise."

It is from this point, from verse 6 and all the way to verse 37, that we read the most brilliant mosaic or collage of Scripture. I use the word "mosaic" to describe this prayer, because when you look closely, you can see each individual tile that makes up the whole image, and when you stand back, you see a beautiful, big picture.

It is evident that the word of God never departed from some of those who were in captivity; it had been fused into their minds. In this prayer, many different passages from God's word poured out from their hearts towards God. Sometimes when we come to God in prayer, we only express our needs. There is nothing wrong with asking God for things, but I want us to learn from this prayer in Nehemiah 9 and see the way that they handled the Scripture. This prayer was a petition, a song of praise and a lament, and all of it was done by assembling passages out of God's book, beginning with the creation. We read from verse 6, "Thou, even thou, art LORD alone; thou hast made heaven, the heaven of heavens, with all their host, the earth, and all things that are therein, the seas, and all that is therein, and thou preservest them all," You give them all life, "and the host of heaven worshippeth thee."

And then we read in verses 7 and 8, "Thou art the LORD the God, who didst choose Abram, and broughtest him forth out of Ur of the Chaldees, and gavest him the name of Abraham; and foundest his heart faithful before thee, and madest a covenant with him to give the land of the Canaanites, the Hittites, the Amorites, and the

Perizzites, and the Jebusites, and the Girgashites, to give it, I say, to his seed, and hast performed thy words; for thou art righteous."

Notice that this prayer jumps immediately from God's power in the creation to Abraham. Whoever the speaker is, he did not waste any time telling us about the twenty generations from Adam to Abraham. He just said, in essence, "Let's cut to the chase: let's talk about God's power in the creation, that He made it all, and that the host of heaven worship Him," and then the speaker doesn't waste time talking about Adam or the fall or the flood; he just goes straight to Abraham. And we know that God gave Abraham many great and precious promises.

The speaker tells us about how God chose Abram, brought him out of a land and changed his name from Abram to Abraham, and He found his heart faithful. I want us to think about those words: "*He found his heart faithful.*" It is remarkable that the prayer immediately jumps over twenty generations to come to the man who is called "the father of faith."

The prayer speaks of the covenant that God made with Abram to give him the land, and it goes on to describe the bondage of his descendants in Egypt, their crying out and being delivered, and God's leading them out and providing for them. We read at the end of verse 15, God brought water "out of the rock for their thirst, and promised them that they should go in to possess the land which thou hadst sworn to give them." Continuing on to the end of the chapter, we read in verse 36, "Behold, we are servants this day, and for the land that thou gavest unto our fathers to eat the fruit thereof and the good thereof, we are servants in it."

This whole prayer, petition and lament, this record of the people's failure juxtaposed with God's love and grace was all to show God's fidelity to His promises. He promised them the land and they indeed entered into that land. Then they were carried out of the land and later they were allowed to return to that land. The concepts of land and of seed are kept at the forefront and are woven into the message. It is as though the speakers were saying, "Can you not see God's faithfulness? Because you are now back in the land that was promised to Abram!" What a remarkable mosaic to tell us about God's faithfulness and man's failure. The prayer itself in one sense is very repetitious, for it says that God did thus, but the people did not; and God did thus, but again the people did not. But the key words that arrested my attention were that God, speaking of Abraham, "*foundest his heart faithful before thee.*"

Let's look at what it means to have a faithful heart, and see if this definition of faithful means what modern-day people would call faithful. Hebrews 11:6 says, "He that cometh to God must believe that he is. . . ." If I could re-punctuate this passage, I would like to put a period right there and read it like this: "He that cometh to God *must believe that he is.*" In other words, that He is who He says He is, that He is the great I AM. "And that he is a rewarder of them that diligently seek him," or "seek after him." We must begin with an understanding that God is, and that He is all-powerful. And God chose this man Abram.

God chose him out of a land whose name is translated "Ur of the Chaldees." The literal Hebrew reads "*Oor of Casdim.*" The name *Casdim* appears to have been Grecianized and later Anglicized into "Chaldean," and the word *oor* looks like the Hebrew word for light. We read in the genealogies at the end of Genesis 11, "And Terah lived seventy years, and begat Abram, Nahor, and Haran. Now these are the generations of Terah: Terah begat Abram, Nahor, and Haran; and Haran begat Lot. And Haran died before his father Terah in the land of his nativity, in Ur of the Chaldees," or *Casdim.* "And Abram and Nahor took them wives: the name of Abram's wife was Sarai," which means "my Princess." He married a woman he called his Princess, however I do believe that was her birth name. "The name of Nahor's wife, Milcah, the daughter of Haran, the father of Milcah, and the father of Iscah. But Sarai was barren; she had no child." I believe that Iscah is actually another name for Sarai. Josephus and others also hold this view that Sarai was thus actually the daughter of Abram's uncle Haran, and not the literal daughter of Abram's father, Terah. In one sense, Abram was telling the truth when he would later say, "She is my sister," for she was at least a half sister.

"Terah took Abram his son, and Lot the son of Haran his son's son, and Sarai his daughter in law, his son Abram's wife; and they went forth with them from Ur of the Chaldees, to go into the land of Canaan; and they came unto Haran, and dwelt there. And the days of Terah were two hundred and five years: and Terah died in Haran."

Genesis 12 begins, "Now the Lord had said unto Abram." There are about thirteen chapters in the book of Genesis that are devoted to the life of Abram/Abraham. There are more chapters about Abram than there are about the creation or the flood or anything else. Here is a man whose journey of faith began with only half-obedience, and it started when he was seventy-five years old, which means you are never too old to start with God. Most of us by the time we are seventy-five are thinking about kicking up our heels and taking things easy, but Abram was just getting started.

We can trace Abram's lineage back to Shem, and we can deduce that he came from a region that had been inhabited for a long time with established villages, though there is much controversy surrounding the identification of the exact location of Ur. God chose this man out of a land inhabited by people who were not, for the most part, God-fearing; they had multiple gods. God called this man out of a place that we might not have chosen someone from. It is an age-old message: God does the choosing. God is the one who turns on the lights. God is able to say, "This one I love and this one I hate." God is able to call you and bring you out of a place, saying, "Hey, you over there, I am specifically calling your name." And the God who called Abraham is the same God who speaks to us today through His word. If you do not see this message against that backdrop, it merely becomes a good little Sunday school story, rather than the message that God still chooses and calls people out.

We read in Nehemiah that God found Abraham's heart faithful, but in response to being called to leave country and kindred, his first response was to go only halfway. He did not abandon his kindred; they went with him. They stopped in Haran, and they may have been there for about six years before they proceeded on. That means when God calls and chooses people, they don't always immediately respond in the way that some people would say they ought to.

I want to bring this message to where we live today. Christianity and the life of faith are not characterized by some perfectionist's standard. We do not serve a puppet-string-pulling God who demands, "Do this and perform like a trained dog. I will teach you how to do this, and you do it on cue." The life of faith requires listening to God and maybe taking two steps forward and sometimes taking twenty steps back. Abram's life depicts that; he only went halfway. He did not rid himself of his relative Lot, which speaks to me of the way we respond to God's calling in our lives; we don't always immediately abandon the things of the flesh. We tend to hold on to certain things for a time. We tend to think that because God's word says something, that will become the norm right away. But the truth is that a transformation will begin to occur over time. God will begin to change us from the inside out. So separation from certain things will not necessarily be an act of the will or something that is worn as a badge. There will be certain things that you once held dearly that will no longer have a hold on you. That is the meaning of the old hymn, "Turn your eyes upon Jesus, and the things of earth will grow strangely dim."

Abram was told, "Get thee out of thy country, and from thy kindred, and from thy father's house, unto a land that I will show thee." At this point, God did not say, "I am going to give you the land," He only said, "I am going to show it to you. Get up and go somewhere and I will show you some land." And then came a series of incredible promises. God said to Abram, "I will make of thee a great nation, and I will bless thee, and make thy name great; and thou shalt be a blessing: and I will bless them that bless thee, and curse him that curseth thee: and in thee shall all families of the earth be blessed. So Abram departed, as the LORD had spoken unto him." This passage at first would give us the impression that Abram listened to God, but did he do it perfectly? No.

A heart faithful towards God does not mean a perfect heart. A heart faithful towards God means that you press on, you keep walking towards God, but it does not mean you are perfect. The life of Abram shows this very clearly.

Abram departed out of Haran, "And Abram took Sarai his wife, and Lot his brother's son, and all their substance that they had gathered, and the souls that they had gotten in Haran; and they went forth to go into the land of Canaan; and into the land of Canaan they came. And Abram passed through the land unto the place of Sichem, unto the plain of Moreh," which means "the place of instruction." "And the Canaanite was then in the land." The Canaanite was in the land that God had promised! That is why I believe that much of modern-day preaching is insanity. Modern-day preaching would have us believe that when God says, "Come and see, and I will show you the land," there will be no hostile people there, and everyone will be happy.

"And the LORD appeared unto Abram, and said, Unto thy seed will I give this land: and there builded he an altar unto the LORD, who appeared unto him. And he removed from thence unto a mountain on the east of Beth–el," meaning, "house of God." And he "pitched his tent, having Beth–el on the west, and Hai on the east." Hai means a "heap of ruins." On one side was the house of God and on the other was a heap of ruins, and right there in the middle, "he builded an altar unto the LORD, and called upon the name of the LORD. And Abram journeyed, going on still toward the south."

Again, everything was not perfect, but this is a type of how we begin our journey with God. God had said, "Go to a land I will show you," and having arrived in Canaan, Abram should have stayed there. But it says in verse 10, "And there was a famine in the land." There was a famine in the very land that God had promised, which should have been flowing with milk and honey and all kinds of good stuff. That is why I say that you have to put flesh and blood on these Bible passages. I believe that God was there the whole time and asking, "Now, what is My servant going to do with this? Will he turn to Me, or will he complain about the circumstances and give up?" But the Bible says that "Abram went down into Egypt." He went down, and the word "down" is the same word that is used in the book of Jonah where it says that Jonah went down into the ship.

So "Abram went down into Egypt to sojourn there; for the famine was grievous in the land. And it came to pass, when he was come near to enter into Egypt, that he said unto Sarai his wife, Behold now, I know that thou art a fair woman to look upon: therefore it shall come to pass, when the Egyptians shall see thee, that they shall say, This is his wife: and they will kill me." So he concocted a lie and told his wife to say, "Tell them you are my sister!" Again, the reality is that by some degree of separation, she would have been his sister, so I am sure that Abram rationalized that it wasn't a complete lie. And when they came into Egypt, the Egyptians beheld that Sarai was very fair, and she was taken into Pharaoh's house.

Abram was tested by God and he flunked. But I want us to notice that it says in verse 17, "the LORD plagued Pharaoh." The Lord did not plague Abram; He plagued Pharaoh. That was God's way of saying, "I am going to show My power and My favor," because He knows our ways. That is not to excuse what Abram did. The failure on Abram's part is the failure that we all suffer from. We often lean on the arm of the flesh before waiting on God, because we think God will not be on time and that He cannot possibly provide for us. Abram did not believe that the same God who had promised him the land and seed could possibly have known that there would be a famine in that land.

God would reiterate the promise of land and seed four times. The next time we encounter this is in Genesis 13:15, and we read it again in Genesis 15:7, "And he said unto him, I am the LORD that brought thee out of Ur of the Chaldees, to give thee this land to inherit it." At that point in time, Abram was worried because he did not yet have any children. He would be one hundred years old by the time he has Isaac. At the age of ninety-nine, the Lord would appear to him and say, "I will come back next year." Isaac's birth was miraculous when you consider the age of his parents. But Abram had received the promise twenty-five years earlier. He had to wait twenty-four years for God to appear again, and a total of twenty-five years for God to do something that He had promised. For the most part, God does not appear to people and speak directly to them today. If someone tells me that God spoke to them, I would probably not listen to them. But here, the Lord actually did speak to him and make him a promise, yet he still had to wait for twenty-five years to receive the promised child.

Considering all of these things helps us to weave together the idea that Abraham, as the writer of Hebrews said, went out by faith without knowing where he was going, but he followed the Lord. In Genesis 15, he asked God, "Is Eleazar my steward supposed to be my heir?" And God said, "No. This is not your heir. But I am promising you that one who will come out of your own loins will be the child of promise." God reiterates His promise in verse 5, telling him, "Look toward the heaven, and count the stars, if thou be able to number them . . . So shall thy seed be." Then verse 6 says, "And he believed," that is, "he *amened* in the LORD; and he counted it to him for righteousness."

Abram's heart was still towards God, but not perfectly. Sarai decided to speed things up and she said, "Listen, you've got to take my handmaid Hagar and produce a child. You've got to take matters into your own hands, because God isn't making good on what He said He would do. You need to fix the problem." When I say Abram was not perfect, I mean that he was acting in the flesh, thinking that God would not make good on His promise.

In Genesis 17, the Lord appeared again to Abram after many years. When we read the Bible, we tend to imagine that the Lord frequently appeared to Abram. But in fact, the appearances were few and they were spread out over a long period of time. And during all that time, Abram waited. He has a better track record than most of us. We tend to get impatient and say, "God is not doing anything. I have been waiting here for ten years and I am not seeing too much go on. What is going on, God?" Imagine having to walk around for twenty-four years without anything happening except for the birth of Ishmael, and that was not accomplished God's way.

"And when Abram was ninety years old and nine, the LORD appeared to Abram, and said unto him, I am the Almighty God," *El Shaddai*, the enough God, the God of provision, "walk before me," the

King James Version says, "and be thou perfect," that is, be upright. "And I will make my covenant between me and thee, and will multiply thee exceedingly. And Abram fell on his face: and God talked with him, saying, As for me, behold, my covenant is with thee, and thou shalt be a father of many nations. Neither shall thy name any more be called Abram," that is "High Father," "but thy name shall be Abraham; for a father of many nations have I made thee." Again, God gave him this promise though he was not yet a father of many nations.

Then God said, "I will make thee exceeding fruitful, and I will make nations of thee, and kings shall come out of thee. And I will establish my covenant between me and thee and thy seed after thee in their generations, for an everlasting covenant, to be a God unto thee, and to thy seed after thee. And I will give unto thee, and to thy seed after thee, the land wherein thou art a stranger, all the land of Canaan, for an everlasting possession; and I will be their God. And God said unto Abraham, Thou shalt keep my covenant therefore, thou, and thy seed after thee in their generations. This is my covenant, which ye shall keep, between me and you and thy seed after thee; Every man child among you shall be circumcised," and God goes on to give Abraham instructions.

We read in verse 15, God said, "As for your wife, Sarai," your Princess, "her name will now be changed to Sarah," which is simply "Princess," and "she will be a mother of nations; kings of people shall be of her." This is pretty staggering considering Abraham was ninety-nine years old. Later Abraham would say to God, "O that Ishmael might live before thee!" But God would say, "As for Ishmael, I have heard thee: Behold, I have blessed him, and will make him fruitful, and will multiply him exceedingly; twelve princes shall he beget, and I will make him a great nation. But my covenant will I establish with Isaac, which Sarah shall bear unto thee at this set time in the next year." If God had not come back at that set time, I could imagine Abraham saying, "Okay, come on. This was just a bad joke, right?" But we know that God did indeed come back at that set time. Abraham laughed at the promise that nations would come out of him, and Sarah laughed within herself as well.

In Genesis 22, towards the end of his life, we read that God did tempt Abraham. Many people say that the Lord does not tempt people, but the Scriptures are very clear on this matter. The word used for *tempt* is the same word that is referenced throughout the whole Bible that means "to see what is in your heart." God tests us to see, "Will you listen? Will you obey?" This tempting is also to show you, like a mirror, what actually is in your heart. It is to show you what you really think concerning the things of God. God told Abraham, "Take your only begotten son and offer him as a sacrifice."

Abraham lived to be 175 years old. I believe that people had great longevity in those days, but less and less as the time went on. I want us to think about the things that Abraham experienced throughout his lifetime, the appearances of God, the promises of God, and all the things that he saw. And after walking with God for so many years, God told him to take this child of promise, this miracle child, and "offer him up in the place where I will tell you." But God did not let him put the knife to his son. God withheld his hand by the angel of the Lord, and then showed him a substitute sacrifice in the distance. God stayed Abraham's hand, knowing now what was in his heart.

Until that point, Abraham had not fully come to cast his all upon God. Abraham was always moving around and twisting a little bit. Abraham was a tent-dweller his whole lifetime. He went out not knowing where he was going, but he went out by faith. And as he went, he made mistakes and he faltered. He told a lie regarding his wife to two different people, and he had relations with his wife's handmaid Hagar, which produced Ishmael. And yet the speaker of the prayer in the book of Nehemiah said that God found Abraham's heart faithful before Him. That was what caught my attention. The speaker of the prayer thought it was important enough to highlight the life of Abraham, the one who was promised the land and seed, to a people who were in fact now in the land. And the end of that verse in Hebrew essentially says that God made good on His promise: He came through; He delivered the goods that He promised to Abraham.

This episode in the history of God's people was being recounted before the people who wanted to hear God's word, and they were caused to understand. It is being recounted today to help us understand that God has never demanded perfection, because He knows we are not able to attain to it, but He asks for trust. He asks for obedience. He asks for us to hear His word. Maybe our first reaction to hearing God's word will be to go to the place where God tells us to go, but then we might keep on going to some other place, because our discernment is not perfect. But when we get off the track, God will steer us back, just like when Abram fled to Egypt and then ended up back between Beth–el and Hai where he first placed the altar. God showed him favor to bring him back to that place to start over again, to start a new journey on a new footing. As we read the prayer in Nehemiah 9, we can see that it was a fantastic jump to go from the power of God's creation to His condescending to call and choose a man and bring him out. God chose a man whom most people in the church today probably would not want to even deal with. God gave His covenant to him, and the close of that verse says that God made good on that word.

We are now standing, figuratively speaking, in the place where God said to His people, "This is yours." Although Abraham may have vacillated, he has a much better track record than most of us. I don't know what your track record is like, but Abraham's is much better than mine when it comes to listening to God's word and parking the self and my own ideas; yet, I take great comfort from this record. God does not want me to be perfect, nor can I be. There is no such thing, by the way. Don't let anybody deceive you into thinking that any of us can attain perfect obedience in this life. There is such a thing as perfect love; and perfect love, that is, God's love, casts out fear and confusion. If you are not sure of what to do, then stand still and wait, as the Psalmist says. Wait for God, wait on God and don't run to the arm of the flesh, which is always the most convenient place to run. When all else fails, stay put. Abraham eventually learned the lesson that God would not fail, but God sure wanted to know what was in Abraham's heart; and that is the heart that He found faithful before Him.

Now let's read from Nehemiah 9:8 again: Thou "foundest his heart faithful before thee, and madest a covenant with him to give the land. . . ." I ask you, did God do it? He did indeed fulfill His promise to give him "the land of the Canaanites, the Hittites, the Amorites, and the Perizzites, and the Jebusites, and the Girgashites, to give it, I say, to his seed, and hast performed thy words; for thou art righteous." In other words, "You did it, Lord. You kept Your word of promise!"

The people who heard those words were standing in a very good place to be, especially if some of them had concerns about the future and wondered how to approach God with the knowledge of their past failures. The way of approach to God is not by performing perfectly. The way is to listen to God. Abraham reflects the heart of God. Sometimes Abraham's heart was wavering and sometimes he did what was flat-out wrong; but his heart was faithful, and that is all that God is asking of you and of me today.

It is a great encouragement to know that the people in Nehemiah 9 were standing in the very place that had been promised to them while the prayer was being spoken. We are standing today on an even greater promise, because all the promises in the Bible are ours to claim. We have the promise and the fulfillment of God's leading, His love, and most importantly His power to enter in to all things and work them out. God is faithful to perform that word.

To be found having a heart faithful towards God does not mean you must be perfect. It means you trust in the One who made the promise, and you run to that voice with the expectancy that God, who does not change and is not a man to lie, will be faithful to perform His word in your life and in mine.

Chapter 12

GOD HOLDS UP HIS WORD

God is not and has never been looking for perfection, but He certainly is looking for people who will trust Him. He is looking for people who will take Him at His word and stand on that word, in the knowledge that He has always made good on His word. Like the children of Israel who looked back on God's leading them for forty years in the wilderness, we should be able to look back on our own lives with wonder and see the grace of God in all things, especially in those things that we thought were impossible, yet somehow God made a way.

We have been looking at the prayer recorded in Nehemiah 9. It is a mosaic of Scripture that contrasts everything that God did with everything that the people did, or failed to do. God is faithful, God is powerful and God will always perform His word, while mankind has a pattern of falling away from God.

I want us to look at the history of God's people and the leading of the Lord, or what I would call God's great deliverance. This prayer teaches us the importance of having a record of the past, and I believe that the lessons in this prayer would benefit the whole church world. You see, the people had gathered and were full of godly grief and sorrow. In the twenty-fourth day of the month, they were assembled and they were fasting with sackcloth and ashes. They must have understood the concept that "for sin comes death," and they must have understood what Isaiah said, "All we like sheep have gone astray." But unlike some churches today, these people did not clobber one another with accusations of each other's sins. Rather, they looked at the corporate body and said, "*We* and our fathers have sinned."

How often do you come into a church or a religious environment where people are talking about sin and singling out one person? That is poor doctrine and it demonstrates a failure to grasp what Paul said in Romans 3:23: "*All have sinned*, and come short of the glory of God." There is not one person who is exempt, whether society views them as the worst sinner or a model citizen.

I have met many people who say of themselves, "I'm basically a good person. Why do I need God?" I am no one's judge, but I know that is what I sounded like when I was out in the world. I thought, "I'm basically a good person. I do good things," but that was just a lie, and a bad lie at best. The more you walk with the Lord and the more you stay in God's word, the more you will come to know the distance between you and God. That is why I often say that John 15 is a pivotal chapter in the New Testament. When you stay in God's word long enough, you begin to understand that without God's light and truth, without His Spirit, you can do nothing. Out in the world, you might be able to do anything you want and have some degree of success; but when it comes to the things of God, you cannot approach them in a fleshly way. That will always end in failure.

Another wonderful aspect of the prayer in Nehemiah 9 is that it is full of history, and everything mentioned in it, save the wickedness of man, glorifies God. Even the passage about God's finding Abram's heart faithful doesn't say that Abram was faithful; it says, "*Thou* found his heart faithful," giving all the credit to God. The prayer is a testimony to God's fidelity. It was vitally important for these people at this juncture to look back into the past and see God's fidelity, to reassure them in the present and to ensure their future. The lesson for us is that if God kept His word with such precision through the centuries, how much more will He fulfill His promises to us? We have the full revelation of all sixty-six books of the Bible, in which we see His handiwork unfolded.

In Nehemiah 9:5, the people were told to "Stand up and bless the LORD your God for ever and ever." Even these people, who had the right attitude and were full of grief and were confessing their sins, even they had to be told to "Stand up and bless the LORD your God." Then we read in verse 6, "Thou, even thou, art LORD alone; thou hast made heaven, the heaven of heavens, with all their host, the earth, and all things that are therein, the seas, and all that is therein, and thou preservest them," literally, You give them life. The word translated "preservest" is a form of the word *chaim;* it is the same word that Jewish people use when they say *"L'chaim,"* meaning, "To life!" In other words, "Lord, You *give life* to them all; and the host of heaven worshippeth thee."

Notice the contrast between these two verses: the host of heaven worships God without needing to be told, but man has to be told to stand up and bless God. There is a chasm, even between two verses, which demonstrates that no matter how good we imagine that our standing is before God, sometimes we need to be told our true standing, either by God's word or by His under-shepherds. I want to emphasize one Hebrew word in Nehemiah 9:5, which is translated "stand up." The word is *koom,* and it will be important to our study.

The verses that follow speak of Abram. "Thou art the LORD the God, who didst choose Abram, and broughtest him forth out of Ur of the Chaldees," or *Casdim,* "and gavest him the name of Abraham." We read in verse 8 that God "foundest his heart faithful" before Him. God looks on the heart, while man sees only the outward performance.

There are many people who call themselves Christians who still think that one's outward performance should somehow reflect what is going on inside, but only God can see what is really going on inside. The reality is that someone who looks like a whore on the outside may have a heart towards God. But the vast majority of people would miss that, because they don't read the Bible and they don't read about people being saved like the prostitute Rahab in the book of Joshua, who was saved out of Jericho. God could see what was in her heart, while the rest of that town most likely could not.

God found Abraham's heart faithful and made a covenant with him to give him "the land of the Canaanites, the Hittites, the Amorites, and the Perizzites, and the Jebusites, and the Girgashites, to give it, I say, to his seed, and hast performed thy words; for thou art righteous." Let's take a closer look at something in the translation of the latter part of that verse. We read in the King James Version the phrase "and hast performed thy words." The Hebrew word translated "performed" is another form of the word *koom*, which means "to stand up." Sometimes we can miss certain subtleties in our English version. But that is not always the translators' fault, for how do you translate something that is really quite difficult?

This word *koom* also means "to arise" or "to be confirmed or established." Looking more closely at the grammar, the word is in the "Hiphil stem." It is declarative, that is, it is a declaration, and it is also causative, which means that God *caused* His word to stand up. It is also reflexive, which means that God performed it for Himself. So when the King James Version says, "hast performed thy words," we might literally say that God *stood up* His word; He uplifted His word. That is more profound than merely saying that He performed it.

There are other places in the Bible where we encounter this concept of God's establishing His word. Psalm 119:89 says, "For ever, O LORD, thy word is settled in heaven." That is a different kind of establishing; nevertheless, it is another example of God's upholding His word. God gives His word and He is faithful to perform it.

I wish that this concept of God's upholding His word would become a reality for some people who seem to be constantly on the brink and never able to settle the issue of completely trusting in God. I do not mean that you can come to a state where you will never have any doubts; I mean that God's word enables us to walk by faith when we see God's fidelity to what He has declared. I heard someone say, "When the waves come, I get a little scared." Instead of looking at the waves, you can say, like David, "What time I am afraid, I will trust in the Lord." Or you can call out to the Lord, "Save me!" like

Peter did. I am not pretending that you will never have any crises or never have to worry, but I am saying that there are plenty of handles to grab hold of in God's word.

This passage in Nehemiah says that God holds up His word, and that same word is a light under our feet to guide our way. God's word provides many great handles to hold on to, and whoever was praying this prayer in Nehemiah recognized this. He spoke of the covenant that God made with Abraham "to give the land of the Canaanites, the Hittites, the Amorites, and the Perizzites, and the Jebusites, and the Girgashites, to give it, I say, to his seed, and hast performed thy words; for thou art righteous." He said, in essence, "You, Lord, held up those words. You caused them to come to pass."

I want us to highlight certain words in verses 9 through 12 that show us how God held up His word and brought about His great deliverance. Still speaking of the Lord, it says that He "didst *see* the affliction of our fathers in Egypt, and *heardest* their cry by the Red sea; and *shewedst* signs and wonders upon Pharaoh, and on all his servants, and on all the people of his land: for thou *knewest* that they dealt proudly against them. So didst thou get thee a name, as it is this day. And thou didst *divide* the sea before them, so that they went through the midst of the sea on the dry land." There are many words in this passage that speak of the activities of God. So far we have highlighted words that say God *saw*, *heard*, *showed*, *knew* and *divided*. "And their persecutors thou threwest into the deeps, as a stone into the mighty waters." We can simply summarize that thought as "God dealt with their enemies." "Moreover thou *leddest* them in the day by a cloudy pillar; and in the night by a pillar of fire, to give them light in the way wherein they should go." So we can add the word *led* to our list.

These are all the things that God did: He saw, He heard, He showed, He knew, He divided, He dealt with the enemies, and finally, He led. In this one brief passage, we see many attributes of the God who delivered these people: we see His great deliverance, we see His omniscience and His omnipotence; we see His power and His presence.

God called Abram out of Ur of Chaldees and promised to give him the land. I want us to remember that there were two things specifically promised: land and seed. Turn to Genesis 15, and let's read beginning at verse 13: God said to Abram, "Know of a surety that thy seed shall be a stranger in a land that is not theirs, and shall serve them; and they shall afflict them four hundred years; and also that nation, whom they shall serve, will I judge: and afterward shall they come out with great substance. And thou shalt go to thy fathers in peace; thou shalt be buried in a good old age. But in the fourth generation they shall come hither again." This prophecy of Abraham's descendants going into bondage in Egypt was given hundreds of years before the event actually occurred. And Abraham was promised that in the fourth generation, the people would come out and return to the land that God had given to Abraham. Yet that land, which was spoken of in Nehemiah 9:8, was inhabited by a people who were cursed.

Back in Genesis 9, after the flood, Noah "planted a vineyard: and he drank of the wine, and was drunken; and he was uncovered within his tent. And Ham, the father of Canaan, saw the nakedness of his father, and told his two brethren without." Shem and Japheth took a garment, and they backed up and covered Noah, so that they would not see his nakedness. But when Noah awoke from his wine, he knew what his younger son had done to him. Then Noah cursed Canaan; he did not curse Ham, who was the guilty one. He cursed Canaan, the fourth son of Ham.

It is important for us to understand where the descendants of Canaan and the descendants of Shem came to dwell. In Genesis 10, in what is called the Table of Nations, we read starting from verse 15, "And Canaan," that is Ham's son, "begat Sidon his firstborn, and Heth, and the Jebusite, and the Amorite, and the Girgasite, and the Hivite, and the Arkite, and the Sinite, and the Arvadite, and the Zemarite, and the Hamathite: and afterward were the families of the Canaanites spread abroad." Here we have the origin of many of the people in the Bible whose names end in *-ite*. It is important to notice that it says in verse 19, "And the border of the Canaanites was from

Sidon." The whole region of what would later become Judea would be inhabited by the descendants of Canaan. When we refer to "the land of Canaan," we tend to forget that these cursed people, who were tribal in nature, inhabited the whole region.

The descendants of Shem include Elam, whose line was the Elamites, and Ashur, whose territory was called Assyria. But the line of Ashur must not be confused with the "Assyrians" who were later brought to that territory, who have more to do with Nimrod and Babylon than they do with the line of Shem. The descendants of Shem lived across a wide swath of land, stretching approximately from the Euphrates all the way down to the lands along the Gulf and to the water's edge of what we now call the Indian Ocean. Abraham was one of the descendants of Shem, and God called him out of Ur of Chaldees, or *Casdim*, and told him, "I am going to give you a land."

Genesis 12:6 says that there were Canaanites in that land, and Genesis 13:7 says that there were Canaanites *and* Perizzites in that land. The answer to the question "Where did these people come from?" is that they were squatters. It is important to view them this way, because they weren't given any territories. In fact, they were of the cursed line. Why would the cursed line inhabit the very place that God would say is dear to Him and that He gave to His promised line? That is the way the devil always works. The devil likes to caricature things; he always takes something that was intended to be used one way and twists it into something else.

In Genesis 10:16, we read of another descendant of Canaan, the Jebusites. In King David's day, David conquered the fortress of Jebus, which became known as Jerusalem, the city of David. The fact that it had been settled by the Jebusites tells us that many generations of these cursed people had established themselves in the land.

When God called Abram out of Ur of Chaldees, it was as though God had let a diamond, His precious stone, be covered up in a cesspool of polytheism. Yet God knew exactly who was His when He called Abram out of Ur. He knew when He called Abram forth and said, "I will show you the land," and when He said, "I will give it to you."

In the Garden of Eden, God gave man everything to keep and to enjoy, except for one tree that they were told they could not touch. But after man's fall and his expulsion from the garden, there is no record of God giving a designated land to His people until this point. Now after many generations, God was saying to Abram, "You, the one I called out of the cesspool, I am going to give you that land, a land that I created and I have a design for." But there were squatters in that land. Some might think, "Well, shouldn't the promised seed have settled immediately in Canaan?" No. God called Abram out and said, "I am going to give you this land, but guess what—you are going to have to fight for it!"

That is a message that is missing from most churches and from most preaching. God is too often depicted as a Santa Claus handing out gifts for His children to revel in. It is true that every child of God can revel in God's goodness and His promises, but if we are really going to walk the walk of faith, there are some things that we have to wrestle down and work through in this pilgrimage down here.

We are talking about the God who holds up His word, and we have a picture of God's delivering His people in four verses of the prayer in Nehemiah. In Genesis 15, God promised Abram, "Know of a surety that thy seed shall be a stranger in a land that is not theirs, and shall serve them; and they shall afflict them four hundred years." God is speaking of those who will go into Egypt's bondage, and they will come out with great substance, and "in the fourth generation they shall come hither again." Abram was standing in that land when God said to him, "Your descendants will come back to this very place."

Now either God saw these things from afar, or the writer of this book was simply telling a bunch of lies. There were hundreds of years between this promise and its fulfillment. Abraham will be one hundred years old by the time that Isaac is born. Isaac will marry Rebekah when he is forty, and they will have two children, Jacob and Esau, who will produce two nations. And out of Jacob's loins, through his two wives and their handmaids, would come the house of Israel. Jacob's name will be changed to Israel, and near the end of his life, his whole family will move down to Egypt, because of a famine in the land of Canaan. And God sent Jacob's son Joseph ahead of them to Egypt in order that Joseph might save them.

When you look at God's fidelity, all of the details are vitally important. Look at the life of Joseph, who was sold into slavery by his brethren who hated him. But God had His hand in everything that happened to Joseph, including everything that happened to him while he was in prison and became the interpreter of Pharaoh's dreams. Joseph was in prison for a purpose. God would enter into every mess and make things come out the way He intended. When the famine hit the land, all the food that Jacob and his children needed could only be bought through Joseph. That is a beautiful type of Christ. As people of God, all the spiritual food we really need, our sustenance, can only come from Him.

The children of Israel went down to Egypt, and many more promises were given to them in the last chapters of Genesis. I would like us to look at one in particular, in Genesis 48. Now Abraham has died and hundreds of years have passed. Jacob was about to die, and we read in Genesis 48:21 that he said to his son, Joseph, "Behold, I die: but God shall be with you, and bring you again unto the land of your fathers." The promise is given again, and it comes right at the end of the book. In Genesis 50, Joseph was one hundred ten years old, and right before he died, he said, "God will surely visit you, and bring you out of this land unto the land which he sware to Abraham, to Isaac, and to Jacob." If we did not know the history of these people as we now do, this would seem like an insane promise.

Joseph had garnered favor with the king of Egypt, who essentially made Joseph ruler over all of that land. When his brothers and his father came to Egypt, this king had said, "I will give you the best of the land of Egypt, and you shall eat the fat of the land." So God's people dwelt in Egypt. But we read in Exodus 1:8, "Now there arose up a new king over Egypt, which knew not Joseph." This new Pharaoh did not know about Joseph, "and he said unto his people, Behold, the people of the children of Israel are more and mightier than we. . . . Therefore they did set over them taskmasters to afflict them with their burdens. And they built for Pharaoh treasure cities, Pithom and Raamses. But the more they afflicted them, the more they multiplied and grew."

Today, people say that if you have affliction, you cannot grow; but I say that you cannot grow without affliction. Spiritually you cannot become what you need to be without some form of affliction, because it is that affliction that either makes you run to God or run away from God. The children of Israel cried out to the Lord in their affliction, and God heard their cry. God did "see the affliction of our fathers in Egypt."

The question is always asked, "Why did God let these people go into Egypt's bondage?" Your answer will depend upon whose side you want to be on, but I would rather be on God's side and I say that this was a demonstration of God's wisdom. He knew that His people would become numerous in that land, and He knew that when He would finally lead them out by means of a deliverer, they would recognize Him and they would recognize their deliverer. They would become one united people. When Moses would speak for God before Pharaoh, he would say, "Israel is my son," referring to His people. In other passages in the Bible, He would call them "the apple of His eye." And God sent Moses to Pharaoh to say, "Let my people go."

Before Moses was born, "The king of Egypt spake to the Hebrew midwives," and told them that if any sons were born to the Hebrew women, the midwives were to take those sons and kill them; but if any girls were born, they would be allowed to live. But the Hebrew midwives refused to obey the king's command, and they let the boys live. "And the king of Egypt called for the midwives, and said unto them, Why have ye done this thing, and have saved the men children alive? And the midwives said unto Pharaoh, Because the Hebrew women are not as the Egyptian women; for they are lively, and are delivered ere the midwives come in unto them." So Pharaoh gave an order that all the sons born to the Hebrew women should be thrown into the Nile. This was a satanic plan to eliminate God's chosen deliverer, and yet God's people prevailed. We know the story of Moses' birth, and how his mother placed him in a basket in the river, and how the daughter of Pharaoh found him and raised him as a prince in Egypt.

Another Pharaoh will come to power after Moses flees from Egypt. We read in Exodus 2:23, "And it came to pass in process of time, that the king of Egypt died." There were actually multiple Pharaohs during Moses' lifetime, and if you study the history of Egypt, you will find that there may have been multiple kings of northern and of southern Egypt as well, depending on the time period. We read in Exodus 2:15 that when Moses fled from Egypt, he went to dwell in the land of Midian. The people of Midian were descendants of Abraham through his second wife, Keturah.

At this point in time, God's people, who had been promised the land and who should have been given the land, were now being held in captivity in a strange land. It does not look like the promise is going to be fulfilled. Now we know that they did in fact come out of Egypt and enter in to the Promised Land, because we have the whole book. But if you were standing at this point on a time line of history, you might say, "I don't see how God can fix this! Pharaoh is too powerful, and God's people are too weak. They don't have any weapons and they can't do anything!" But the Scripture says, "And God heard their groaning, and God remembered his covenant with Abraham, with Isaac, and with Jacob."

God holds up His word. Now, it may take God a few hundred years. He had said it would be four generations for these people, but God made good on His word. During those four hundred years, many people lived and died, because people did not live as long as they did before the flood. Maybe the first generation died thinking, "God didn't do anything," and they are now gone. And then the second generation may have said, "God still is not doing anything," and they are now gone; and the third generation may have said likewise. But in the fourth generation, they could look back as they were leaving Egypt and say, being reminded of the covenant that was made with Abraham, Isaac and Jacob, "This is what God said He would do!"

Now you might think, "Well, of course God would do this," but how many times have *you* forgotten, having the Bible in hand and seeing all His glorious promises? Looking back at the history of God's people, for forty years God led them through the wilderness where they lacked nothing. In the book of Nehemiah, we see the people who are now back in the Promised Land and have rebuilt the city of Jerusalem. Looking back, we see that the promise was doubly fulfilled. They entered in to the land, but later they were carried away into captivity. Then they came back to the land, and they were standing in the land and were told, "Do you see how God holds up His word?"

I want you to think about God holding up His word, especially those of you who are grappling with things that are just beyond comprehension. You may get tired and weak, and you may even lose faith along the way. These people were in bondage in Egypt for a total of four hundred thirty years. Now I don't know about you, but I can get disheartened in only an hour. I am just being honest. And that is why I say that you always need to come back to these lessons. They are lessons to establish the principle of God's fidelity.

This prayer in Nehemiah speaks volumes, though most of us are familiar with the Exodus and the deliverance of God's people. Moses might seem like an unlikely choice, because he was brought up in a palace with all the pleasures of Egypt, yet God chose that man. Again, I go back to the analogy of a cesspool with a diamond hidden somewhere in it. God knows where things are, even though they are covered up and soiled. I do not believe that most people see themselves in that light. Let me make an analogy to a young child who has been given a treat or a piece of chocolate and has just made a mess of things. The child is all covered in a gooey, sticky mess. Where the analogy breaks down is that a messy child can still look cute. But I want you to envision yourself in that way for a moment. And God looks down on His children and says, "My kids are just covered in a filthy mess," except what covers us is sin. That is why we need to understand the concept of "crossing over," just like the children of Israel crossed over the Red Sea. God parted the sea and made a way; we cross over the sea and are covered with the shed blood of Jesus Christ. We are washed and cleansed and made whole. And God looks at us as we now are in Christ, as though we were just like Him. We are now clean in His eyes.

So when we talk about a great deliverance, there could be no greater type than God's delivering His people out of Egypt's bondage. God chose an unlikely person and spoke to him in an unlikely place, on the backside of the desert. God spoke out of the burning bush, and we read in Exodus 3:8, "I am come down to deliver them out of the hand of the Egyptians, and to bring them up out of that land unto a good land and a large, unto a land flowing with milk and honey; unto the place of the Canaanites, and the Hittites, and the Amorites, and the Perizzites, and the Hivites, and the Jebusites." Moses was warned in advance that there would be squatters in the land.

God gave instructions to Moses and said, "Go, and gather the elders of Israel together, and say unto them, The LORD God of your fathers, the God of Abraham, of Isaac, and of Jacob, appeared unto me, saying, I have surely visited you, and seen that which is done to you in Egypt: and I have said, I will bring you up out of the affliction of Egypt unto the land of the Canaanites. . . ."

If someone had told me that I would be going into a land where I would have to fight a whole bunch of enemies, I really don't know what I would do. But if I had to choose between living as a slave in bondage or living free and fighting for my freedom, there would be no choice. This is why the spiritual moorings of this country are so off, because no one can see the concept of fighting for freedom and how important that has always been. God did not hand freedom to His people on a silver platter. He said, "Here is the land. Get in there and go fight. And as you fight, I will be with you to fight your battles with you. But you still must fight for your freedom." I don't know what is wrong with this country today, where many people don't understand that there are men and women fighting for our freedom in foreign lands, not just one day a year, but 24 hours a day, 365 days a year. Why can't we as Americans have the same mindset that God had concerning these people? If something is worthwhile, it is worth fighting for, and freedom is one of those things, for these people and for us as well.

Everything comes at a price, and you must be willing to pay the price. Don't ask for God's blessings in your life if you are not willing to walk through the storms. Don't ask God to remove the storms. But when the storms come, say, "Thank You, Lord, for those storms, because I know that You are with me. I know that the rainbow which will appear after the storm will be Your doing, and I know that the sun that will come out and keep me warm and the shelter that You will provide are all of Your doing." The freedom that will be obtained will be worth going through the storm with God.

We read in Nehemiah 9:10 that God "shewedst signs and wonders upon Pharaoh, and on all his servants, and on all the people of his land: for thou knewest that they dealt proudly against them." God plagued the Egyptians and turned their water into blood; He sent frogs and lice and flies, plagues of boils, plagues of hail and locusts. There were three days of darkness and the deaths of the first-born. The Passover was instituted and the people killed the paschal lamb and applied its blood to the lintel and the doorposts of their houses. And then finally, the people were led out of Egypt.

Now let me ask you something. If you were a part of those people who were with Moses, and you saw all of those things happen with your own eyes, wouldn't you say, "Okay, Moses, I am reporting for duty! Where are we going? I don't care; I am following you!" That is what I would have said if I had seen all of those things. What is even more remarkable is that it says very clearly in Exodus 12:40–41, "Now the sojourning of the children of Israel, who dwelt in Egypt, was four hundred and thirty years. And it came to pass at the end of the four hundred and thirty years, even the selfsame day it came to pass, that all the hosts of the LORD went out from the land of Egypt." And again in verse 51, "It came to pass the selfsame day, that the LORD did bring the children of Israel out of the land of Egypt by their armies."

They were delivered out of the land of Egypt, but they were not yet in the Promised Land. They were not only greatly delivered, but to top it all off, when Pharaoh and all of his army pursued the people, the sea was parted, the people crossed over on dry land, and then God closed up the water and drowned the enemies. The people who had seen these miracles were obedient for a time, but that did not last very long.

Since God did all of this, why did the people have to go wandering for forty years in the desert? The number forty in the Bible is symbolic of a period of complete testing. It was as though God was saying, "I don't think they are ready yet." The people might have been saying, "Are we there yet? We are tired. We are hungry. We need this. We need that," but I think that God was saying, "You need to walk a little bit more." You can follow their wanderings on a map and see all of the places that they went, when they could have just made a beeline and gone straight into the Promised Land. We cannot tell exactly how long it would have taken them to go there by a more direct route, but we do know that it wasn't a journey that required forty years.

God had made a promise. Remember it would not be Moses to lead the people in, it would be Joshua. Most of those who followed Moses were the ones murmuring and complaining. When they were hungry, God fed them, and when they were thirsty, He sweetened the waters in one place, and He made water come out of a rock in another place. Everywhere they went, God provided for them and sustained them and protected them, even in their first encounter with the Amalekites. This history of God's deliverance was not simply recounted as a history lesson for the people in Nehemiah's day. It was given to a people who needed encouragement. They were standing in that land and they needed to be reminded that it was indeed the land that was promised. It was a promise obtained in the past, and was a future promise, which we know was fulfilled in the coming of Christ, and there is also a future promise which will be fulfilled when Christ will return. That part of the land will play a pivotal role in history at the end of days, when Christ comes.

We are speaking of God's great deliverance, His leading and providing for His people. It should not be too difficult for us to take hold of this concept by faith and make an application to our own lives. God was leading His people the whole time. We read in Exodus 13 that God did not lead them through the way of the land of the Philistines, even though it would have been a more direct route. He avoided that land, "Lest peradventure the people repent when they see war, and they return to Egypt." The danger was that the people always teetered on the edge of going back to Egypt.

Egypt is a symbolic type of bondage to the world or bondage to sin and the flesh. So when we see the children of Israel's wanting to return to Egypt, it is a warning that there is always the danger of your looking back and thinking that there is something better out there for you than what God is doing inside you. Most of the time, you cannot see or even discern what God is doing in you. These people had an open display of God's deliverance. They had signs and wonders. God sent a deliverer equipped with words and equipped with power and the knowledge of God. God had revealed Himself to Moses, saying, "I am." And all the way through the wilderness they had another sure sign: there was a pillar of cloud by day and a pillar of fire by night to guide them in the way.

The children of Israel had a visible manifestation of God's presence; they could have looked at any time and seen God's deliverance. In our day, there are many people who, if they could see a miracle, it would never be enough, because they could always say, "Well, that one could have been a hoax." They will never come to the faith through that means, which is why God does not often do those types of outward miraculous signs today. But God performs inward miraculous signs every single day. These people needed to have signposts everywhere that said, "I am the Lord your God. I will lead you. I will take care of you. I will feed you when you are hungry. I will give you water when you are thirsty. I will provide for you." They wanted visible and tangible signs—but it was never enough. In the New Testament, Peter speaks of Jesus Christ, and says, "whom having *not* seen, ye love." Romans 8 and Galatians 5 talk about being led by the Spirit. There are no fancy displays of God's power today, no signposts, but every day great miracles occur. God still delivers people in the same way, and He delivers them from the world, the flesh and the devil, in an ongoing, lifelong battle.

Isn't it interesting that after the enemies are drowned in the sea, Exodus 14 ends with these words: "Thus the LORD saved Israel that day out of the hand of the Egyptians; and Israel saw the Egyptians dead upon the sea shore. And Israel saw that great work which the LORD did upon the Egyptians: and the people feared the LORD, and believed the LORD," that is, they *amened* the Lord, "and his servant Moses."

We know that that only lasted for a time. It only took a few days of journeying before they forgot what God had done, and they started to complain and wanted to go back to Egypt. How quickly we do the same thing and forget about God's goodness in our lives and all the things that He has spared us from. We forget about those accidents that we narrowly avoided as a result of His angels encamped around us. We forget about those times when God provided for us when it seemed like we might not make it. How often are we just like these people; we experience a great deliverance and in that moment, we say, "Of course, amen!" But give us a week or a month away from walking with the Lord and acknowledging Him in all things, and we revert back to the same old faithlessness, and we say, "I doubt God will do this thing." The whole Bible is a history that reveals God's faithfulness and His long-suffering with His people.

We have seen in the Scriptures how God performed His word, He upheld His word, He kept His word and He wrought a great deliverance. He saw, He heard, He showed and He knew. He did divide the sea, He dealt with the enemies and He led His people.

The prayer in Nehemiah continues to chronicle the history of God's revelation and instruction, His coming down and giving the law and speaking forth His commandments, God's giving supply and provision to His people, giving them bread and water. Yet we read in Nehemiah 9:16–17, "But they and our fathers dealt proudly, and hardened their necks, and hearkened not to thy commandments, and refused to obey, neither were mindful of thy wonders that thou didst among them; but hardened their necks, and in their rebellion appointed a captain to return to their bondage."

Think on these words that were spoken at a celebration of God's great deliverance. If there is some exclamation mark to put on this prayer, God's great deliverance was confirmed by history! The people were gathered together and whoever was praying was saying, in essence, "Don't forget that! God delivered you from such a great death!" This is echoed in the New Testament in 2 Corinthians 1:10, where it says that we had a sentence of death upon us, but we were delivered; God did deliver us. He delivered us in the past, He is delivering us in the present, and He will deliver us in the future! That is the promise for those who stand recognizing that God upholds His word. He hasn't put His word behind His back and He hasn't covered it up, though many people do, because they do not want to hear about God's word.

God is still holding up His word, and His church is still holding up His word and declaring, "Look to that word, because God has not changed and His promises have not changed." It just takes one thing, and that is looking with faith to what He said He will do. The history of these people in the book of Nehemiah confirms it. And I believe that if you were to look back on all the way the Lord has led you thus far, your history confirms it too.

I can look back on my life and see God's great deliverance and recognize He was there all along the way. It may have taken me a little bit longer than some to acknowledge and recognize His leading, but I do not need any signposts. The greatest signpost is what He has done inside my heart, causing me to understand that He was with me, that He was for me and not against me, and that He loved me and took me to Himself for a special purpose. How privileged and how honored I am that I could be His servant! I pray that that attitude would prevail among His people. What a great deliverance God has wrought, especially when we think about what might have happened to us had God not reached down to rescue us. There is the cesspool of life, and then there are the diamonds. He calls you His treasured people, so think on that. And if you are still faltering and trying to figure out what to do, remember that God holds up His word.

Chapter 13

THE LESSON OF THE MANNA

We have been preaching on Nehemiah 9 and what is one of the longest prayers in the Bible. It is a prayer that reflects back on all the goodness of the Lord and all the ways that He led His people, from the time of creation to the period when the children of Israel entered into the Promised Land. Everything in this prayer is centered on God; it speaks of His faithfulness and also of the failure of His people, which are concepts that we can take into the New Testament frame and apply to the church today.

Today we will be starting from verse 9. The prayer speaks of God who did "see the affliction of our fathers in Egypt, and heardest their cry by the Red Sea; and shewedst signs and wonders upon Pharaoh, and on all his servants, and on all the people of his land: for thou knewest that they dealt proudly against them. So didst thou get thee a name, as it is this day. And thou didst divide the sea before them, so that they went through the midst of the sea on the dry land; and their persecutors thou threwest into the deeps, as a stone into the mighty waters. Moreover thou leddest them in the day by a cloudy pillar; and in the night by a pillar of fire, to give them light in the way wherein they should go. Thou camest down also upon mount Sinai, and spakest with them from heaven, and gavest them right judgments, and true laws, good statutes and commandments: and madest known unto them thy holy sabbath, and commandedst them precepts, statutes, and laws, by the hand of Moses thy servant: and gavest them bread from heaven for their hunger." A few verses later, we read that God "withheldest not thy manna from their mouth, and gavest them water for their thirst. Yea, forty years didst thou sustain them in the wilderness, so that they lacked nothing; their clothes waxed not old, and their feet swelled not."

When we read passages that recall the history of God's people, the subject matter is so familiar that we are often tempted to believe that the lessons are not applicable to us today. Or we only selectively take the lessons that we would like to take. I want us to understand that there are principles embodied in these passages that are not strictly limited to the laws and commandments in the Old Testament. If we pay close attention to this prayer, we can see that these people understood something about God's nature that we can carry with us today, something we can chew on as "soul food." So I want you to underline in your Bible two statements from these passages: in verse 13, it says God came down and *"spakest with them from heaven"* and made things known to them; and in verse 15, it says God *"gavest them bread from heaven."* God had more than one way to teach His people. He did not only teach them by means of "Thou shalt" and "Thou shalt not," He also taught them by means of the manna. The lesson of the manna is very important, though it is evident that most of God's people did not learn this lesson.

Let's look at the background in the book of Exodus. God had delivered the children of Israel out of Egypt. He parted the Red Sea in order that the people could go through, and then He closed up the waters and drowned the Egyptians. And as the people began their journey, the first place they came to was a place where the waters were bitter. When you spend time in God's word, you begin to see patterns. Notice that after the people were delivered, their first stop was at a place where there were bitter waters. There are too many preachers who will tell you that when God delivers you, everything will become sweet. But God's method of delivering His people has never been by simply transporting them away from their trials so that they might not experience the bitterness and harshness of life.

When the people murmured about the bitter waters, God instructed Moses to fell a tree into the waters, and the waters were made sweet. That tree was a type of Christ. Everything in the Old Testament points to Christ, but there is something about this particular episode that strikes me. Count the number of miracles that occurred leading up to the Exodus out of Egypt. Depending on how you count them, there were at least twenty-one or as many as twenty-five miracles. That is a whole lot of miracles! Now I don't know about you, but I know that I have not seen that many miracles in my life. But if we had seen all of those miracles, I would hope that our reaction would not be like that of these people recorded in Exodus 16. "They took their journey from Elim, and all the congregation of the children of Israel came unto the wilderness of Sin, which is between Elim and Sinai, on the fifteenth day of the second month," which means this was just a few weeks after they had exited Egypt. "And the whole congregation of the children of Israel murmured against Moses and Aaron in the wilderness."

It is unfortunate, but you will always find examples of people who are ungrateful. The children of Israel did not understand that Moses and Aaron did not have to be perfect. In fact, no one whom God has chosen is perfect, except Jesus Christ. Jesus came in the likeness of sinning flesh, yet He knew no sin.

After this great deliverance from Egypt, after all of those great miracles, the people murmured against Moses and Aaron, as if it were Moses and Aaron who came up with the plan to deliver the people. And eventually these people will murmur directly against God. "The children of Israel said unto them, Would to God we had died by the hand of the LORD in the land of Egypt, when we sat by the flesh pots, and when we did eat bread to the full." In other words, "You brought us out into this wilderness to kill us!" This is a problem with some people today. They come to church broken and bowed down, and life has eaten away at their vitality. When they first hear God's word, they get comforted for a while. But then all hell breaks loose on them, and they say to God, "What did You do *that* for?" Remarkably, the children of Israel were complaining that they got better food when they were slaves in Egypt. Then the Lord said unto Moses, "Behold, I will rain bread from heaven for you," I am going to cause bread to come down from heaven, "and the people shall go out and gather a certain rate every day, that I may prove them."

God did not say, "I am going to give you free food and create a welfare state." He said, "I am going to *prove* these people." The Hebrew word for "prove" here is the same word used in Genesis 22:1, where it says, "God did *tempt* Abraham," that is, God tested or tried him, concerning Isaac.

God said, "I will rain bread from heaven for you; and the people shall go out and gather a certain rate every day, that I may prove them, whether they will walk in my law, or no." He gave them further instructions to gather twice as much manna on the sixth day in preparation for the Sabbath, when they would not go out and gather. "And Moses and Aaron said unto all the children of Israel, At even, then ye shall know that the LORD hath brought you out from the land of Egypt: and in the morning, then ye shall see the glory of the LORD; for that he heareth your murmurings against the LORD." Moses and Aaron said to the people, "You are not complaining against *us*, you are complaining against God!"

This should be the quintessential lesson for the church. Too many people have their own ideas of what God's leaders ought to be doing. And it is unfortunate that many pastors end up like Aaron, who succumbed to the pressure from the congregation to please the flesh and made an idol of a molten calf. When God calls a person to the pulpit, though he or she is frail and faltering, they are called to deliver the word of God, not to cater to the flesh and not to make you feel good. They are called to educate you, to help you come to know, as the New Testament says, the one true living God and Jesus Christ His Son whom He has sent.

When the people murmured against Moses and Aaron, it came right back at the people because Moses said that the Lord heard their murmurings against *Him.* And Moses said, "And what are we, that ye murmur against us?" Anyone who feels inclined to complain about their pastor should read this passage. The apostle Paul makes it very clear that God gave some gift ministers to the church "for the perfecting of the saints," and not the other way around. Moses could have said, "God, blot them out now," and later on God would be ready to blot them out. But Moses will plead and intercede for them, and say, "Lord, please don't kill them. If You kill these people, then those who know that You delivered them out of Egypt will ask why You delivered them in the first place!"

Moses said to the people, "What are we? your murmurings are not against us, but against the LORD. And Moses spake unto Aaron, Say unto all the congregation of the children of Israel, Come near before the LORD: for he hath heard your murmurings. And it came to pass, as Aaron spake unto the whole congregation of the children of Israel, that they looked toward the wilderness, and, behold, the glory of the LORD appeared in the cloud. And the LORD spake unto Moses, saying, I have heard the murmurings of the children of Israel: speak unto them, saying, At even ye shall eat flesh, and in the morning ye shall be filled with bread."

There is something about bread that God really likes, because it is mentioned throughout the Bible. What did God say to Adam when He cursed him? "You are going to eat bread all your life." What is the name of the town where Jesus was born? Bethlehem, which means "house of bread." When famine hit the land, Joseph's brothers did not ask, "Where can we buy milk?" They asked, "Where can we buy bread?" And even as Jesus was about to feed the multitude, He asked Philip, "Where can we buy bread?" God told the children of Israel that they "shall be filled with bread; and ye shall know that I am the LORD your God. And it came to pass, that at even the quails came up, and covered the camp: and in the morning the dew lay round about the host. And when the dew that lay was gone up, behold, upon the face of the wilderness there lay a small round thing, as small as the hoar frost on the ground. And when the children of Israel saw it, they said one to another, It is manna." Literally, they said, "What is this thing?" That is what *manna* means; it was a "whatchamacallit." "For they wist not what it was. And Moses said unto them, This is the bread which the LORD hath given you to eat."

For forty years this supply of food did not fail. The number forty typifies a time of complete testing. So you would think that after all those many years of faithful provision, someone would have said, "I get it! We can depend on God to supply all of our need!" The lesson was that we can trust Him to take care of us and supply our need, and that is not limited to just physical hunger.

God is teaching us other things in this lesson. We know that God said He would provide manna for a time and then the supply would cease when the people entered into the Promised Land. But what is remarkable is that God knew exactly where to rain down the manna even though the people moved around from place to place for forty years. Now that may seem to be self-evident, but it demonstrates that God knew exactly where they were at every point in their journey. Anywhere the camp moved, that was where the manna fell. God was not only a faithful God, He was also with them everywhere they went. God through this lesson was making a point, and we always tend to miss the lesson that is right in front of us. When the psalmist asks, "Can God furnish a table in the wilderness?" the answer is, "Of course!" And He can do it anywhere. The manna fell in close proximity to where the people were; they did not have to go to another town to get it.

God told the people, "Each man has to gather the manna, and he will not gather too much or too little." The people brought whatever amount of bread they gathered that day to their tents, and they had to consume it all. Now God could have dumped the manna all in one place and all at one time. He could have said, "I am giving you a one-time meal that you can carry around for forty years!" But God knew that if He had done that, some people would gather more than they needed, and some probably would have become covetous of what others had, even if they were given enough. Remember that they had to consume all the manna that fell each day, and if they didn't, it would spoil. And they could not gather any on the Sabbath. So God laid out a plan, and He was teaching them through the manna. They received precepts and commandments at the hands of Moses to understand God's ways, but the manna taught them the lesson that He would provide. God didn't have to respond to their murmurings. The people left Egypt "spoiling" the Egyptians, which means they not only went out with silver and gold, they went out with cattle and other livestock. They were in the wilderness and had provision, yet they said, "Oh, would to God we could die right here. We miss the food of Egypt. Give us that food!"

There is a description of what the manna looked like. It was round and it had no jagged edges; there was nothing rough about it. You might say that it had no beginning and no end. It was white, symbolizing God's purity, and it was a gift from God. It is evident that the manna was a type of Christ.

There is another lesson being taught here. God wanted to instruct the people about His Sabbath. But He was not emphasizing the Sabbath day as we understand it today. When He told them to "keep My Sabbath," it was to remind them of what the Sabbath originally was: God created everything, and then He rested. It was not so much given as a day for them to rest; rather it was in commemoration of God's resting after the creation.

Try to imagine what these people might have done on a day when they did not work and did not gather. They probably discussed things about their families or about the people within the community. They probably talked about the goodness of God and what He had done for them. By putting that emphasis on the Sabbath, God was forcing these people back to a recognition of His power in all creation.

The people were told not to take more manna than they needed, and not to keep it overnight. Yet we read in verses 20–21, "Notwithstanding they hearkened not unto Moses; but some of them left of it until the morning, and it bred worms, and stank: and Moses was wroth with them. And they gathered it every morning, every man according to his eating," sufficient for each day.

Now if we were only talking about bread for the stomach, we see that God did in fact provide them with manna and with quail, and He also sweetened the waters so that they could drink. That in itself is pretty amazing. All of this provision was a free gift from God, unmerited; no one could work to obtain it, and each person had to appropriate it for himself. The Bible says, "Taste and see that the Lord is good," which talks about the concept of bread for the soul. I want us to notice that this bread remains merely bread until it is individually appropriated and consumed.

Another lesson is being taught here in a subtle way about the concept of God's sovereignty and God's election. Many denominations tend to polarize around their own definition of "election." I have said that God is sovereign: He can call whom He will. He can make someone hear who has ears to hear, or He can take someone who was born out of due time, turn him around and give him the capacity to hear. But God chose a people and He revealed His greatness to them by means of this miraculous provision.

The miraculous provision of the manna was unlike any other provision by God. God provided for Elijah through the ravens that brought him food that they found. When that supply came to an end, He told Elijah to go to Zarephath where God provided through a widow who was able to feed him and her house for many days with the little food she already had. Even when Jesus fed the multitude, He used the loaves and fish that the boy already had in his possession. But for the people in the wilderness, the manna was not produced from anything that already existed; it rained down from heaven, and it was produced by God.

God gave the people specific instructions on how much manna to gather every day, "that I may prove them." And clearly, they failed the test. God said, "I will rain down bread that I may prove them, whether they will *walk* in my law, or no." Notice He did not say, "whether they will *keep* my law, or no." Distinguish between *keeping* the law, which no man is able to do in its entirety, and walking in God's law, which essentially means at least going in God's direction. The history of these people is not very good. Based on the total population chronicled during that time, there were somewhere between 600,000 and 2,000,000 people in the wilderness who did not get the lesson! God was trying to teach His people that He loved and cared for them, and that He would provide for them. And this lesson is summarized in the prayer of Nehemiah 9. The fact that God spoke to them from heaven and rained bread from heaven says that they were very special people, a chosen-out people.

As we move into the New Testament, we still encounter the concept of bread everywhere. What was the first thing that happened after Jesus was baptized and then led by the Spirit into the wilderness where He was tempted by the devil? The devil commanded Jesus to turn stones into bread. But Jesus replied, quoting from Deuteronomy 8: "Man shall not live by bread alone, but by every word that proceedeth out of the mouth of God." Wasn't that the same lesson that God was trying to teach the people in the wilderness? If you read Deuteronomy 8, that was exactly what God was saying: "Listen to Me. There is more than just your belly to be fed; your soul needs to be fed." And when Jesus taught His disciples to pray, He said, "Pray ye: Our Father. . . . Give us this day our daily bread." God is saying, "I am sufficient for you."

All sixty-six books of the Bible declare God's provision, sufficiency, fidelity and love. You can only really come to know about God and His ways by spending time in His word and understanding that God wants to nourish hungry souls. Jesus tells us to not worry about the food for our bellies, but to strive for the things that do not perish. He is speaking of Himself and His word.

We saw in Exodus 16 how God's people failed to learn the lesson of God's provision. You can also read about it in Numbers 11. But I would like to juxtapose the record of these people in the Old Testament with the events recorded in John 6, so please turn there. Jesus was about to feed the multitude, and He asked Philip, "Whence shall we buy bread, that these may eat? And this he said to prove him: for he himself knew what he would do." Jesus asked the question *to prove* him. The word for "to prove" in the Greek is *peirazo.* It is the same word that is used in the Septuagint in Exodus 16 and in Genesis 22, but we see a different type of testing here, unlike the testing in the wilderness. Christ was testing His disciples to see if they would trust Him. But Philip answered, "Two hundred pennyworth of bread is not sufficient for them." He told Jesus that there wasn't enough money to buy bread for all the people. Philip's answer should have been, "Lord, You can make it enough!" But he had not yet made that connection, even though the disciples had already seen Jesus perform many great miracles.

Jesus miraculously fed the multitude, and there were enough fragments left over to fill twelve baskets. Then He performed another miracle in which He walked on water. Now we read beginning at verse 25, "And when they had found him on the other side of the sea, they said unto him, Rabbi, when camest thou hither?" When did You get here? "Jesus answered them and said, Verily, verily, I say unto you, Ye seek me, not because ye saw the miracles, but because ye did eat of the loaves, and were filled." Earlier, they wanted to make Him king because He fed the people. But they were not thinking of Him as king, in the sense of the Messiah. They wanted to make Him king so that He could be their provider of free food. So He said, "Ye seek me, not because ye saw the miracles, but because ye did eat of the loaves, and were filled. Labour not for the meat which perisheth, but for that meat which endureth unto everlasting life, which the Son of man shall give unto you: for him hath God the Father sealed." Jesus was referring to the true soul food. We must quest after that food for the soul! Even the prodigal son, when he came to his senses, said, "In my father's house there is bread enough to spare." God really likes *this* Bread, for John 3:16 says that He gave His only begotten Son: that is the true Bread.

The people asked Jesus, "What shall *we* do, that *we* might work the works of God?" Notice the emphasis is on *we*. "Jesus answered and said unto them, This is the work of God, that ye believe on him whom he hath sent." Every time we read the word "believe," it translates the Greek verb *pisteuo*, which means "to trust." Our English word "believe" is inadequate to translate *pisteuo*, because "belief" only involves the mind, whereas *pisteuo* is an action word. It conveys the meaning of putting one's weight completely upon something. Dr. Gene Scott translated the word *pisteuo* by coining the expression "to *faithe.*" So Jesus said, "This is the work of God, that ye *faithe* on him whom he hath sent. They said therefore unto him, What sign shewest thou then, that we may see, and believe thee? what dost thou work?" They wanted Him to perform another miracle to prove He really was who He said He was!

This is a warning to people who are not well-versed in the Bible. We are not to put our focus on miracles. When the Antichrist comes in the end times, he will perform great miracles and the people will be amazed. Antichrist means "false Christ," and Paul warns us that the spirit of Antichrist is already at work. That is why it is important that we study God's word to understand that God is looking for people who will trust Him, not because He performs miracles, but because He is faithful to His word. Most of today's churches are so caught up in teaching people about what God can do for them here and now, that they have no breath of eternity on them. When Jesus returns, will people even recognize Him? Or will they readily run to Antichrist because of the great miracles that he will perform?

The people demanded that Jesus perform miracles to prove who He really was. "What sign shewest thou then, that we may see, and believe thee? what dost thou work? Our fathers did eat manna in the desert; as it is written, He gave them bread from heaven to eat." Jesus' reply was not subtle at all: "Verily, verily, I say unto you, Moses gave you not that bread from heaven." Moses was not the one who fed them. Remember back in Exodus 16:4, it was God who spoke to Moses, and said, "*I* will rain bread from heaven for you." Jesus said, "Moses gave you not that bread from heaven; but my Father giveth you the true bread from heaven." The people who ate the manna still eventually died. But Jesus said that if you eat of this true Bread, you will never be hungry and never die.

Now these verses of Scripture were tremendously twisted during the period prior to and straight through the Reformation, where the concept of eating God's flesh and drinking His blood became the doctrine of transubstantiation. Christ referred to His body and blood as meat and drink, and Satan managed to deceive the people into fixating on a literal interpretation of those words. They failed to see the spiritual food that God provided for them. But Jesus said, "For the bread of God is he which cometh down from heaven, and giveth life unto the world." In other words, while the manna was strictly for the children of Israel in the wilderness and not for other people in some other place, this Manna, which is the true Bread, is food for the world. God was trying to teach a lesson that those people in the wilderness failed to understand. That is why John said earlier, speaking of Jesus, "He came to his own, and his own received him not. But as many as received him, to them gave he the power to become the sons of God." But the people still said, "Lord, evermore give us this bread." They were telling Jesus, "We will stay with You if You give us free food." They were still focused on receiving free food! "And Jesus said unto them, I am the bread of life: he that cometh to me shall never hunger; and he that believeth on me," or "*faithes* on me shall never thirst. But I said unto you, That ye also have seen me, and believe not. All that the Father giveth me shall come to me; and him that cometh to me I will in no wise cast out."

That is a bold statement! Someone says, "I'm going to lead someone to the Lord today." That is not how it works. The Lord can open a person's eyes and ears and position you at the right time and the right place to be a conduit for that person to learn about God and His word. But as the saying goes, you can lead a horse to water, but you cannot make it drink. The soul must be hungry to eat of this Bread. When someone casually says, "I'd like to know a little about God," they are really saying, "I'm still not hungry for that Bread." But when someone says, "I want to know everything I can know about God," that is a person who is hungry to eat of this Bread. That is someone who understands that this Bread has the power to give life.

Nehemiah 9 says that God spoke from heaven and gave them bread from heaven. Here in John 6, the Son of God says, "I came down from heaven, not to do mine own will, but the will of him that sent me. And this is the Father's will which hath sent me, that of all which he hath given me I should lose nothing, but should raise it up again at the last day. And this is the will of him that sent me, that every one which seeth the Son, and *faitheth* on him, may have everlasting life: and I will raise him up at the last day. The Jews then murmured at him. . . ." There is a pattern of people constantly murmuring whenever God declares something of His nature. They did not murmur when He performed the miracles of feeding the multitude and of walking on water. But they murmured when He said, "I am that bread of life. Your fathers did eat manna in the wilderness, and are dead. This is the bread which cometh down from heaven, that a man may eat thereof, and not die. I am the living bread which came down from heaven: if any man eat of this bread, he shall live for ever: and the bread that I will give is my flesh, which I will give for the life of the world."

The people who were praying in Nehemiah 9 did not yet know what the manna symbolized, because Jesus had not yet come in the flesh to be revealed to them. The manna symbolized something better to come, which was fulfilled in Christ. The book of Hebrews says that at different times and in different ways, God spoke to the fathers through the prophets, including Moses. And in these last days, He has spoken to us through His Son Jesus Christ. From Moses' day in Exodus 16, to Nehemiah's day and straight to the time of John's writing of his Gospel, God is showing us that not everyone has an appetite for spiritual food.

This is probably one of the simplest lessons, but one of the more profound ones: I cannot make people have an appetite for this Bread. I can tell you about the love of God, about how God fixes the broken, how He heals the sick and how He will raise the dead. I can tell you about the things that happened on Calvary. I can tell you about all those things, but I cannot make you eat of this Bread. Some people simply do not have an appetite for this Bread. They want something else that Paul warned about: a "gospel" which is not really a gospel at all. But there is only one gospel, there is only one Bread, there is only one Source of life revealed to us in the New Testament, and that is in Christ Jesus. And if you do not eat of this Bread, your soul will remain hungry and impoverished.

There are some preachers who, after delivering their message, will ask their congregations if they are ready to "make a commitment" and "come up to the altar." They will tell the people that they must "accept" Christ and say the "sinner's prayer" to be saved. I can tell you that there is no such thing as the "sinner's prayer" in the Bible. I do find many sinners praying in the Bible. They cried out in a wilderness place; they cried out in their misery. And they learned that their cries were met with God's attentive ear, and that God takes care of His creation.

The appetite for this kind of food does not come from one moment at an altar. It comes when you spend time with God and study His word. Not only will you learn about God, you will also learn about yourself and about your wretched state. Without that spiritual food, you cannot exist. You may be able to exist out in the world, but you cannot become a new creature in Christ merely by glancing at God's word. You must approach God, learn about Him and learn about yourself. Then you will realize that without this Bread, you have no hope. This is a simple lesson, but the people in Nehemiah's day did not think about that. They saw the manna merely as a provision of food for the body. But the lesson for those people was that God would see His creation through, and that He would be enough. God is sufficient.

As a pastor, I do not have "altar calls." Rather, I teach you about God. I teach that if you have a hunger and you know you are broken, then you know you are broken. And if you know you are a sinner, then you know you are a sinner. We are not sinners because of what we say or how we act; we are all sinners because of what Adam did. When we come to the knowledge of who Jesus Christ is, when we understand what He did at the cross when He shed His blood to die for a sinning and lost world, then we can begin to understand that the way God makes possible is the way of faith. And His provision for us is the Bread of Life called Jesus Christ.

The only thing an altar call does is put a giant target on people's backs. The devil probably already knows the ones who have stepped forward in their hearts before they even step forward to the altar. The devil takes pride in soiling those testimonies as quickly as he can. You see a man who comes forward and says, "I'm a sinner and I know I'm a sinner, but from this day forward, I will walk with the Lord and I will keep His law and be holy and righteous." Yet six months later you might find that same man being dragged out of a bar by the cops. That is why I do not have altar calls or testimony services.

You should never make the mistake of basing your faith on someone else's "testimony." There have been a number of famous preachers who testified that they lived a pure and holy life, and they preached a perfectionist doctrine exhorting their listeners to do the same. And then it was discovered that they were living lives of hypocrisy. They would condemn others, while behind the scenes they were frauds. Not only did that cause some people to fall away from the faith, it also managed to make some people be hesitant to even approach the things of God. These days, many people think that any preacher who has a program on television must be a charlatan. Do not place your trust in a man or a woman who is in the pulpit; rather you should trust that God's Spirit is operating through that man or woman to deliver the word of God. Love the Lord and get to know His word, so you will not be deceived. And let no one condemn you with their perfectionist doctrine.

For those who are in bitterness or grief, this Bread is comfort and sweetness to the soul. If you have never known what it is to be needed and to be loved, you will begin to understand once you get into God's word. You will be able to say, "I am loved and I have a reason to get up every day, and that reason is found in the Bread of Life called Jesus Christ."

To the soul that is hungry, Jesus says, "Eat of this bread and you will never hunger again." To the soul that is thirsty, He says, "Drink of this water and you will thirst no more." Taste and see that this Bread is good. And those who are able to taste and see can say, "The Lord has given me enough strength and provision for this day according to His word, according to this Bread." The Lord is sufficient. The people in Nehemiah's day did not have this promise, but we have it, and thank God we have it!

Chapter 14

THE GOD OF FORGIVENESSES

We are continuing our study of the staggering prayer and petition recorded in Nehemiah 9. We read about the lesson of the manna, and how the people in the Old Testament did not recognize what it was. They did not call it "God's bread," they called it a "whatchamacallit." Likewise in the New Testament, when Jesus came, He had to ask, "Who do people say that I am?" In both cases, there was a failure to recognize God's true gift. We saw how God chose and called Abraham and found his heart faithful. And we reviewed a myriad number of verses that showed us God's deliverance: how He heard, protected, led and fed His people. Now we read beginning at verse 16, "But they and our fathers dealt proudly, and hardened their necks, and hearkened not to thy commandments, and refused to obey, neither were mindful of thy wonders that thou didst among them; but hardened their necks, and in their rebellion appointed a captain to return to their bondage: but thou art a God ready to pardon."

If you are reading from a King James Version Bible, you should see that the word *art* is italicized, indicating that it was added by the translators and is not in the original Hebrew text. There is an alternative translation in the margin of my Bible that says, "a God of pardons."

The phrase "but thou art a God ready to pardon" is a translation of only three words in the Hebrew. The first word is *attah*, meaning "you," or *thou* as it reads in the King James Version. The next word is a name for God; it is *Eloah* in this case, and not *Elohim*. In the Hebrew there is no definite article before the word for God, but the rules of grammar dictate that you translate it with a definite article because it is a proper name, hence "*the* God." And the third word, in its root form, is *selach*, which means "forgiveness." But its ending here is in the plural, so we could translate this phrase as "You [are] the God of forgivenesses."

Pay close attention to the subtle change in meaning that results from our correction to the text. I do not disagree with the concept that God is "ready to pardon." The fact of the matter is that God *is* always ready to pardon, but that is not how the original language reads. It makes a statement that God is *the God of forgivenesses*, and "forgivenesses" is in the plural.

Let's look more closely at this Hebrew word for forgiveness, *selach*. It can be used as a verb or an adjective, but here it is used as a noun. Looking at the verbal and adjectival usage in the Bible gives us important clues to its meaning. When *selach* is used as a verb, the subject of the verb is always God; it is God who forgives. The word *selach* is used only once as an adjective, and that is in Psalm 86. An adjective describes something or gives it color, and in this case, it gives you an attribute of God. So the grammar helps us to understand that this forgiveness comes from God. It is not something magical as though someone could wave a wand and suddenly you are forgiven; rather *selach* describes a characteristic of God. It may sound strange to us in the English language frame to refer to "the God of forgivenesses," but I want us to consider this concept first within the backdrop of the history of the children of Israel, and second in terms of what it means for us today.

Many people wrestle with the concept of God's forgiveness. We can read in the Bible about the nature of God and know that this is what He does. We can read about how He dealt with His people in the Old Testament, and how in the New Testament the sacrifice of Christ was sufficient: Jesus paid it all. But then we go out into the world and multiple things happen. I call it the "unfortunate recall," whether it be something in your own mind or something triggered by friends, enemies or the devil. Something stirs the soul and brings back memories of all of those storms that caused you to crash into the rocks. Those memories set a new course of frustration, and your mind starts spinning as you begin to question, "Will God forgive even this? *Can* God forgive even this?"

Now this concept of forgiveness seems like a simple thing to discuss, but in fact, it is quite challenging and it shows the importance of doing studies using the original languages. And if you will give God the opportunity, He will show you that there is a lot more in His book for your soul to feed on than you might otherwise see if you are only reading an English translation.

There are three important words in the Hebrew for "forgiveness." We looked at *selach*, which can be a verb, a noun or an adjective. Another word that expresses the concept of "forgiveness" that you will see quite often is *kappor* or one of its related forms. It is the root of the word translated "atonement." When the word ends with a *th*, it becomes the word for "mercy seat," *kapporeth*. It is translated by other words that convey the idea of "to be covered." For example, it is the root of the word translated "pitch," which is used when God told Noah to build an ark and "pitch it within and without with pitch." A form of the same word is found in the name of the Jewish Festival *Yom Kippur*, the great Day of Atonement. So it was long established that this word *kapporeth* would specifically lead us in type to Christ becoming our *Kapporeth*, our mercy seat and the atonement made by the blood being sprinkled on that mercy seat.

The third word for forgiveness is *nasa*, which means "to carry" or "to bear." This word is specifically used in Isaiah 53, which speaks of how our burdens were laid upon Christ and He took them up and carried them away. There is something else vitally important about this word *nasa*. In Exodus 28, we read about the high priest's garments. Aaron wore two stones, one on each shoulder, that were engraved with the names of the tribes of Israel, as well as twelve stones that he wore on his breastplate when he went into the holy place. And it says, "Aaron shall *bear* the names of the children of Israel . . . before the LORD." So the high priest lifted up and carried before God the names of the tribes of the children of Israel. The *Urim* and the *Thummim* were placed in a pouch behind the "breastplate of judgment," and we read, "Aaron shall *bear* their judgment upon his heart before the Lord continually," which means that the high priest carried their judgment as well, and again it uses this same word *nasa*. The word *nasa* is also used in Leviticus 16:22 to describe what happened when the sins were laid upon the scapegoat.

These are all very important words, but I want us to concentrate on *selach* and *kappor*. We can see that these two Hebrew words function together. In the book of Leviticus, God laid out a system of sacrifices that included the sin offering and the trespass offering. The command was given to slay a bullock, and in Leviticus 4:20, it says that the priest will make an atonement for them, *kappor*, and it shall be forgiven them, *selach*.

The Scripture says that without the shedding of blood, there is no remission of sin. From the Old Testament to the New Testament, and as unfolded in the book of Hebrews, we realize that God had set up a system. Death had come because of sin, and man was separated from God beginning right in the garden. After the fall, when Adam and Eve would be driven out of the garden, they covered themselves with leaves. But God slew an animal to cover them with skins. For the first time, blood was shed to cover sins, and throughout the Bible you will find God doing the same thing. This system will become clarified when the law is given, and Leviticus 17 plainly states the purpose for the shedding of blood. There are prohibitions against eating blood given in Leviticus and Deuteronomy, which is why to this day the Jews do not eat anything containing blood. But in the New Testament, Jesus said that all things are made clean.

The words *selach* and *kappor* usually function together, but even when the word *selach* occurs without *kappor*, it was understood that there was no forgiveness of sin without the shedding of blood. The concept of the shedding of blood for the remission of sin was already assumed by the people in Nehemiah's day. They understood that this was the manner or the method to restore communion between God and man.

The part of the prayer we have been looking at through Nehemiah 9:17 covers a period of time from the exodus of the children of God out of Egypt, to their rebellion in the wilderness. So it speaks of a time when the children of Israel had already celebrated the first Passover. They had already applied the blood once, and the death angel had passed over. They were now heading into the time when Moses would climb up the mount to receive God's commandments written on the first tables of stone. Nehemiah 9:18 goes on to describe the events recorded in Exodus 32, where Aaron made a molten calf and claimed that it had magically appeared.

Because of the time frame covered in this prayer, we can assume that the speaker already understood about sacrifices and the shedding of blood, and that nothing was forgiven without the shedding of blood. And to this day we still understand this. The book of Hebrews, in chapters 9 and 10, gives the greatest summation of Christ's sacrifice once and for all, for sins that the blood of bulls and goats could never cover or wash away. But under the sacrificial system of the Old Testament, the people could at least temporarily appease their consciences from year to year. They would perform their daily and weekly sacrifices by bringing an animal and laying their hands upon it to transfer their guilt to that animal before it was slain.

Again, we are looking at the verse that speaks of "the God of forgivenesses," first to look at God's forgivenesses of the children of Israel. If you can grab hold of that history without making it too much of a caricature through familiarity, you are on a good path to understanding the concept that God is long-suffering, "gracious and merciful, slow to anger, and of great kindness, and forsookest them not."

Let's look more closely at what is said in Nehemiah 9:16–17, to help us wrap our minds around what a big statement this was for the children of Israel and is for us today. We can break this passage down into six things that chronicle the failure of God's people. First, it says, "But they and our fathers dealt proudly." Pride is first on the list. Second, they "hardened their necks." God called them a stiff-necked people. Third, they "hearkened not to thy commandments," which for them meant that they did not listen to God's commandments, but more generically we could say that they did not listen to God's word. Fourth, they "refused to obey," and fifth, "neither were mindful of thy wonders that thou didst among them." They were not mindful of everything that God did. And sixth, it says, "And in their rebellion appointed a captain to return to their bondage." In essence, they said, "We want to go back into slavery," if we can even comprehend the insanity of that declaration.

God's people had been delivered out of Egypt. While Egypt was a real place, Egypt also represents the type of bondage to sin. Now, I want you to think about this. Our eyes are often too fixed on the past or too fixed on the world. We get delivered by God: He opens up our eyes, our heart is open and our ears are open to His word. But then suddenly, the "old man" in us rises up and we rebel against God's deliverance. You will find that all of these Old Testament verses apply to us, and in some ways we are not that different from the children of Israel. You can read these verses as a caricature or you can read them as a true history and a reflection of our sinning nature.

God had delivered these people, and He did it all. I preach today that God still does it all. Salvation is a gift of God. Salvation is not something we can do. It is not the result of saying, "I'm going to try to do a little bit better today." Most people fail to understand that there are two fundamental things we all have to confront. First there is yourself in your natural state, which is the condition of fallen man in Adam. After Adam, there was no perfect communion with God. In fact, when God drove Adam and Eve out of the garden, the curse put upon them and on the ground was not as bad as what befell all mankind, which was separation from God. That is why when Jesus was hanging on the cross, He said, "My God, my God, why hast thou forsaken me?" while the sin of the world was being placed upon Him. And for the first time, He knew separation from the unity that He had with the Father.

The fall of Adam resulted in the condition of all mankind. When I hear people say, "Well, but I am basically a good person," that just tells me that they have not looked in the mirror called the Bible. Now according to the world's standards, I may appear to be basically a good person, but how do you know what goes on in my mind and in my heart? You do not know. And the Bible tells us repeatedly that the thoughts of man and our imaginations are continually evil. That doesn't mean that you are thinking right now of robbing a bank, but there are other devices in the mind that are constantly functioning. That is the natural mind that is at enmity with God.

I have met people who say, "Do you really believe in all that God stuff?" The Psalmist said in Psalm 14, "The fool hath said in his heart, There is no God." It is your decision what you choose to believe, but God's word says that Adam was created with free will and was in perfect communion with God at first. But both Adam and Eve were separated from God by sin, and now we are all born into the condition of sin. It is imprinted on our DNA, plunging all of humanity into the darkness of that condition.

The second fundamental issue we have to deal with is what I would simply call the consequences of living. Each person in their lifetime will have issues they have to deal with. There are too many people who want to inspect what you are doing and judge you by means of a behavioral checklist. If you have time to inspect someone else's issues, that means you have not yet looked at yourself. Jesus said in Matthew 7 to be careful about how you judge, who you judge and how much you judge; because by that very measure in which you sit in judgment of others, by the very measure you decide, "Oh, they are just no good," by that same measure *you* will be judged. I love God because He says, "Come unto Me, whosoever will, and I will take you as you are." He doesn't ask me to recite a formula or perform certain practices. Yet there are many people who have not looked at themselves in the mirror. They are still busy trying to find out "What is that in your eye?" so they can say, "Let me pick it out for you."

We have man's condition of sin and we have the circumstances that go along with life and living. When I talk about "sin," I am not referring to whether or not someone drinks, smokes or cusses. Those are the superficial things that God can easily deal with. We are talking about the things that occur in the darkest chambers of the heart and mind, the things that are the hardest to cope with and to come to terms with. And there is not a human being alive that does not have to grapple with what goes on in the mind, even if you live in God's word. We can live in the word, while our thoughts are still corrupt because of man's condition of sin.

Romans 3:23 says that *all* have sinned and have fallen short of the glory of God. The glory of God is this new creature, Christ Jesus. No one has lived up to this Person; therefore, all have fallen short, and therefore, all need forgiveness. And 1 John 1:10 says, "If we say that we have not sinned, we make him a liar." I am not trying to condemn anybody. I am just trying to shake the tree so that some stuff finally falls off that has been hanging there for too long, because God has given us this beautiful picture of His mercy. But I cannot help you if you keep holding on to what you think you must keep holding on to, whether you have been persuaded by the devil, by the people around you, or by yourself.

Again, 1 John says if we say that we have not sinned, the truth is not in us; we are liars. But it goes on to say, "If we confess our sins, he is faithful and just to forgive us our sins, and to cleanse us from all unrighteousness." It is an attribute of God to forgive. When we look at God's way with man, we see that His forgivenesses are not limited to a single event. And His forgivenesses are not expressed as some kind of remote possibility. The Bible does not say, "God *might* pardon you—but only if you act good enough, if you clean up, if you change your clothes, if you talk differently, etc. If you would just stop doing something, then He will work it out for you." That is *not* the God we are looking at here in the Scriptures. How can we be assured of this? Take a look at the children of Israel and how God related to them.

We read in Nehemiah 9 that they "dealt proudly," they were full of pride. What exactly did they have to be proud of? I wonder if some of them thought to themselves, "Well, we are God's oracle people! He called us, and He didn't call those other people. In fact, we are the only people that have the right message. We are pretty important!" That may be somewhat of an exaggeration, but I want you to make an application to what goes on in churches when people who have been Christians for many years forget how they started with God.

These people, who began to rebel and to murmur, still had the scars on their backs from being whipped during their slavery in Egypt. And yet because that was behind them, they couldn't even remember what the feeling of the whip was like. They just craved the food and demanded, "Bring us back to that place." They would have preferred to follow the rebels Korah and Dathan. When Korah and Dathan rebelled, the people said in essence, "We would prefer a leader whom God did *not* talk to. We would prefer a leader who wasn't chosen." Korah and Dathan and the other two who went with them led a sedition, and the people said, "We don't like Moses. We don't even like Aaron. Give us Korah!" And God opened up the earth and swallowed them up!

They were so full of pride, they "hardened their necks." It seems self-evident that if you harden your neck, you are not being malleable in God's program. You are refusing to follow God's leading. Have you ever met someone whom you would label as stiff-necked? Try to show them the right way to do a job, and they will say, "Leave me alone. I know what to do and how to do it!" Then you come back later to check on their work and it is a complete mess!

Next it says that they "hearkened not to thy commandments." They wouldn't listen. Again this is speaking of the children of Israel, but let's apply this message to ourselves. If you refuse to listen to God's word, how can faith come? Romans 10 says that faith comes by hearing, and hearing by the word of God. And if there is no faith, then it is impossible to please God, so you end up like the people who say, "I don't need to listen anymore. I have heard it all."

There are many people who become like that. All they want to do is talk about the past and how great it was when they were connected to God's work. But now they have completely disconnected themselves. How did that happen? Because they are not hearing, they are not listening, they are not even connected by faith. Let me tell you that yesterday's faith will not buy you tomorrow's anything.

They "refused to obey." I am not speaking of the laws and commandments. They refused to listen to God's word. God had said, "Moses is the deliverer and Aaron is the mouthpiece. They are leading." Chronicle everything that happened from Exodus 15:24 through Exodus 32, and consider how many times the people murmured, how many times they disobeyed and ultimately how many times they rebelled. Now take that concept into the modern church. When people refuse to obey God's leading, they are in essence saying that God does not know what He is doing. The word "obey" simply means "to run to the voice of the sayer." That means if Moses said, "Follow Joshua," then the people should have followed Joshua. The people had a choice: they could either follow Joshua into the Promised Land, knowing that there would be battles to fight and work to do, or they could die and rot in the wilderness.

This is not strictly an Old Testament concept; it still goes on today. There are people who refuse to listen to their God-ordained leader. As long as your pastor is declaring the word of God and not telling you to do something crazy, God's word says to follow. As a pastor, I am following God's leading. God has not spoken to me in some great revelation. I have not heard His voice audibly speaking. All I am saying is that I am acting in faith, and I am telling you to do the same. So when you look at these people in the Old Testament, do not judge them too harshly and say, "They didn't do thus and so," because the reality is that there are many today who refuse to follow. These lessons are timeless.

Next it says that the people were not "mindful of thy wonders that thou didst among them." Look at the catalogue of God's miracles and wonders. Imagine that you were living in Egypt in those days and that you saw all of those incredible things happen: the water turned to blood, the plague of locusts and the horrific hail. Imagine standing by the Red Sea when Moses stretched out his rod and the water parted. If we had seen all of this, I think we would consider being a bit more mindful of all the things that God had done.

We are talking about God's wonderful provisions, so much so that later on in Nehemiah 9, it says, "Yea, forty years didst thou sustain them in the wilderness, so that they lacked nothing; their clothes waxed not old, and their feet swelled not." God gave them forty years of great provision, protection and guidance, yet they were not mindful of that. What earth denied, heaven supplied; God supplied the whole way for forty years. Now if you or I were led for forty years and our shoes never wore out, if God took care of us that way, I think we would be mindful, but they were not.

And last but not least, in what may be the most incredible passage, it says that the children of Israel "in their rebellion appointed a captain to return to their bondage." Just think about that for a moment. I do not share this often, because it is so easy to be misunderstood, but there are two goals or standards by which I try to live my life. The first one is that you should live every day as if it were your last day. Then you will not have any regrets about what you should have prayed for, what you should have read, what you should have done, or even whom you should have told, "I may not like you, but I am going to love you for Christ's sake." The second one is that you should live free. Live free in Christ, and live free as an American. Live free and fight for your freedom, and fight for your freedom because it is a freedom worth dying for. I do not mean that you should go out and be a martyr; I am just saying that some things are worth standing up and fighting for. That is what makes it staggering for me to think that these people wanted to go back. And it is not just that they wanted to go back to Egypt, it says they wanted to go back to their *bondage!* Who in their right mind would want to go back to Egypt, back to the taskmasters and the forced labor? Who in their right mind would say, "We need to appoint someone who will lead us back to Egypt," instead of following the one whom God appointed to lead them into the Promised Land?

These lessons from the past give us the pathway for the future. It doesn't mean we will not make mistakes, because we will. But what I glean out of this book is that God is the God of forgivenesses. Consider all of this history that we have just chronicled concerning these six things that the people did. Think about the forty years of murmuring, rebelling, provoking, tempting and trying God, that is, putting Him on trial, and yet the Scripture still says that God is the God of forgivenesses.

Maybe you do not have a track record of forty years of walking with the Lord and trusting Him. But you can look at the track record of these people in the Old Testament and see that God, in spite of these people and their complaining, had a plan all along to provide them with forgivenesses. After all, if there were no forgiveness in God's book, why would God implement a system of sacrifices? Why would He appoint a high priest? And why would He instruct Moses to build a tabernacle where the high priest could enter in to the holy of holies to bring the blood of the sacrifice? If there were no forgiveness, why on earth would God in His holiness even deign to come down and commune with the people? But all of these things were shadows and types pointing to Christ, who is our High Priest and the sufficient Sacrifice. Everything about the tabernacle speaks of Christ in some way, shape or form. So all along, God was saying, "I have a way." But the book of Hebrews teaches that the sacrificial system of the Old Testament was not perfect, because the blood of bulls and goats could never permanently take away sin.

We have covered God's forgivenesses towards the children of Israel, but I would like to talk more about God's forgivenesses of us. There are conditions of pardon given throughout the whole Bible, starting essentially in Genesis 3 and going all the way to the book of Revelation. The conditions of pardon include having a personal awareness of the reality of your state before God. In other words, one must have a right view of oneself. Too many will read a passage about the Old Testament saints and say, "But those people were terrible!" Were they really that bad? Or were they God's oracle people, concerning whom God had said, "You are My people, and

I promise you this land"? Yet God still stayed with them in their sinfulness, in their repeated rebellion.

From cover to cover in God's book, we are taught about having a right view of ourselves, and acknowledging it before God through confession to Him. I have heard many people say that Christians should confess to one another. The only place in the Scripture where you find that is in James, and if something occurs in only one place you probably are going to be a little hard-pressed to make it doctrine. But we have sound doctrine repeated throughout Scripture of confession to God, for example, in Psalm 41 and in Psalm 51, where the Psalmist says to the Lord, "Against thee, thee only, have I sinned."

If it makes you feel better to confess to someone, go right ahead. But that will not save you. You must talk to God, knowing that He does forgive. It is one thing to say, "I can see and read that God is the God of forgivenesses." But knowing that God does forgive, knowing the kind of God that He is by His track record throughout the Bible, enables you to approach God by faith and say, "God did that for these people; He also did it for me." Those are the conditions, and that is the whole premise of John 3. And again, 1 John says, "If we confess our sins, he is faithful and just to forgive us our sins, and to cleanse us from all unrighteousness."

Forgiveness or pardon has these characteristics: it is unmerited, unlimited and permanent. It is unmerited because we do not deserve to be forgiven. I do not deserve that God the Father would send His only begotten Son to die on a hill for me in my sins. We are saved by grace. And when I say it is unlimited, I would include a caveat: as Romans 6 says, we must not say that if grace abounds, then let's sin all the more. Rather, it is unlimited in the sense that God's forgiveness not only deals with our condition of sin, it also deals with all of our specific trespasses. Christ bore each and every individual sin that I have ever committed—past, present, and those I have yet to commit. Christ dealt with it all on Calvary. They were all laid upon Him. Isaiah 53 says, "The LORD hath laid on him the iniquity of us all," not the iniquities of only some of us. Some people have the strange idea that they are qualified to judge who is worthy to receive this gift. But let me ask you, who *is* worthy to receive this? No one is worthy, which is why it is called grace, unmerited favor.

There are changes that come as a result of having been a recipient of this grace. I have turned towards God, in what we call repentance, *metanoia*, which is acknowledging my condition before Him and recognizing that I do not deserve it. Then the changes come, including a sense of gratitude and a new way of looking at your life. You will begin to change your focus from the perpetual storms that keep crashing on the rocks and the resulting turmoil of the mind. You will no longer be focused on those things, because you have confidence that God is the God of forgivenesses. That is what He does. And you will be less apt to judge or criticize other people. That is one of the marks or emblems by which you may know whether or not you understand what forgiveness means and whether or not you have received it.

I love what Jesus said to Peter as recorded in the last chapter of John. Jesus told Peter to follow, and Peter saw John and said, "What about him?" And Jesus replied, "If I will that he tarry till I come, what is that to thee?" In other words, "What business is it of yours what I do with John?" To say it more colloquially, Jesus was saying, "None of your business! Don't even go there. That is between Me and him." Your issues are between you and God.

What is another mark of a person who has received this forgiveness? In Luke 7, Jesus went to the home of a Pharisee called Simon, where a woman washed His feet with her tears, wiped them with her hair and kissed His feet. And Jesus said to Simon, "Do you see this woman? Since I entered into your house, you have not done any of these things that this woman has done. You have not washed My feet nor given Me kisses. When you have been forgiven much, you love much."

That is another emblem, once a person wraps their whole being around this concept of forgiveness. That is when you know it is not fake love, not coerced loved, not love that is worn like a Christmas tree ornament; rather it is a love that radiates from the inside out when you know you shouldn't be here, but for the grace of

God. And suddenly, the servant's heart of love, worship and devotion radiates out, which is what this woman embodies. And these are the marks of knowing you have received this forgiveness.

Now there are many other things I could say on this subject, but what I want to tell you is this: there are many people who wrestle with issues or maybe an ongoing issue. It happens more often than most people would even admit, but I have heard people say, "I know the Bible teaches about God's forgiveness, but somehow I just cannot forgive myself." It is not up to you to forgive yourself. That is what Christ did, and He did it all at Calvary.

Now some other religions propose that you must do some extra penance in an imaginary place where you serve out your punishment. But if that were true, it would mean that Calvary did not complete it all, the work was not done and the words He spoke from the cross, "It is finished," only concern Christ Himself and not the work that He came to do. Either that is true, or "It is finished" means exactly that. He said that He came to do His Father's will, and He accomplished it. The New Testament says, "If Christ be not raised, your faith is vain; you are yet in your sins."

But Christ is risen. God has provided abundant proofs of the Resurrection of Jesus Christ. If you have doubts on this matter, I invite you to read one of the many outstanding messages on the evidence for the Resurrection of Jesus Christ as taught by Dr. Gene Scott.* Concerning our sins, God has not only declared that they are blotted out, He also said, "I will remember them no more." How can this be? Because Jesus carried it all; He paid it all. Remember those words the next time the accuser of the brethren, your friends, your enemies or even people who love you become the catalyst to try and bring something back to your mind and heart that you have committed to Christ.

That is the God that the people in Nehemiah's day were referring to: the God of forgivenesses. He is not the God of only a single, one-time forgiveness. He is not the God of some remotely possible forgiveness conditioned upon your somehow acting good enough or changing your outward behavior to please other Christians. You

*See, for example, *The Pulpit*, Vol. 9, "The Resurrection: A Factual Basis for the Christian Faith," pp. 207–230 and also *The Pulpit*, Vol.10, "The Resurrection of Jesus Christ," pp. 155–175. (Dolores Press, Inc., Glendale, CA)

are not gambling on whether or not God forgives. The word of God declares that God forgives *by virtue of His nature.* There is no reason to preach any other message than this message of salvation. And the message of salvation encompasses the whole work that Christ did when He said, "It is finished." If Jesus came only to save, but He did not come to deliver and to heal and to fix what was broken, then we only have half of what He claimed was finished. But the reality is that He did the total work.

I would encourage you to read again these verses in Nehemiah and the related chapters in Exodus in your devotions. When you read them, you will discover something quite remarkable: These people did not deserve one more second of God's attention. They did not deserve another miracle; they did not deserve any more of His provision. And yet, it says He did not forsake them. How much more will He forgive us and care for us, who have this wonderful promise? And how shall we escape if we neglect so great a salvation? What shall we say when we are confronted with the question concerning why we didn't look to Him who is the Author and the Finisher, the Alpha and Omega of our faith? Christ said, "It is finished. Sins are forgiven. I bore them for you at Calvary." Now get up just like those in the New Testament and know that your faith in Him has made you whole!

CHAPTER 15

THE GIFT OF GOD'S SPIRIT

Nehemiah 9:20 says, "Thou gavest also thy good Spirit to instruct them. . . ." We are going to look at the gift of God's Spirit. In the New Testament, God gave His Holy Spirit to equip the church. Jesus promised the disciples that they would receive the Spirit of God, which was poured out on the Day of Pentecost. That Spirit would help them to be witnesses, first in the place where they were and later in every place they would go. We know the history of the disciples spreading out and taking the Gospel message to distant lands.

Every so often you will hear sermons by people who want to make the person of the Holy Spirit something other than what the Scriptures declare. That is disturbing, because Christ made some very clear statements about the gift of the Spirit. There are whole denominations that essentially believe that the emphasis should only be on the Spirit. But that goes against what Christ said, because He said, speaking of Himself, "When the Spirit comes, He will speak of Me. He will glorify Me. He will point you to the things concerning Me." The Spirit was not given to testify concerning the Spirit.

There are some people who say that speaking in tongues is the mark of salvation. They believe that you can tell whether or not you are saved by your ability to speak in tongues. That viewpoint is born out of ignorance, and it has even caused some people to fall away from the faith, because they felt that if they did not speak in tongues, then there must be something wrong with them. The people who hold that doctrine have obviously not read 1 Corinthians 12:8–11, where Paul teaches that all the gifts of God are given through the same Spirit, but they are dispersed to individuals as the Spirit sees fit. In other words, not everyone receives the Spirit in the same way. Paul said, "For to one is given by the Spirit the word of wisdom; to another the word of knowledge by the same Spirit; to another faith . . . to another the gifts of healing . . . to another the working of miracles; to another prophecy; to another discerning of spirits; to another divers kinds of tongues; to another the interpretation of tongues: but all these worketh that one and the selfsame Spirit, dividing to every man," literally, "to every person severally as he will." So how could speaking in tongues be a mark of salvation if it is given to one person but not given to another? Yet people have made that into a doctrine.

We read, especially in John's Gospel, about how the Spirit is given to us. Sometimes the Spirit is called the "Holy Ghost," if you are reading the King James Version. Other names include the Holy Spirit, the Spirit of grace, the Spirit of truth, the Spirit of promise, the Spirit of glory, the Spirit of Christ and the Spirit of God.

Jesus said in John 14:26, "The Holy Spirit, whom the Father will send in my name, will teach you all things, and He will bring to your memory all the things that I have said to you." That does not mean that the Holy Spirit teaches all things to everyone. All Scripture must be read in context, and just a few chapters earlier, the same idea is recorded in a different way, so there should be no misunderstanding. In John 12, Jesus was making His entry into Jerusalem and the people were crying, "Hosanna! Hosanna to the King!" We read, "And Jesus, when he had found a young ass, sat thereon; as it is written, Fear not, daughter of Sion: behold, thy King cometh, sitting on an ass's colt. These things understood not his disciples at the first: but when Jesus was glorified, then remembered they that these things were written of him."

Many people have wondered, "How was it possible for the writers of the New Testament to have remembered everything that happened?" Jesus' words in John 14 explain to us how the disciples would be able to recall everything: it was through the gift of the Spirit given to them.

There are many references in God's word concerning this gift and why He gave it. For example, we are cautioned to not grieve the Spirit, to not quench the Spirit and to not quiet the Spirit. There is a warning in Stephen's sermon in Acts to not resist the Spirit. We are told in Hebrews 10 to not "do despite" to the Spirit, which is called the Spirit of grace. And the most important warning is one that is most often misunderstood. In Matthew 12, Jesus said, "All manner of sin and blasphemy shall be forgiven man, even sin against the Son of man; but one sin that will not be forgiven is blasphemy against the Holy Spirit." Many have misinterpreted that warning. It must be read in its context, where Jesus was casting out demons and the Pharisees said, "He does this by the power of Beelzebub." The sin, in essence, was the failure to recognize God's Spirit at work, failure to recognize God's truth at work, failure to recognize the truth and then to call the truth a lie.

Throughout the Bible, in both the Old and New Testaments, God gave the Spirit to certain people at certain times to accomplish His purpose. Many times it was to teach, to guide, to instruct or to lead. In the book of Judges, it says that God clothed Gideon in His Spirit, and the Spirit of God also came upon Jephthah and Samson. We read in 1 Samuel 16:13 that the Spirit of the Lord came upon David from that day forward. Saul had a good spirit put upon him, but God took it away. And in 1 Samuel 18:10, God placed an evil spirit upon him because he was evil.

When we study these passages, we begin to see that God's Spirit was not given as a mark of salvation; it was a mark that God was going to do something, and that He was going to use human vessels to accomplish His purpose. I do believe in a charismatic faith; I just do not believe in all of its caricatures, which I think the devil has had such a good time with. The devil takes things that are serious and makes them into caricatures. A perfect example of this is how unbelievers picture the devil as someone wearing a red leotard and having horns and a tail. People are perfectly happy to think of the devil that way, just as people are perfectly happy to think that all charismatics are like what is seen on religious TV. When a person on TV really wants to show that they are Spirit-filled, it is like they can flick a switch and start spouting off in tongues, and flick a switch to turn it off just as quickly. That is unbiblical. First of all, we are told to pray in our closet and not show off. But if you are in the church and someone prays in an unknown tongue, then there must be an interpreter.

God gave the Spirit on the Day of Pentecost for the specific purpose of equipping the saints. The Pentecost, the harvest of souls, began on that day, and it will not be finished until God says He is finished. So the Spirit is still at work, acting and moving and guiding and leading and instructing. That is why it grieves me to hear people say that they would prefer a church that has more entertainment or social activities or other things. In other words, people want less of what is needed, because you cannot know God or the Spirit of God without knowing His words. These two things go hand in hand, no matter what anyone tells you. If you say you are a Christian, then you must be word-based, because the only way to know Christ is through His book. We do not live in the dark ages, when the word of God was hidden for a time. We have access to the word of God, and like the description in the book of Romans, we are "without excuse."

With that understanding, I want us to lift out those words in Nehemiah 9:20, "Thou gavest also thy good Spirit to instruct them," and see what they represent in the context of the prayer that is prayed in Nehemiah 9. Then we will look at the gift of the Spirit throughout time, as God has ordained it.

The background is found in Numbers 11, where we can begin to see what type of gift God gave. God had just finished raining down the manna, and the people were complaining about what God had provided for them. We read starting from verse 10, "Then Moses heard the people weep throughout their families, every man in the door of his tent: and the anger of the LORD was kindled greatly;

Moses also was displeased. And Moses said unto the LORD, Wherefore hast thou afflicted thy servant?" Moses was saying, "Why have You done this to me?" "And wherefore have I not found favour in thy sight, that thou layest the burden of all this people upon me? Have I conceived all this people? have I begotten them, that thou shouldest say unto me, Carry them in thy bosom, as a nursing father beareth the sucking child, unto the land which thou swarest unto their fathers? Whence should I have flesh to give unto all this people? for they weep unto me, saying, Give us flesh, that we may eat. I am not able to bear all this people alone, because it is too heavy for me. And if thou deal thus with me, kill me, I pray thee, out of hand," God, wipe me out, "if I have found favour in thy sight; and let me not see my wretchedness," or "my misery." Some translations read, "my evil."

"And the LORD said unto Moses, Gather unto me seventy men of the elders of Israel, whom thou knowest to be the elders of the people, and officers over them; and bring them unto the tabernacle of the congregation, that they may stand there with thee. And I will come down and talk with thee there: and I will take of the spirit which is upon thee. . . ." Moses is one of the few men in God's book of whom it simply states that the Spirit was upon him. It does not specifically say when the Spirit was placed upon him. God did tell Moses in Exodus 3, "Certainly I will be with thee," and in Exodus 4, "I will be with thy mouth," but there is no specific reference where God says, as He does in other places, "The Spirit of the LORD was upon such a one." It simply says in Numbers 11:17, "I will come down and talk with thee there. I will take of the spirit which is upon thee, and will put it upon them; and they shall bear the burden of the people with thee, that thou bear it not thyself alone."

I want you to think about this. God being God, He could have said, "Gather the seventy, and I will place my Spirit upon them," but instead He said, "Gather the seventy, and I will take the Spirit that is upon you and give a little bit to each of them." God is able to do whatever He wants to do. That is the sovereignty of God. It is as though God said, "It may not be by the usual way, but this is the way I am going to do it."

Then the Lord told Moses to say to the people, "Sanctify yourselves against to morrow, and ye shall eat flesh: for ye have wept in the ears of the LORD, saying, Who shall give us flesh to eat? for it was well with us in Egypt: therefore the LORD will give you flesh, and ye shall eat. And you are going to eat not one day, or two days, or five days, or ten or twenty; but even a whole month, until it comes out of your nostrils, and it be loathsome unto you: because that ye have despised the LORD which is among you, and have wept before him, saying, Why came we forth out of Egypt?"

Moses will reply to God and say in essence, "Really? You are going to feed flesh to all these people? We would have to sacrifice every animal we have!" But God said to Moses, "Is the LORD'S hand waxed short?" Is the Lord's arm too short? Is there anything that God cannot do? In other words, "Are you going to tell Me what I am *not* able to do, Moses?" Remember, Moses was the man who raised the rod and the Red Sea parted, and here he is talking back to God about what God can and cannot do!

But Moses "gathered the seventy men of the elders of the people, and set them round about the tabernacle. And the LORD came down in a cloud, and spake unto him, and took of the spirit that was upon him, and gave it unto the seventy elders: and it came to pass, that, when the spirit rested upon them, they prophesied, and did not cease." If you are using a King James Version Bible, you should make a correction in the margin because that is not how it reads in the Hebrew. Literally it says, "They prophesied, but they did not do that again."

"But there remained two of the men in the camp, the name of the one was Eldad, and the name of the other was Medad: and the spirit rested upon them." So the Spirit not only came down to where the seventy were gathered, but it also rested on two other men who were standing in the camp, and they began to prophesy. "And there ran a young man, and told Moses, and said, Eldad and Medad do prophesy in the camp. And Joshua the son of Nun, the servant of Moses, one of his young men, answered and said, My lord Moses, forbid them. And Moses said unto him, Enviest thou for my sake?

would God that all the LORD'S people were prophets, and that the LORD would put his spirit upon them," or it should say, "upon them all!" Moses didn't have a messiah complex and didn't act like he was the only one God dealt with, though Miriam and Aaron would accuse him of that in the next chapter. But God gave the Spirit, and the method that He used here was to take a little of what was on Moses and give it to these seventy. In this case, the purpose of giving the Spirit was to equip the elders in the camp to handle the burdens of the daily ministry of the congregation. God gave the Spirit as an instructor and teacher to equip the people, because what God requires, He gives. And He will give the sufficient measure that is required for each person.

One of the best examples in the Bible of how God equips a person for service is found in a man who is rarely spoken of. He might seem unimportant, yet God deemed him important enough to not only tell us his name, but also to make sure we understand how God would equip him for service. You see, Moses received all the instructions from God for building the tabernacle, but Moses didn't build it himself. The builders are named in Exodus 31: "The LORD spake unto Moses, saying, See, I have called by name Bezaleel the son of Uri, the son of Hur, of the tribe of Judah: and I have filled him with the spirit of God, in wisdom, and in understanding, and in knowledge, and in all manner of workmanship, to devise cunning works, to work in gold, and in silver, and in brass, and in cutting of stones, to set them, and in carving of timber, to work in all manner of workmanship. And I, behold, I have given with him Aholiab, the son of Ahisamach, of the tribe of Dan: and in the hearts of all that are wise hearted I have put wisdom, that they may make all that I have commanded thee."

Moses had been commanded by the Lord, "See to it that you make the tabernacle exactly according to the pattern that I gave you." That is one of the reasons why God called these men, Bezaleel and Aholiab. These two would be given God's Spirit to take the instructions and carry them out, to craft and to design. Notice that we do not have any indication that these men were already craftsmen.

Look at all the things that they are going to build: "The tabernacle of the congregation, and the ark of the testimony, and the mercy seat that is thereupon, and all the furniture of the tabernacle, and the table and his furniture, and the pure candlestick with all his furniture, and the altar of incense, and the altar of burnt offering with all his furniture, and the laver and his foot, and the cloths of service, and the holy garments for Aaron the priest, and the garments of his sons, to minister in the priest's office, and the anointing oil, and sweet incense for the holy place: according to all that I have commanded thee shall they do."

That is a whole lot of stuff for these two men and their helpers to do, and that is why God put His Spirit upon them, in order that they would be able to carry out His instructions. The tabernacle would be the place where God's presence would come down. This was the tent of meeting, God's place, and everything in the tabernacle represented Christ, except perhaps the table of shewbread, which was an offering from the people to God. Everything in the tabernacle had to be precisely built according to the pattern that God had given. Now God could have said, "Just get any couple of guys to throw this thing together." But without the Spirit of God, the ability to hear the words and to carry them out, it would not have been a work of God. This is a clear example of being equipped for service, though it is a different kind of service than we would normally think of. And God saw to it that about 160 verses were devoted to this man Bezaleel and all the work he did.

Turn now to Exodus 35:30. "Moses said unto the children of Israel, See, the LORD hath called by name Bezaleel the son of Uri, the son of Hur, of the tribe of Judah; and he hath filled him with the spirit of God, in wisdom, in understanding, and in knowledge, and in all manner of workmanship; and to devise curious works, to work in gold, and in silver, and in brass, and in the cutting of stones, to set them, and in carving of wood, to make any manner of cunning work. And he hath put in his heart that he may teach, both he, and Aholiab." In the Hebrew, it clearly says that God's Spirit taught them how to do these things. It goes on to say, "Them hath he filled with wisdom of heart, to work all manner of work, of the engraver, and of the cunning workman, and of the embroiderer, in blue, and in purple, in scarlet, and in fine linen, and of the weaver," everything imaginable!

Then we read in Exodus 36, "Then wrought Bezaleel and Aholiab, and every wise-hearted man, in whom the LORD put wisdom and understanding to know how to work all manner of work for the service of the sanctuary, according to all that the LORD had commanded." And remarkably, when we get to verse 10, Bezaleel's name will disappear, but everywhere that we read, "And he coupled five curtains. . . . And he made loops of blue. . . . And he made fifty taches. . . . And he made curtains. . . . And he coupled five curtains. . . . And he made fifty loops," it is speaking of Bezaleel and his associates.

I want us to notice that Bezaleel will not get any credit for all of the work that he did. When Moses spoke to the children of Israel, he said, "Bring an offering," and they brought an offering and instructions were given and men were assigned to do the work. But afterwards, we do not hear anything else about Bezaleel and the workers. There will be one reference in 1 Chronicles 2, because Bezaleel, descending from the line of Judah, becomes important in the genealogies. But other than that, no more is said about him.

We read in Exodus 37:1, "Bezaleel made the ark of shittim wood: two cubits," and then in verse 2, "he overlaid," and in verse 3, "he cast," and in verse 4, "he made." In Exodus 38 and 39, you will repeatedly find the words "he" and "they," referring to these men. We read in Exodus 38:21–22, "This is the sum of the tabernacle, even of the tabernacle of testimony, as it was counted, according to the commandment of Moses, for the service of the Levites, by the hand of Ithamar, son to Aaron the priest. And Bezaleel the son of Uri . . . made all that the LORD commanded Moses." Then comes a chronicle of all that they made; and at the conclusion of Exodus 39, ultimately "Moses did look upon all the work, and, behold, they had done it as the LORD had commanded, even so had they done it: and Moses blessed them."

The message is that God equips people for the task. God will never put you in a place without giving you the things that you need to make what He requires according to His design, whether it is in your personal life or in anything pertaining to Him. People like to talk about the Holy Spirit as some type of a badge or mark of achievement, but in reality, first and foremost, the Spirit is given to build up God's program.

Back before the flood, God said in Genesis, "My spirit shall not always strive with man," because He saw the evil that was in man's heart. And from that time to the coming of Christ, we have a long series of events in which God at diverse times used people as human conduits to accomplish His purpose.

We say that God can do anything because He has all of this incredible power. God could have just said, "Moses, this is what I am going to do, and this is exactly what it will look like. Now, you and all the people go and hide behind a rock, and when you come out, you will see this amazing tabernacle." But that is not the way He does things. If He had done it that way, it would no longer be the representation of man as touching the things of God. It would only have been a representation of God, and not of man. God gives His Spirit to men and women to accomplish His work, and He has not changed His ways.

We read in 1 Kings about all of the work that Hiram did in the days of King Solomon. Solomon prayed for wisdom, and he was supposedly the wisest man, though he did not necessarily act very wisely concerning women. But he would build the temple that David had not been allowed to build, because David had shed blood. And Hiram of Tyre (not to be confused with Hiram the king of Tyre) was filled with the spirit of wisdom and of knowledge to be able to carry out the work.

I do not believe that any human being could, on their own, carry out all of the instructions for building the tabernacle or the temple. And after the temple was completed, the glory of the Lord filled that place. God must have been satisfied with the temple's design and construction, for we have no record of God saying, "Well, no, it wasn't exactly the way I originally designed it, so I cannot enter it." Throughout God's book, this is the way He accomplishes things, through diverse people like Gideon, Jephthah, Samson, Saul,

Samuel and David. God placed His Spirit upon people for a set time to carry out specific things.

The people on whom God placed His Spirit were not perfect and they made mistakes. In Saul's case, his sins were so egregious that the Spirit was removed. David committed an egregious sin, and yet the Spirit did not depart from him. And we know in his great psalm of repentance, Psalm 51, he cried out to God to not take His Holy Spirit from him, because David felt that he had committed such an egregious act that God might do just that. But he went to God with a heart repenting and asking for forgiveness, and of course, God would not deny such a request. As we saw in the previous message, God is a God of forgivenesses.

All of this ultimately brings us to the book of Acts. Jesus had told the disciples about the Comforter yet to come. He said in John's Gospel, "Howbeit when he, the Spirit of truth, is come, he will guide you into all truth: for he shall not speak of himself; but whatsoever he shall hear, that shall he speak: and he will shew you things to come. He shall glorify me." Throughout God's book, that is consistently the way God has given gifts to His people to instruct, to teach, to lead and to guide.

We read in Acts 1:5, "For John truly baptized with water; but ye shall be baptized with the Holy Ghost not many days hence." If you want proof that the disciples still did not understand, verse 6 says, "When they therefore were come together, they asked of him, saying, Lord, wilt thou at this time restore again the kingdom to Israel?" They didn't get it. And Jesus said, "It is not for you to know the times or the seasons. . . . But ye shall receive power." The Greek word translated "power" is *dunamis,* which is a cognate of our word for dynamite. "But ye shall receive power, after that the Holy Ghost is come upon you: and ye shall be witnesses unto me both in Jerusalem, and in all Judaea, and in Samaria, and unto the uttermost part of the earth." And we know that what was said came to pass in Acts 2, which says, "When the day of Pentecost was fully come." It should read "was beginning" or "was starting," because the day of Pentecost is the day of harvest, and the harvest is not over.

Peter began to preach. He was the impetuous apostle, and he was quick to say foolish things. Yet he was the one who stood up and preached the sermon that brought the church into existence. I am reminded again of John 12:16, where it says that the disciples did not understand until after Jesus rose from the dead, and then they remembered all the things written about Him. That was indeed the gift that was promised to them in John 14:26, which says that the Spirit "shall remind you of all things." "All things" does not mean every memory about everything; it specifically means all the truth concerning Christ, the truth concerning God's word.

Peter quoted from the prophet Joel in the Old Testament, saying, "And I will shew wonders in the heaven above, and signs in the earth beneath; blood, and fire, and vapour of smoke: the sun shall be turned into darkness, and the moon into blood, before that great and notable day of the Lord come." These words are also reminiscent of Christ's words in Matthew 24.

Think of how remarkable it is that the disciples could instantly recall all the things that Christ said and did. They were with the Lord every day, and so much had happened: How many people did He heal? How many sermons did He deliver? So we can even see in Peter's sermon how God stirred up the memory of the things the disciples had heard, and He enabled them to preach them with the conviction to persuade men's hearts. When Peter reached the conclusion of his sermon, some thought it was a joke, some could not believe what they heard; but of others, it says, "When they heard this, they were pricked in their heart, and said unto Peter and to the rest of the apostles, Men and brethren, what shall we do? Then Peter said unto them, Repent, and be baptized every one of you in the name of Jesus Christ for the remission of sins, and ye shall receive the gift of the Holy Ghost."

I said earlier that when God gave a gift to the church, it was not like a light switch that may be switched on or off as a mark of salvation. For if speaking in tongues is the mark of salvation, please tell me what do people who are mute do? Does that mean they can never be saved? You can understand why I am so appalled by the utter nonsense that is peddled to people who are really just looking to have some tangible external sign of their salvation. And just as Christ rebuked those people in His day by saying there will be no sign except the sign of Jonah, today, there will be no sign except for this one thing: you will hunger and thirst for this bread and this water, and you will be satisfied with it. You won't go questing after other things; you will desire the things that are eternal. That is what speaks to me about God's working in a person. When God calls you, He will put that hunger in you. He does not call you by an "altar call." He does not call you by something that man designed. As John said in the opening of his Gospel, we were born not by the will of the flesh, but by the power of God, by His Spirit.

In Nehemiah's day, they did not have the knowledge that we now have concerning the Spirit of God. We can read the whole book. We can look at how God accomplished many of His great acts through men, through the giving of the Spirit. In the New Testament, we can see how He accomplished the birthing of the church, and that the Great Commission could only be fulfilled by giving the capacity to men and women to bear witness of Christ.

We should be glad that we are able to hear and receive the knowledge of the truth. For there will come a time when people will be reminded of days past, and they will cry out and ask, "Where is God's Spirit?" I am speaking of a future time that is prophesied in Isaiah 63.

Isaiah prophesied of many things that are now past, like the birth of Cyrus. He also prophesied of many things that have not yet been fulfilled. Isaiah 63 opens with a picture of Christ. Many have made the mistake of identifying this prophecy with Christ at His first coming, but this prophecy fully fits into the events that are foretold in the book of Revelation. Verses 1–6 present an eschatological view and a vision of the adequacy of the Lord in a final battle, the day of vengeance. Then verses 7–10 speak of the Lord's care in relation to human inadequacy.

We read, "I will mention the lovingkindnesses of the LORD, and the praises of the LORD, according to all that the LORD hath bestowed on us, and the great goodness toward the house of Israel, which he hath bestowed on them according to his mercies, and according to the multitude of his lovingkindnesses. For he said, Surely they are my people, children that will not lie: so he was their Saviour." Notice it is written in the past tense: He *was* their Saviour. "In all their affliction he was afflicted, and the angel of his presence saved them: in his love and in his pity he redeemed them; and he bare them, and carried them all the days of old. But they rebelled, and vexed his holy Spirit: therefore he was turned to be their enemy, and he fought against them." Think about this. Not the Assyrians, not the Babylonians, but God's people themselves became His enemy by failing to listen to Him, by turning their backs and looking away from Him when He said, "I only ask this of you." But they said, "We don't want to do that."

"Then he remembered," and the "he" in this case is Israel, "he remembered the days of old, Moses, and his people, saying, Where is he that brought them up out of the sea with the shepherd of his flock? where is he that put his holy Spirit within him?" The question will be asked at the end of days by those who remain who failed to recognize the Lord when He was here. They will ask, "Why will He not put His Spirit upon us? Why will He not lead us?"

We have looked at God's gift of the Spirit in the past, to enable people to make it through, to give them understanding and wisdom to do His bidding. And we have looked at the Spirit in the age of the church, which is the Day of Pentecost until the present time. But in a future time, in the end of days, there will be a people who remember "the days of old, Moses, and his people, saying, Where is he that brought them up out of the sea with the shepherd of his flock? where is he that put his holy Spirit within him? That led them by the right hand of Moses with his glorious arm, dividing the water before them, to make himself an everlasting name? That led them through the deep, as an horse in the wilderness," as a surefooted horse, "that they should not stumble? As a beast goeth down into the valley, the Spirit of the LORD caused him to rest: so didst thou lead thy people, to make thyself a glorious name." The "rest" does not speak of a final rest, rather it was the rest obtained when they finally entered into the land.

In the end of days, but before the end of time, there will be a people crying out, "Lord, where are You? Why aren't You leading us anymore? Why aren't You helping us?" These questions will not come from the mouth of a Christian. There are some people who believe that God will save everyone. In fact, there was a preacher who used to say that even the devil will be saved. But my Bible says that the devil will be cast into a lake of fire, and that doesn't look very much like salvation to me.

God's Spirit is still working in the church today. The evidence is that you desire to know, you desire to learn and you haven't turned your back on God, even on the days when you have not felt like moving a finger, let alone even getting up out of bed. You still have said, "The Lord Jesus Christ is my Savior. His works and His ways are perfect, and I am just a messed up container. But I shall not neglect the gift He has given, neither shall I resist or quench it."

God's Spirit does not make me disorganized; it does not make me flop around on the ground like a fish out of water. Rather, when God's Spirit is upon men and women, it is an organized Spirit, because He ordains men and women with a commission to do His work. This same concept is repeated everywhere you look in the Bible, and when things are confirmed repeatedly in Scripture, you can be assured that you have good, sound doctrine.

This is also a message for those of you who, like Jonah, are trying to run away from your calling, because you think that it is too great a demand on your life. God sent His Holy Spirit to instruct, and He sent His Holy Spirit into some gift ministers to equip you to do the things that you are called to do. We are all operating by that one Spirit, though He does indeed give out different gifts at different times to different people, severally and as He wills.

But many still say, "Well, I don't feel like I'm being led. I don't know what to do or how to do it." Such language sounds like Gideon in the book of Judges, talking back to God and saying, "Who? What? Where? Why?" The answer is clearly spelled out by Paul in Galatians 5: if we are led by the Spirit, that is, if we are coming under the Spirit, let us also walk in the Spirit. "Walking in the Spirit" does not mean doing crazy things like rolling around on the ground; it simply means listening to God's word and aligning our lives with His book.

I am not perfect, you are not perfect, but in our hearts we can say, "God, I am going to be obedient and listen and follow hard after Your word, and not be like those who had the opportunity but failed to take it." His oracle people had that opportunity, and they will stand one day and remember the days of old.

To those of you who have said, "What is the point?" the point is a warning about that attitude, which was the attitude of the children of Israel. Our attitude should be grateful acknowledgement that God has given us this great gift. The New Testament says you are the habitation of the Holy Spirit, and you remain the habitation simply *by faith*, not by some funny, mysterious stuff. Recognize that God has been gracious to give you that gift.

Now when I say that the Spirit was given to instruct and to lead in all manner of truth, I am talking about the word of God. That is the Spirit bearing witness to the truth being declared. If you want to know what the Spirit of God really looks like in a person, I will tell you. It is seen in people who desire to grow in their relationship with Him. It is seen by their desire to gather together to hear the teaching of God's word and grow in the knowledge of the truth.

You might say, "But I don't feel anything! How do I know that something is really happening to me?" You don't have to feel anything. God never said that you would feel something, but He did say that you would come to a knowledge of the truth about Him. And that knowledge and truth comes through the opening up of the word, through the preaching and the hearing of faith. It comes through a deposit of God's nature in us, which Paul calls in his letter to the Ephesians "the earnest of our inheritance," a part-payment of what we will fully receive over there. It is the Spirit of promise given to you and given to me.

Do not neglect the gift. Do not try to stir up your own idea of what God is trying to do. Rather, you should graciously take the gift that has been with you ever since your eyes were opened and your heart was turned to God. Recognize that even on the days when you don't feel very good or when you have messed up pretty badly, God is still looking at you and saying, "I know, and that is why I sent My Comforter to equip you, to instruct you and to guide you. I am with you always." What do you think these words mean, "I am with you always and to the end"? Is it just some random thought? No, it is an assurance of His presence with you and in you.

God gave His Holy Spirit to the people in Nehemiah's day to instruct them. He has given His Spirit to us today to equip, instruct and guide us, and we are blessed recipients of that Spirit. If you do not feel like you are honored to be a recipient, I do not know what else I can say to you. But if you are one of those who understand what I am saying, you do not need to have any mystical experience or crazy contortions. You can simply say from your heart, "Lord, what a wonder that You would condescend to come into this container, which You have washed and cleansed—though it is still filthy; I am still a sinner. It is a great miracle, and I will not frustrate, quench or resist the Spirit. I desire more of You and less of me." Let the knowledge of that gift settle in your mind: Jesus died for me, He died for you to give us that great gift, and we should rejoice and be glad.

Chapter 16

PUT GOD'S HOUSE FIRST

The Greek word for "church" is *ekklesia*, which simply means those who have been called out, or you could say "the out-called ones." In New Testament times, a caller would go out on the street and call people out for different purposes. When Jesus said, "I will build *my church*," He was specifically speaking of those called out to worship Him.

The church is not a building; the church is a people who are called out to worship the Lord. But there is a paradox, because there is still the need for a place for the people to assemble and worship. It would not make sense for Paul to say that God gave some gift ministers to the church to teach the word of God, if there were no place for the people to gather together to hear the word. And the purpose of that gathering is "for the perfecting of the saints," until we all come in the unity of the faith, and of the knowledge of the Son of God, to grow unto the perfect man, Jesus Christ.

Today's message out of Nehemiah speaks of something that has been going on in churches throughout the ages. It first needs to be applied to our hearts individually, and then be applied to the church as a body. Turn in your Bible to Nehemiah 10:39. The last part of this verse reads, "and we will not forsake the house of our God." In the Septuagint, the Greek word translated "forsake" is *egkataleipsomen*, which may also be translated "desert" or "abandon." We could simply say, "we will not *leave behind* the house of our God." Some English translations read "we will not *neglect* the house of our God." I looked for other translations that might help us to understand the sense of this word, starting with two different Portuguese translations. In the Portuguese translation of the King James Version Bible, the word for "forsake" is *desleixada*, which means "to be slovenly" or "to be sloppy" about something. In another Portuguese Bible, the word is *negligenciarmos*, which means "to be negligent." The French Bible uses the word *abandonner*, which means "to abandon." These different translations give us a point of departure to help us understand the meaning of the verse.

Before going forward in Nehemiah 10, we need to set the context and briefly review the prayer in Nehemiah 9. It is a prayer that reflects back on God's goodness, from the time of creation to the time when His people entered into the Promised Land. It begins with praise to God; it speaks of the creation, and then it jumps right to the calling of Abraham out of Ur of the Chaldees, and God's promise to give him the land of Canaan. The prayer focuses on God's faithfulness in delivering His people from bondage, bringing them through the Red Sea, being with them in the wilderness, providing them with manna, quail and water, and making sure that they had enough. For forty years God took care of them, "so that they lacked nothing; their clothes waxed not old, and their feet swelled not." We described this prayer as a mosaic of Scripture being poured out in reflection of God's faithfulness and grace. We said in a previous message that God is "*the God of forgivenesses.*" Think about how many times the children of Israel slipped back and fell away from following God. But when they cried out to Him, He heard their cries and delivered them. He multiplied the people and gave them children as numerous as the stars of heaven. And He led the people under Joshua into the Promised Land. The whole passage speaks of the goodness of God and His faithfulness to His promises.

Near the end of Nehemiah 9, the people were lamenting. We read beginning at verse 36, "Behold, we are servants this day, and for the land that thou gavest unto our fathers to eat the fruit thereof and the good thereof, behold, we are servants in it: and it yieldeth much increase unto the kings whom thou hast set over us because of our sins: also they have dominion over our bodies, and over our cattle, at their pleasure, and we are in great distress." In essence, they were saying, "We are now in the land that was promised to us. We have rebuilt the temple and the walls, and we have read the law. This is a great time of celebration, and yet there is still one problem: we don't own our land and we don't own ourselves." Although they had returned from captivity, they were still under the rule of another empire. They were still not a free people. They were so close to being completely emancipated, but attaining that freedom was like the proverbial brass ring, just out of reach.

Notice what happens in Nehemiah 9:38. Remember that the chapter and verse divisions in the King James Version Bible were not in the original text. Nehemiah 9:37 should really be the last verse of the chapter, and Nehemiah 10 should start with verse 38, where the people make a covenant, an oath to obedience. We read, "And because of all this we make a sure covenant, and write it; and our princes, Levites, and priests, seal unto it." Then the verses that follow enumerate a long list of people who signed the covenant. We might wonder, "Why on earth would all of these people sign a covenant?" Because they knew their state and they desperately wanted to serve and please God.

I pause to say that it is easy to think of ourselves as being far removed from these people, when in reality we are not. No, we are not under the law; we are under grace by Jesus Christ. The law was a schoolmaster and served its purpose to bring us to Christ. And now that faith has come, we are free, as John 8 says, because of the Son. But there are principles taught in these verses that apply to us today.

Nehemiah 10:28 is the close of the list of those who agreed to the oath of obedience, including "the rest of the people, the priests, the Levites, the porters, the singers, the Nethinims," or servants, "and all they that had separated themselves from the people of the lands unto the law of God, their wives, their sons, and their daughters, every one having knowledge, and having understanding." The Hebrew word translated "understanding" is *been*, which we covered in a previous message. It means understanding or spiritual insight that only comes as a gift given by God. "They clave to their brethren, their nobles, and entered into a curse, and into an oath, to walk in God's law, which was given by Moses the servant of God, and to observe and do all the commandments of the LORD our Lord, and his judgments and his statutes."

The people made a covenant to walk in God's law and to do all His commandments, and they said "that we would not give our daughters unto the people of the land, nor take their daughters for our sons: and if the people of the land bring ware or any victuals on the sabbath day to sell, that we would not buy it of them on the sabbath, or on the holy day: and that we would leave the seventh year, and the exaction of every debt. Also we made ordinances for us. . . ." The rest of this passage talks about certain other responsibilities that the people understood and willingly accepted.

God's people had made an incredible journey across the desert to return to Jerusalem to rebuild. They overcame obstacles, rebuilt the temple and the walls, and celebrated a great victory. When Ezra read from the book of the law, they were gripped with godly sorrow and they wept. They had come to their senses and turned their eyes unto God. After they prayed the prayer in Nehemiah 9, they made a covenant and said, "We will keep this covenant because we desire to please God. We don't want to be like our forefathers who drifted away from Him." Then they made the bold declaration: *"We will not forsake the house of our God."*

The tragedy here is that the people will not keep this covenant. Just three chapters later, we read that Nehemiah had to return to his official post in Babylon for a time, and he will come back to Jerusalem only to find that the house of God will once again be in disrespect and disrepair. The people will have completely abandoned their covenant with God.

The people had only momentarily come to their senses and made that bold declaration and then they went right back to doing all the things that they said they wouldn't do. I do not have to belabor the point; this is just human nature.

In our day, when something tragic happens, whether it is a natural disaster, war or the threat of war, it shakes us to the core and we say, "Oh my, let's get vigilant!" Then after a time, the feeling just fades away. We no longer feel like we really have to be vigilant because nothing has happened for a long time. And this is exactly what happened in Nehemiah's day. After making their incredible prayer testifying of God's fidelity, they heard the word of God and completely turned around. But after making an oath to return to God's ways, shortly thereafter they completely abandoned their resolution. It is just like many of us who have made a vow to God to be more faithful, more diligent and more disciplined, to pray more or to study more. Then over time, whether it is by the power of the devil or the power of laziness or just plain being tired, we find every excuse for not doing what we had committed to do.

Let's look more closely at the last words in Nehemiah 10:39, "the house of our God." Whose house is it? It is the house of *our God.* We can trace this expression "house of God" throughout the Bible. Now, God did not erect a physical structure for Himself. In Genesis 28, God brought Jacob to a place where he put his head down on a rock for a pillow and fell asleep. Jacob saw the vision of the angels ascending and descending a ladder, and he heard the Lord speaking to him. And when he awoke out of his sleep, he said, "Surely the LORD is in this place, and I knew it not." He called the place *Beth–el*, which means "house of God." God deigned to commune with Jacob and give him instruction and a sense of comfort. The presence of God was there with him.

As we move through the Bible, "the house of God" becomes more clearly defined. In Exodus 25, God gave instructions to Moses and said, "Make me a sanctuary." We are reminded in the New Testament book of Hebrews that Moses was specifically told that he must build it "according to the pattern shewed to thee in the mount." God put His Spirit in the builders to build His house, which later on will be called "the tent of meeting" or "the tabernacle." But in

Exodus, he said, "Make me a sanctuary, that I may dwell among them."

Did God really need a place to dwell? This was the God who appeared in the pillar of cloud by day and the pillar of fire by night! Did He really need a place of residence with a street address? Yet God said, "Build it," and not man's way, but God's way. And this would be the place where God and man would meet.

Solomon would later build a temple, though God did not ask him to build one. What is so beautiful about this is that the Lord's presence, His *Shekinah* glory, filled that temple. When God's glory descended into the temple, the priests could not even enter in. In all of these references to "the house of God," we have the concept of God meeting man, of God being in communion with man at a designated place. Further, that meant that some people would have the privilege of being exposed to God's presence, while others would not have that privilege.

Notice that God met Jacob in Beth–el. Jacob became Israel, and from this man Israel came the house or community of Israel. But the house of God, as it pertained to the tabernacle, moved with the people wherever the community of Israel moved. And the tabernacle was always in the center of the community. No matter where they went, the center of their community pointed to the worship of God, communion with God, and service to God.

In most of today's churches, instead of putting God at the center of all things, He is put somewhere else. Jesus said in Revelation 3:20, "Behold, I stand at the door, and knock." This verse is usually misinterpreted to suggest that Jesus is standing outside your heart's door, begging to come in and save you. Jesus is not begging to be let in; He is standing outside because the church in the last days has locked Him out!

When the people would camp in the wilderness, each tribe had its assigned position in the camp, with the tabernacle at the center. Again, that means God's presence and the worship of God was always at the center of their community. If you look back at the history of our nation and look at the layout of principal towns that were built in each state, the churches were always in the center of the town. They were purposely designed that way to bring people into the heart of the town, to bring people to God. Anywhere the people went in the town, they found their direction by where the church was located.

For the children of Israel, the presence of God was at the center of the community, and worship went on no matter what. To make a ludicrous comparison to our modern day, imagine an Israelite saying, "Okay, I've set up my tent exactly the way I'm supposed to. But I'm not feeling this 'God-thing' today, even though it is my time to go to the tabernacle and make a sin offering. So I think I'll just stay in my tent today and find something fun to do." People have lost their sense of purpose today, and too many say, concerning the church, "What does it matter?"

Eventually the temple would replace the tabernacle, and it became the stationary place where the people would bring their sacrifices and offerings; they would bring what was prescribed in the law. But in Jesus' day, "the house of our God" had become "a den of thieves." Although the people gathered in the temple, they were only going through the motions and their hearts were far away from God. Had their hearts been towards God, they would have seen Christ and recognized that He was indeed the Son of God, the Messiah who came to save His people from their sin. But they did not recognize Jesus. As John said, "He came unto his own, and his own received him not."

So the concept of the house of God is well established from the Old Testament and into the New Testament realm. We quoted Jesus saying, "I will build My church, My *ekklesia*, My out-called ones," and the house of God is now in man. We become the house of our God by being the house of faith. Paul said to the Corinthian church, "You are not your own; you are bought with a price." You are Christ's. You belong to Christ, you are bought with His blood and have become the habitation of His Spirit by faith. And if you want to take this one step further, Jesus said in John 14:2, "In my Father's house are many mansions." Jesus was speaking of the place

He was going to go, where He would prepare a place for us, which we refer to as heaven, a kingdom not on earth.

But I want to return to the concept of the house of God on earth, because in the text of Nehemiah 10:39, "we will not forsake the house of our God," there are certain things we can know. First of all, it is God's house and He is the Proprietor. We read in Psalm 127:1, "Except the LORD build the house, they labour in vain that build it." But as the Proprietor, God says, "I will build *My* church." The church is His. If the church is His and we are His, then we should be surrendered to Him. He is indeed the King of the kingdom.

Why do people pray the so-called Lord's Prayer, which is really the Disciples' Prayer? It begins, "Our Father in heaven," and it says, "thy will be done." Why pray "thy will be done" if you are not interested in knowing what "thy will" is? A prayer has to mean something. That is why the Bible cautions against praying with "vain repetitions." Ask yourself, do you really want His will on earth?

Psalm 84 says, "Blessed are they that dwell in thy house." I want us to connect these concepts, from Beth–el to Solomon's temple, to the temple in Christ's day, and to understand that the house of our God is the dwelling place of our God. Why do churches struggle so much to get people to be faithful and committed? If you are going to commit to something, commit to being faithful to serving God and then stick to it. But why is that so difficult? Because the church is no longer looked at as the center. What good is a lighthouse if there is no light in it? It is just a house. It will not protect anyone who is sailing from having a shipwreck or a disaster, because it has no light to guide. And what good is the lighthouse if the light is not lifted high enough to see? I am speaking about the word of God and Jesus Christ.

How is the Light lifted up? It is not sufficient to simply preach a little sermon that is punctuated every few minutes with an "Amen" or "Hallelujah." It is the pastor's responsibility to lift up the banner of Jesus Christ and proclaim that He is the salve for the disease of mankind. You who are in darkness, look unto the Light. Look unto the One who is lifted up and understand that He is the salvation of your soul. He is life eternal.

The house of God on earth, the dwelling place of God, also suggests the picture of a family and a householder. Jesus said in a parable in Matthew 21, "There was a certain *householder.*" And Ephesians 2 says, "Now therefore ye are no more strangers and foreigners, but fellow-citizens with the saints, and of *the household of God,*" where God is the Householder, "and are built upon the foundation of the apostles and prophets, Jesus Christ himself being the chief corner stone; in whom all the building fitly framed together groweth unto an holy temple in the Lord: in whom ye also are builded together for an habitation of God through the Spirit."

In summation, the church is God's house, His dwelling place. God is the Proprietor or Householder of the family and the King of the kingdom. That is the first concept I want us to understand.

The next concept I want us to understand is the *design* of the house of our God. I am not talking about the shape of the building or the size of its platform. Let's return to Nehemiah 10 to help us see what we mean by the design of the house. We read in verse 30, "And that we would not give our daughters unto the people of the land, nor take their daughters for our sons." These people vowed that there would be no intermarriage between their daughters and sons and the people of the land. You might say, "Well, that's an Old Testament concept. We don't have to worry about that." But I want you to comprehend the scriptural basis for this instruction.

God was concerned about His covenant people and their faith. God was not saying, "I do not want this race to be intermixed with that race." He was concerned about apostasy, the falling away of His people because they got involved with others who did not worship Him. Solomon had wisdom and incredible riches, and he built the temple of God. His downfall was not that he refused to worship or pray; it was the foreign women who led his heart astray. These women worshiped Ashtoreth and many other gods; they worshiped every god *except* the living God, and they lured Solomon's heart away from Him. Ahab's union with Jezebel also had terrible consequences because she worshiped Baal. It does not matter whether Ahab started out good or bad, because in the end Baal worship won out.

Now there have been a few exceptions. One of them was Ruth, the Moabitess. She turned from the gods she worshiped and said, "Your God will be my God." She turned to God and never looked back.

So when the people in Nehemiah's day said, "We would not give our daughters unto the people of the land, nor take their daughters for our sons," the point is not so much that under God's law there was a prohibition against intermarriage. The essential point is that the people desired to do God's will. We could go even further by making the case about the need to protect the line descending to Christ. But our subject is the house of our God and its design, and the first element in its design is the desire to carry out *His will.* What is His will for us today? It is very simple: that we come to the faith in Jesus Christ, to know who He is. That is not simply having faith in faith itself, or simply believing with your mind. Jesus said in His high priestly prayer in John 17:3, "This is life eternal, that they might know thee the only true God, and Jesus Christ." His will for us today is to have faith and to trust in Him. If God did all of those things that He said He would do, we can count on Him to do the things that are yet to be fulfilled; but He only wants us to trust Him.

People pray the Disciples' Prayer and say, "Thy will be done." I have heard many people say, "How can I know God's will?" Before you can know the will of God for your life, you need to read His book. Before you start looking for some kind of personal revelation of God's will for your life, you need to learn His clearly stated will already revealed for us in the Bible. Otherwise you will not know anything more than the subjective things people will try to plant in your head. You must get into the book. That does not mean you have to live like a hermit or a monk and never come up for air. But you do have to learn His word to know His will. That is the first element in the design of the house of God.

The second element is in Nehemiah 10:31: "And if the people of the land bring ware or any victuals on the sabbath day to sell, that we would not buy it of them on the sabbath, or on the holy day." We will label this *His day*. In Nehemiah's day, the Sabbath needed to be kept. Its first purpose was to honor God. Remember that the people lived in a close community and you could see everything. You could clearly see the distinction between the people who were honoring God by keeping the Lord's Day, and those who were chopping wood and selling it. Secondly, the Sabbath served as a stark and beautiful reminder that God created everything, and at the end of His creating, He rested. Therefore, keeping the Sabbath helped them to remember the Lord. And lastly, the Sabbath was a day of rest. There were no desk jobs in that day; all of their work involved hard physical labor, so the Sabbath was a day of rest for them. But keeping the Lord's Day was primarily a demonstration of honoring God.

How do we apply this concept of "His day"? I have had many people ask me, "What day is the Sabbath day?" and "Should I celebrate a particular day?" My answer is that I "Sabbath" daily. That does not mean that I rest every day, it means that I remember God every day; I celebrate Him every day. But there are some who say, "Well, I can't do that just yet. I'm not ready to do that, because on some days I work, and then Sunday is football day, and Monday night is a teachers' meeting or something for the children, etc." But you need to be honest and do a reality check. We are so busy making excuses, but the reality is that our hearts and minds are constantly coming up with ways to fill the time with all the other things we could possibly do. That is why I said that I Sabbath daily. I do not need to have a special day. It is wonderful to gather in one place once a week as the family of God to open up the word and learn together, but there is nothing better than to recognize God on a daily basis.

The next element in the design of the house of God is found in the latter part of verse 31, which says, "that we would leave the seventh year, and the exaction of every debt." We will label this *His way*. We read in the book of Leviticus that the people were instructed to not till the ground in the seventh year, but to leave the ground to rest. But this required that they trust God implicitly to provide an abundant harvest in the sixth year that would be sufficient to carry over into the seventh year. His way was to teach His people to trust Him for provision. He would take care of them if they kept this prescribed part of the law. God was saying through His word, "I will take care of you. Because you are doing things My way, I will take care of the rest."

I want us to think about this because it is very profound. We normally think of God's law in the Old Testament in terms of its stringent demands. But God provided this law of the cancellation of debts to show His love, as if to say, "I will extend My love and My mercy to show you and teach you about loving and forgiving your neighbor, including those who owe you, and those to whom you are debtors." Doesn't that remind us of "forgive us our debts, as we forgive our debtors"? You no longer have to wait for a seventh year to forgive, because, as Jesus taught His disciples, this is something to do daily, sometimes hourly.

The last item we will look at in the design of God's house is shown in verse 32: "Also we made ordinances for us, to charge ourselves yearly with the third part of a shekel for the service of the house of our God." Let's label this *His work*, and we will come back to this concept in a moment.

I want us to look at all of these elements in the design of the house of God: His will, His day, His way and His work. God made these things known in order that the people should teach them to the community and that they should implement them. And in the old dispensation, God said that if you do these things, "For this I will bless you."

The design of the house of our God is not how you or I think it ought to be, or how it might be. The design of the house of our God today is still His will, His day, His way and His work; and it should still be all about those elements. A church calling itself a house of God that is void of Christ, void of the word of God or void of Bible teaching is just an empty house.

When the Spirit of God comes in and fills our hearts and minds, we become the habitation of God, both individually and when we come together corporately as the body called the church. As Paul wrote in 1 Timothy 3:15, the church is "the pillar and ground of the truth." That is the house of God, the church of Jesus Christ.

Now let's return to our last element in the design, His work. Under this item there could be a number of subheadings, but at the top of the list would be systematic, proportionate and sacrificial giving. All of these are woven into the service of the house of our God. We read in verse 32, "Also we made ordinances for us, to charge ourselves yearly with the third part of a shekel for the service of the house of our God." Now you might say, "But you're quoting from the Old Testament. How do I make an application today?" God has never changed. He has been saying the same thing through the ages. God through the prophet Malachi said to a disobedient people, "Return to me, and I will return to you." The last prophet of the Old Testament was still crying out for God's people to turn back to God's ways.

In Zerubbabel's day, the king had given an edict allowing the people to return, and no doubt the people had to be subsidized. A lot of money was given to them to enable them to rebuild. But after all the work was done, after the altar, the temple and the walls were rebuilt, the temple would have to continue to function. Clear directions had been given in the law for this, and it started with the shewbread.

When God rained down the manna in the wilderness, the people would gather it up for food, but they would also give a portion back as an offering to God. After the temple was rebuilt, the equivalent of the manna, the shewbread, was the first requirement in the temple. The people gave offerings "for the shewbread, and for the continual meat offering, and for the continual burnt offering, of the sabbaths, of the new moons, for the set feasts, and for the holy things, and for the sin offerings to make an atonement for Israel," which was for the entire community as well as for each individual. There were many required offerings. That is why I say that they gave systematically, proportionately and sacrificially, and all to His work.

"We cast the lots among the priests, the Levites, and the people, for the wood offering. . . ." Note that there is no prior reference to a "wood offering," but it is obvious that the people needed wood to keep the continual fire burning. Someone had to go cut the wood and bring the wood. While there was no prescription in the law for a wood offering, they simply understood that they had to keep the fire burning. They brought the wood "into the house of our God, after the houses of our fathers, at times appointed year by year, to burn upon the altar of the LORD our God, as it is written in the law: and to bring the firstfruits of our ground, and the firstfruits of all fruit of all trees, year by year, unto the house of the LORD: also the firstborn of our sons, and of our cattle . . . the firstfruits of our dough, and our offerings, and the fruit of all manner of trees, of wine and of oil . . . and the tithes of our ground unto the Levites, that the same Levites might have the tithes in all the cities of our tillage. And the priest the son of Aaron shall be with the Levites, when the Levites take tithes: and the Levites shall bring up the tithe of the tithes unto the house of our God." The Levites received a portion of the offerings, and they in turn gave a tithe of the tithes that were collected for them. So no one in the community was exempted from participating in giving. Each member of the community had a responsibility.

I have met homeless people who would collect empty bottles and sell them just so they would have money to give an offering, as if to say, "No matter what, I am putting God first." If a homeless person can do that, we need to examine ourselves in order to make sure that we are still putting God first.

The priests were to bring "the tithe of the tithes unto the house of our God, to the chambers, into the treasure house," into the storehouse. "For the children of Israel and the children of Levi shall bring the offering of the corn, of the new wine, and the oil, unto the chambers, where are the vessels of the sanctuary, and the priests that minister, and the porters, and the singers: *and we will not forsake the house of our God.*"

Remember that during the time of captivity in Babylon, the people were not regularly taught about God's law and the ways of God. But when they heard God's word, they declared, "This is what we will do." And suddenly, God's word, God's way, and anything that pertained to God became front and center in their lives, and they made the resolution: "We will not forsake the house of our God."

Now it seems self-evident what this word "forsake" means, whether we use the definition "to leave behind," or from the Portuguese language, "to be slovenly" or "to be sloppy," or from the French language, "to abandon" or "to leave."

When the edict came allowing the people to return to Jerusalem, very few returned, so we can be sure that when they said, "We will not forsake the house of our God," that was a vow from the heart. Did the vow last? No. Nehemiah would return to Babylon for a time, and when he came back to Jerusalem, he found God's house again in disrepair. He also discovered that the tithes were not being brought into the storehouse. And the chamber of the temple that was supposed to house the offerings was being used to house the enemy Tobiah!

God was faithful to His people. In Deuteronomy 4:31, He made a promise that He would not forsake His people. He made a promise to Moses, He made a promise to Joshua, He made a promise to David, and He made promises to many others, saying, "I will be with you." So to a God who had been so faithful to do all of this, it seems terrible that the people would fall away again, even though they made the promise in good faith, "We will not forsake the house of our God."

What can we glean from this today? Let me tell you that there are still people today who forsake the house of God, despite all of these reasons we have given for the house of God to exist. The book of Romans speaks of the need for a person to be called and sent to preach the gospel. "How shall they hear without a preacher? And how shall they preach, except they be sent?" That is what the church exists for. You don't come to church to be a Christian, but you come to church to hear faith spoken into your ears, so that more faith comes, because "faith comes by hearing, and hearing by the word of God." You come to church because God, the One who gave the minister as a gift, also gives the minister the ability to open up a passage. You come to church to make a testimony that God is still front and center in this community of faith.

Some people do not want to listen to a long sermon. Some only come to church on holidays. How can people say, "Jesus is my

Lord and Savior and He washed and cleansed me with His shed blood," and how can they read, "You are not your own, you are bought with a price," and then leave and remain completely indifferent as to whether or not they ever come back? Because the house of God is no longer respected, and the position of the pastor is no longer respected in the church. I am not asking you to respect the pastor personally, I am saying that you ought to respect the position.

Even though these people made the declaration, "We will not forsake," they still fell back. Don't imagine that somehow if we make a similar resolution that we will always be able to keep it. It can only be maintained by abiding in the word. When you abide in the word, the word abides in you. That is what will keep you from departing from the way. You know that this word is all the spiritual nutrition that you need.

The resolution that these people made was an indication of their spiritual life, an acceptance of a burden, a declaration of priority and an acknowledgment of the importance of the house of God. When the church puts God front and center and says, "This is what matters," the community of faith comes together and recognizes the opportunity for God to work His will in our lives and demonstrate His power.

Those who neglect God's house say, "I'll get to it when I get to it," and we know what God says about that attitude. God says, in essence, "When you make time for Me, and as much time as you make for Me, I will make for you." He is looking at us as His children and wondering, "What is wrong with some of those who will not recognize My love and care and become committed?"

If you are just beginning your study of the word of God, I would tell you to give God a chance, and see if this word does not begin to spring up new life inside your heart. It doesn't happen in a day, and it doesn't happen at an altar. It happens as you go along, saying, "I need this word of God, and I need the house of God, and I will not forsake it. I will not be so quick to draw back."

Jesus had to say to His disciples, "Will you also go?" I am not asking that question, I am forging forward full of faith. I know what my God can do. My God can do anything; my God can fix the problems you made or the problems you didn't make. My God can raise you up from the shambles and put your feet on solid ground. He can give you vision when you thought you would never have any. He can give you a way where you thought there would never be a way, because you thought that God couldn't possibly be listening to your little prayers. And I am standing here to tell you yes, He will, and yes, He can, because He is faithful.

This whole book of Nehemiah demonstrates God's fidelity. May some of us have the courage to not only say, "We will not forsake the house of our God," but to also say, "We will stand on God's fidelity." Let that kind of faith spill over into your life and your walk. And as you go, recognize that God is in the mix; and whatever problems and issues you may have, God is going to take care of them, because He is faithful. And while others may forsake, we will not forsake the house of our God. My God can do anything, including fulfilling His promise to build His church. His word will not return void. Stand on that promise and rejoice.

CHAPTER 17

GOD WILL FIGHT FOR YOU

Have you ever confronted a problem or situation that seemed so gargantuan, so large in terms of its depth and complexity, that all you could do was just shake your head and say, "I just don't know what I am going to do about this"? The life of faith is not what is commonly preached in modern Christendom, which too often teaches that God will strew rose petals in your pathway. The Christian walk is full of contradictions: we are living, yet dead. It is a life full of paradoxes: the life of faith seizes things that the seen circumstances absolutely deny.

Over the years I have faced many challenging and difficult circumstances. I believe that there will never be a stopping point down here, as long as we are acting in faith and grabbing hold of the promises of God. There is no letup in the battle. There will never come a time when you will be granted a special respite. You may have seasons of rest from the attacks of the enemy, but on the whole, it is Satan's goal to shake you out of your faith life.

But we know this: God gave us His precious promises, and we can lift ourselves up by remembering the truth of God's word that has ministered to us over the years. His name is Emmanuel, the "*with-us* God." He will never leave us nor forsake us. And 2 Corinthians 1:20 says that all the promises of God in Him are yes and in

Him Amen. That means that all the promises of God are ours to claim, so long as we are acting in faith. We are not saved by works, but by faith.

In the New Testament, Peter writes that "the Lord is not slack concerning His promise, as some men count slackness." Jeremiah in the Old Testament says essentially the same thing: when God says something, He brings it to pass. Both the Old and the New Testaments say, "The just shall live by faith." But it is a battle and we must stay vigilant in God's word. The book of Hebrews specifically warns that if a person draws back from that life of faith, God says that His soul shall have no pleasure in him. God does not take pleasure in seeing people draw back. We are not talking about people who backslide, we are talking about people who completely let go because they think that the challenge before them is just too tough and looks impossible. Maybe you are facing multiple challenges. For some people, it doesn't have to be something gigantic in size; it could be that your greatest challenge is just being able to pay your rent.

The message throughout God's book is that He is faithful, and when we stand on His word of promise, He brings it to pass. Now it does not say how quickly or how slowly. That is why we studied the life of Abraham. I take great comfort in the fact that after God told Abraham that He was going to change his whole life by making him father of many, it took twenty-five years for God to make it come to pass. That should give us hope.

Abraham speaks to us because he is a type and pattern of faith. He was called out of a strange land, and the book of Hebrews says he was called to a place he knew not. I think that is true of most of us. We take a step of faith, and we do not necessarily know where we are going. We ask, "How is this going to work out?" That is not to say that when you start out on a course, you will never falter. Abraham did falter. That is why I love him; he faltered, he went down to Egypt and he lied and did other things that he should not have done. But eventually we see his faith blossom, and he is not only called "friend of God," but he is also memorialized in Nehemiah 9, where it says that God found his heart faithful before Him. That was not said of any other individual in Nehemiah, let alone most of the Old Testament. So Abraham is an example for us.

Romans 4 says that when God spoke to Abraham and gave him the promise, "he staggered not at the promise of God," but he had strong faith and he "*amened*" that promise, and God imputed to him His righteousness; God placed His righteousness in him. Abraham was made in right standing with God for his faith. I do not believe that we normally have to face the kinds of things that Abraham faced. We are not faced with the impossibility of being told in our old age, "You will have a child, a promised seed to repopulate as the stars in the sky and the sand on the seashore, and abundant land will be given to you." Since I am not confronting those types of issues, perhaps I need to make sure that I am not exaggerating the things that seem impossible to me, because we know that with God, nothing is impossible.

So with that backdrop of focusing on the promises of God when facing something impossible, we are returning to Nehemiah 9 and the great prayer concerning God's faithfulness in relationship to His chosen people. The prayer opens with a blessing, an exaltation of the Lord for all that He wrought in creation. When God declares something, "God is not a man to lie." He doesn't say, "Let's see if this will work." When He says something, it is. God delivered His people time and time again. He heard their cry in their affliction in bondage, and He had promised Abraham that they would come out of the land of their captivity in the fourth generation. This whole passage is saying, "I am God. I do not lie. I am faithful. When I say a thing, it will come to pass. If I say, 'You will take the land,' then you *will* take the land. I will make a way for you where there is no way." Abraham said, "Is Eleazar my steward supposed to be my heir?" And God said, "No." Then Abraham and Hagar produced Ishmael and that was a disaster. The problem is that we grow impatient and say, "Oh God, hurry up! I am running out of time!" But whose time is it anyway, if you think about it?

What happens if you are sick or have other needs, and you have been hanging on to God and His word but your deliverance does not come to pass in the now? Then you will wake up in eternity, standing before Him with your eyes open. That means you crossed what I call the beautiful yellow-tape finish line, saying, "Lord, I am claiming it now." There is nothing wrong with that. I think that too much time is spent down here lamenting about what God has not yet done, when in fact, we are simply told to claim a promise and stand until God brings it to pass. If it is fulfilled in this lifetime, then you had better start looking for another promise to claim in God's book so that He may bring it to pass.

We read in Nehemiah 9:22, "Moreover thou gavest them kingdoms and nations, and didst divide them into corners: so they possessed the land of Sihon, and the land of the king of Heshbon, and the land of Og king of Bashan." You could very easily read right by those names and they would not mean anything to you, unless you took the time to go back and study who these people were. Sihon was the king of Heshbon, who seized the Moabite territory and made it his. Sihon was an Amorite. The Amorites came out of the line of Canaan. Noah had cursed Canaan, Ham's son. Canaan's descendants were a cursed people who appear in a myriad number of passages, and some of them appear to be giants. Amos 2:9 tells us of the destruction of the Amorite, which happens much later, "whose height was like the height of the cedars, and he was strong as the oaks." These were a mighty big people. Og's name means "gigantic" or "long-necked giant." Deuteronomy 3:11 records that King Og of Bashan had a bed that was about thirteen and a half feet long by six feet wide, which suggests that the man was perhaps twelve feet tall and who knows how wide.

Both kings, Sihon and Og, were essentially blockading the gateway into the Promised Land. The land of the Amorites was controlled by these two kings. And their dominion was vast: King Og of Bashan, for example, ruled over sixty fortified cities. So the children of Israel would first have to get past these two kings before they could cross over the Jordan River and enter into Jericho, which we know happened in the book of Joshua. There are a remarkable number of references to these two kings, Sihon and Og, and when something is repeated in the Bible over and over again, we had better pay attention.

God had promised Abraham the land and said that His people would go into a land for four generations and then come out. Then He said, "For the iniquity of the Amorites is not yet full." The Scripture says that the Canaanite and the Perizzite were in the land; a plethora of *–ites* were living in the land. These were enemies of the people of God and there was great animosity. And if you keep traveling through Genesis, you will find an increasing number of times that these people appear, until the time when God's people will attempt to pass through some very hostile territory.

Before the children of Israel under Moses' leadership tried to enter the land, they had to pass through the king of Edom's territory. God recorded this in two different places. One record says they went through, but the longer record says they were denied entrance and they turned back. Does that sound like something God's people would do, turning back? But they did.

There is another wonderful picture of the children of promise versus the children of works. The Edomites, who were the descendants of Esau, and the Horites and other *–ites* were against the children of God. The book of Galatians speaks of the clash between the promised child, Isaac, and the child of the flesh, Ishmael, who was mocking him. It is age-old to be hated without a cause, to be hated for your commitment to God. The children of Israel weren't that committed, we know that. But they were still hated, so we can take comfort in the knowledge that this is not something new.

We read in Numbers 21, beginning at verse 21, "Israel sent messengers unto Sihon king of the Amorites, saying, Let me pass through thy land: we will not turn into the fields, or into the vineyards; we will not drink of the waters of the well: but we will go along by the king's high way, until we be past thy borders. And Sihon would not suffer Israel to pass through his border: but Sihon gathered all his people together, and went out against Israel into the wilderness: and he came to Jahaz, and fought against Israel. And Israel smote him with the edge of the sword, and possessed his land from Arnon unto Jabbok, even unto the children of Ammon: for the border of the children of Ammon was strong. And Israel took all these cities: and Israel dwelt in all the cities of the Amorites, in Heshbon, and in all the villages thereof. For Heshbon was the city of Sihon the king of the Amorites, who had fought against the former king of Moab, and taken all his land out of his hand, even unto Arnon." Sihon had dispossessed the people and taken over their land. "Wherefore they that speak in proverbs say, Come into Heshbon, let the city of Sihon be built and prepared: for there is a fire gone out of Heshbon, a flame from the city of Sihon."

Verse 31 says, "Thus Israel dwelt in the land of the Amorites." Deuteronomy 1 says that they encamped there in the fortieth year, on the first day of the eleventh month. Though they had spent forty years wandering in the wilderness, the battles against Sihon and Og would be fought within only a short period of time. All of these events happened very quickly.

So we see them encamped here, and then it says, "And Moses sent to spy out Jaazer, and they took the villages thereof, and drove out the Amorites that were there. And they turned and went up by the way of Bashan: and Og the king of Bashan went out against them, he, and all his people, to the battle at Edrei. And the LORD said unto Moses, Fear him not: for I have delivered him into thy hand, and all his people, and his land."

I want us to think about this. Moses and his band, regardless of how few or how many, would have looked like ants in comparison to these men and their army. Yet God said, "Fear him not: for I have delivered him into thy hand, and all his people, and his land; and thou shalt do to him as thou didst unto Sihon king of the Amorites, which dwelt at Heshbon. So they smote him, and his sons, and all his people, until there was none left him alive: and they possessed his land."

What this says is very profound. God made a promise, saying, "You are going to enter into that land. This is the land I have promised to give you." But there were giants on the border of the land, and God said, "Go get them!" We have a second record of these events in Deuteronomy 2, which also lists other enemies like the

Emims that "dwelt therein in times past, a people great, and many, and tall, as the Anakims." These were all giants, sometimes called Zamzummims. But imagine God saying to you, "Go and possess that land." Imagine receiving this command and having to come against men who were twelve feet tall! I am sure that God did not think that the children of Israel were able, but He knew that *He* was able. And as long as the people went according to what He said, "Fear not," they would get the victory over their enemies.

We read in Deuteronomy 2, beginning at verse 24, "I have given into thine hand Sihon the Amorite, king of Heshbon, and his land: begin to possess it, and contend with him in battle." Again, God said, "Go get him!" And God is still telling us the same thing, so we should start making an application.

Canaan, the Promised Land, is not a symbolic type of heaven. Canaan to us represents the life of faith. God said, "Go in there and possess it," which is living the life of faith. During this walk down here, we are living the life of faith; and as we go from "faith to faith," we will encounter things that seem impossible. They are the Sihon and Og and Anak and Emims and Zamzummims and whatever else you want to call them, of your life and of mine, whatever they may be. And they are overcome only by one way: by God giving a word of promise, and His people acting on that. That does not mean taking an independent action; it does not mean performing "works." You do not achieve God's victories by saying, "I can do this in my own strength." God must first send us.

He said, "Go to possess the land, and contend with him in battle. This day will I begin to put the dread of thee and the fear of thee upon the nations." And we know that this came to pass, because when Joshua went into the land and he encountered Amorites and other hostile kings, it says that when they heard they were coming, their hearts melted. The enemies did not look so big after all, because they had heard of all the great things that God had done for His people.

So everywhere we turn in the Bible, God is saying, "This is what I am going to do," and He makes it come to pass. Note also that

God said He would not remove the enemies in one day. Many times over He said, "I will do it little by little," because if He had emptied them all in one fell swoop, it would have created other problems.

Many things come our way that seem awful at first, and we ask, "How do these things happen?" But I am praying that this message brings encouragement to those of you who are still looking at the things which seem too gigantic and too impossible. I want us to recognize that when God calls us and sends us, He makes a way. As Dr. Gene Scott would often say, "Whom the Lord calls, He enables." He not only gives you the ability, He gives you the strength and might—not your strength, but His.

We have more detail given in Deuteronomy 2:30, where it says that "Sihon king of Heshbon would not let us pass by him: for the LORD thy God hardened his spirit." Doesn't that remind us of what God did to Pharaoh? It tells me that when I am dealing with people who are enemy-like, maybe God is hardening them. Maybe God is doing the very thing that He did with Pharaoh, with this king and with others, to show that He is still in control, and all of this was by His hand to make something else come to pass.

When you start putting things in perspective, you might say, "Well, maybe it is not so gargantuan. Maybe it is not so difficult. Maybe it is not going to be so terrible after all." As long as the Lord is there, as long as He will go with me, I am okay. I just don't want to go by myself, because if God is not with me, I know I am going to be defeated. That is the reality of living the faith life.

"Sihon came out against us, he and all his people, to fight at Jahaz. And the LORD our God delivered him before us; and we smote him, and his sons, and all his people." Not only did they wipe out the enemy, they took all of their possessions. God has a way of saying, "I will take care of your enemies and make sure that you don't have any lack at the same time."

We read in Deuteronomy 3 of how Og the king of Bashan and all his people came out against God's people at the battle at Edrei. "And the LORD said unto me, Fear him not: for I will deliver him, and all his people, and his land, into thy hand; and thou shalt do unto him as thou didst unto Sihon king of the Amorites, which dwelt at Heshbon. So the Lord our God delivered into our hands Og also, the king of Bashan, and all his people: and we smote him until there was not one remaining."

If you have a concordance, you can look up how many times this battle is referenced in the Bible. It was memorialized because it was such a great victory over these giant Amorite kings. It would have been very easy for us to have just read right by that reference in the prayer in Nehemiah 9, but even the one who was praying recognized how important the victory over these two kings was. It was essential to penetrate the defenses of those two gate guardians who were hindering God's people from entering into the Promised Land.

God uses some interesting words to describe what He was going to do to these kings and the enemies of God. The word for "hornet" or "hornets" appears only three times in the Old Testament, and it is used in connection with these two kings, and on one occasion in reference to Pharaoh or other enemies of God's people. Exodus 23:28 says, "I will send hornets before you, to drive them out." It is as though God is saying, "You need to get up and go by faith," like when He said to Moses, "You have tarried at this mountain too long; it is time to move on." God is also saying, "But before you get there, I am going to send something their way." God will send something against the enemies first, but you still have the responsibility of going out against them. And we can be assured that the Lord will be there before we get there.

Now I want us to look at some promises in God's book that show us how the battle is won. Throughout this whole book, God is saying the same thing: the life of faith requires leaning on the promises of God, knowing God's fidelity and being confident that God will do what He said He would do; He will make His word come to pass. But at the same time, He also says, "I am going to be with you and I am going to help you do the very thing that I am asking you to do." That is the heart of the message.

God has been saying the same things over and over again. We have promises from God for every occasion in the life of faith, whenever you are trying to enter into the Promised Land and you encounter enemies hindering you or blockading you. Let's look at some of these promises. Deuteronomy 1:30 says, "The LORD your God which goeth before you, he shall fight for you, according to all that he did for you in Egypt before your eyes." Deuteronomy 3:22 says, "Ye shall not fear them: for the LORD your God he shall fight for you."

Again, when God says something over and over again, I pay attention. Deuteronomy 20:4 says, "For the LORD your God is he that goeth with you, to fight for you against your enemies, to save you." Joshua 23:10 says, "One man of you shall chase a thousand: for the LORD your God, he it is that fighteth for you, as he hath promised you." There are many more promises like these in God's book, and we can see the repetition.

God is saying, "I am going to do this thing." It still requires that we get up in faith. It still requires facing the giants, whatever they are. But when you face them, go in the knowledge that you are His, you belong to Him, and He is going to be there fighting the battle. God is going to be there before you get there. He asks that you still stand and face the enemy and not run away like they did the first time when they encountered the king of Edom; but rather, look at the giants that you face, and ask the question, "Who else but God?" And "If God be for us, who can be against us?" Who can bring us down if God is for us? That is not to say we will never have problems or times of sorrow, but we can be fortified with might from God.

Now we can see why the reference to these two kings was included in the prayer in Nehemiah 9. It was included to show that God had promised the land and not even these giants could hinder. And if you read on, you will see that they entered in and possessed the land. In fact, there is a great passage in Joshua that puts a capstone on the victory. Joshua 21:43–45 says, "The LORD gave unto Israel all the land which he sware to give unto their fathers; and they possessed it, and dwelt therein." God makes good on His word. "And the LORD gave them rest round about, according to all that he sware unto their fathers: and there stood not a man of all their enemies before them; the LORD delivered all their enemies into their hand. There failed not aught of any good thing which the LORD had spoken unto the house of Israel; all came to pass." I want us to highlight those last four words: "*all came to pass.*"

The message is simple: when you come into the kingdom of God as a child of God, you will have obstacles. Some will have more obstacles than others. Not everybody is a walking magnet for trouble or giants, but you and I know, especially those of you who have been walking with the Lord for a long time, that trouble is part of the journey. That is why I love the message that Dr. Gene Scott would preach on Deuteronomy 33, that God provides "tough shoes for a tough trip." Or that he would oft quote the Australian preacher Jack White, saying, "Cheer up, saints, it's going to get worse!" But when I read this particular passage and read what happened to these two kings, I say, "My God will fight for me." He will go before me. I will not fear those things that are in front of me. Why? Because God's hand is in it; and just like it happened for these people in Nehemiah's day, all will come to pass according to His word, because we serve a very faithful God.

Now let me take you back to Nehemiah, just so you can see that God has not changed, not through hundreds of years. In Nehemiah 4, while the enemies were coming against the people and doing whatever they could do to hinder the work, we read in the last part of verse 20, "our God shall fight for us." I want you to think about how many times, if you comb the book, you will find those words, or something like those words, which say that God will fight the battles for His people.

The one who prayed the prayer in Nehemiah 9 knew about that in his day. We should know about it in ours. That means no matter what comes against us, we can say, "If God be for us, who can be against us?" I am speaking faith to myself and saying that no matter what I face, it is nothing in God's hands, because God is with us. And I am claiming all of the other promises that He has declared: No weapon formed against us shall prosper. Greater is

He that is in me than any other power that could be lobbed at me. And I will be fortified as a consequence of the very thing that the devil intended to use to cripple me; because when I am weak, then I am strong, because it is God's strength in me, and by that strength I can do all things.

Our God shall fight for us! The apostle Paul was alone in prison, and he said in 2 Timothy that no one stood with him, but the Lord stood by him and strengthened him. And He is the same God yesterday, today and forever. He is the same God who will be with us as we meet the challenges of the coming week and the coming year, and maybe the challenges of our lifetime. The devil has been trying for years to hinder the work of God and break our faith, and now it seems like he just increased the pressure. The devil will try to frighten you away and convince you that you are not going to make it, sometimes by attacking your mind or attacking your finances. Whatever it is, I have seen it and I recognize who the enemy is. Whatever the source of the attack, recognize who the enemy is. The enemy is the devil and he will try anything to make you afraid or confused, or cause you to lose your focus. Hang on to God's word and declare, "My focus is here." Instead of saying, "God, You can't possibly fix this," say, "God, there is no problem so great that You cannot solve it!"

I am not being cocky about it, but I am looking ahead and I am thinking to myself that maybe the enemy has enlarged the way I see things. Maybe the enemy is trying to make himself look much bigger than he really is. But there is a much greater Person, somebody bigger than all the giants and demons and forces that come against God's people and His work.

The Bible says, "Resist the devil, and he will flee from you." You rebuke Satan, in Jesus' name. You recognize that the enemy doesn't care how he causes you to disconnect from faith. Look at the opposition as though they were a King Sihon or a King Og, with the certainty that our God is greater than any problem we may encounter. Our God will fight for us, and all of the things that He has said, just like we read out of Joshua, they will all come to pass.

Those will be the final words on that day, and there will come a day. It might not happen down here, but I believe it will be when we all get to heaven: "And it came to pass," God made good on all the things that He said He would.

Now when we encounter the heinous attacks of the enemy, instead of saying, "How awful!" we can say, "We glory in tribulation!" We glory in the fact that God has seen us to be more than honorable vessels to give us the challenges that He metes out; and no matter how great those challenges appear, I know my God will fight. God will fight for you and for me and for His work, and we will get the victory, because the victory is ours, in Jesus' name.

CHAPTER 18

GOD RAISED US UP FOR A PURPOSE

We have been navigating through the extraordinary prayer in Nehemiah 9, which is a mosaic comprised of verses of Scripture and history patched together. Today we will begin at Nehemiah 9:23, which looks at the period when the children of Israel were just about to enter into the Promised Land. Verses 23 through 25 capture what happened at the end of the Pentateuch and describe events that are recorded in the book of Joshua.

"Their children also multipliedst thou as the stars of heaven, and broughtest them into the land, concerning which thou hadst promised to their fathers, that they should go in to possess it. So the children went in and possessed the land, and thou subduedst before them the inhabitants of the land, the Canaanites, and gavest them into their hands, with their kings, and the people of the land, that they might do with them as they would. And they took strong cities," which are named in the book of Joshua, including Jericho, Ai, Libnah and Lachish. They came in and took possession of "a fat land, and possessed houses full of all goods, wells digged, vineyards, and oliveyards, and fruit trees in abundance: so they did eat, and were filled, and became fat, and delighted themselves in thy great goodness."

This part of the prayer describes the period from the time of Moses' death to the time of Joshua's death. For those who are new to studying the Scriptures, it helps to view the books of Joshua and Judges as a bridge between the Pentateuch and the time of the kings. By analogy, in the New Testament, we can view the book of Acts as a bridge between the Gospels and the Epistles. If you took the book of Acts out of the New Testament, you would have a hard time understanding the connection between the events recorded in the Gospels—including Jesus' death, Resurrection, Ascension and the commission to the disciples—and the planting of the churches that produced the Epistles. The books of Joshua and Judges may be looked at in the same way. God raised up Moses and his successor, Joshua, to lead the people into the Promised Land. Saul later became the first king, followed by David, who united the kingdom, and then by Solomon, David's son. Then the kingdom was torn apart into two kingdoms. Without the books of Joshua and Judges, we would have a hard time understanding how all of that happened.

The book of Joshua is the confirmation of what God promised to the people. Joshua's name means "the Lord is my salvation" or "the Lord is salvation." The Greek form of the name *Joshua* gives us the name "Jesus," which embraces the same principle. The book of Joshua can be divided into two parts: twelve chapters that talk about the conquest of the land, and twelve chapters that talk about the partition and distribution of the land. Alternatively, if you were to view the book of Joshua in terms of a time frame, it would be comprised of a period of about one month to enter the land, followed by a period of perhaps seven years of conquest, and then another period of eighteen years of dividing the land between each respective tribe. So the events recorded in the book of Joshua span a total of twenty-five or more years.

As we go into the book of Judges, there is an important question before us: who would be God's mouthpiece? We know that God spoke directly to Moses, and that God was with Joshua as He was with Moses. God's people had come out of Egypt and for the first time, they did not have a mouthpiece like Moses or Joshua to go to anymore. But one of the purposes of the book of Judges is to show us how God related to His people during this time between the period of the deliverers and the kings.

Nehemiah 9:26 and 27 take us straight into the book of Judges, so today we will skip over the book of Joshua and talk about the book of Judges. I suggest that you read the book of Joshua in your own time; it is not especially complicated and it is straightforward reading. We read in Nehemiah 9:26, "Nevertheless they were disobedient. . . ." That is how we know that we are talking about the book of Judges and not the book of Joshua, because Joshua and his people were obedient unto the Lord: they harkened diligently to the voice of the Lord. But these people were disobedient and they rebelled against the Lord.

Here begins a tragic pattern of the people in the book of Judges. We will read many times over: "the children of Israel did evil in the sight of the LORD." There is a pattern of apostasy and a pattern of returning to the Lord. And it is not just simply a pattern of apostasy and returning, rather it is a whole series of events: God raises up a deliverer to deliver the people out of their oppression, the people are delivered, and then the deliverer dies and the people return to their evil and apostasy. But we should not make the common mistake of caricaturing the book of Judges based upon the more familiar figures such as Gideon or Deborah. You cannot adequately survey the book of Judges without looking at the twelve judges strung across a period of time, encountering a concept that God still has to deal with today: people doing what is right in their own eyes.

"Nevertheless they were disobedient, and rebelled against thee, and cast thy law behind their backs, and slew thy prophets which testified against them to turn them to thee, and they wrought great provocations. Therefore thou deliveredst them into the hand of their enemies, who vexed them: and in the time of their trouble, when they cried unto thee, thou heardest them from heaven; and according to thy manifold mercies thou gavest them saviours, who saved them out of the hand of their enemies."

What grips my attention is that at this time there was no more Moses, there was no more Joshua, and there was not yet an appointed king. Although appointing a king may have been in God's plan, He would appoint the first king only because the people had rejected Him when they rejected Samuel, God's chosen vessel. Therefore a king was raised up who started out good and ended up bad. But what I found interesting here in the prayer in Nehemiah 9 was the expression "thou gavest them saviours." This caught my attention, first and foremost, because we tend to exclusively use the term "saviour" to refer to our Lord and Savior, Jesus Christ. I was also caught off guard by the appearance of the word "saviours" in the plural, which forced me to do a little digging. The Hebrew word translated "saviour" or "savior," using the modern spelling, is a form of the word *yasha*. It is the basis of the name *Joshua*, which again in the New Testament Greek becomes the name "Jesus." So from the Old Testament into the New Testament we have the concepts of deliverance, a savior and salvation.

Our English word "salvation" can be traced all the way back to the Greek word *soterian*. It is interesting that this word was not used exclusively within Christendom or even Judaism. The Bible says, "Thou gavest them saviours," that is, God gave them saviors. But in the course of history, we know that there were men who appointed themselves as saviors on earth, and that was clearly seen in the days after Alexander the Great's death when his four generals took up the four quarters of the conquered land. We read of names like "Ptolemy I Soter" and "Antiochus I Soter." The word "Soter" is a title that they gave themselves; it means "savior." Ptolemy also wanted very badly to be referred to as "Pharaoh." He wanted to be seen not just as *soter*, "savior," but also as the god of the people. So we see that there were men in the course of history who considered themselves to be the savior of people. It is not unusual for a man to declare himself savior. In fact, the book of Revelation shows us that is exactly how the people will be deceived in the end times, when someone will come as a substitute deliverer, the Antichrist.

Nehemiah 9:27 says, "Thou gavest them saviours." Please write in the margin of your Bible that the word for "saviours" in Nehemiah 9 is *Strong's* number 3467. I would like us to look at those saviors whom God gave for a very good purpose, so please turn to the book of Judges.

Judges 2:16 says, "Nevertheless the LORD raised up judges, which delivered them out of the hand of those that spoiled them." The word translated "delivered" is a form of that same word translated "saviours," again, *Strong's* number 3467.

God raised up judges and deliverers. We will talk about the term "judges" shortly, but first I want us to read Judges 2:18: "And when the LORD raised them up judges, then the LORD was with the judge." This is important to the understanding of the whole book: the Lord was with the one whom He raised up, whether we have only one verse telling us about a judge like Shamgar, or we have a hundred verses telling us about Gideon. When God raised up the judge, He "was with the judge, and delivered them," and again the word is *Strong's* number 3467. He "delivered them out of the hand of their enemies all the days of the judge." And we read, "for it repented the LORD," or the Lord had compassion, "because of their groanings by reason of them that oppressed them and vexed them. And it came to pass, when the judge was dead, that they returned, and corrupted themselves more than their fathers, in following other gods to serve them, and to bow down unto them." Again we see the pattern: Israel sins, God is angry, Israel is subjugated to an oppressor, a deliverer is raised up by God who delivers and rescues the people, the deliverer dies, and then the people return again to their evil ways.

God raised up these judges to save or deliver the people. We cannot understand the book of Judges unless we understand this one point. In Judges 11, Jephthah was wrestling to understand how God was going to do something, but he appealed to God and he referred to "the LORD, the Judge." That means when God raised up a judge, He did not just arbitrarily hand over the reins and say, "Okay, now it's up to you." When He raised up a judge, He was with the judge, but God Himself always remained *the* Judge.

When we talk about the concept of judges in the Old Testament, it should not convey an image of our modern judicial system, with a judge in a black robe saying, "Order in the court!" The

Hebrew term carries with it the sense of "to decide," "to govern," "to vindicate" and "to deliver." If the word were simply thought of as "to judge," as in "rendering judgment" alone, that would be rather unfortunate, because it would conceal the meaning of the Hebrew word. God is the Judge; literally in the Hebrew, He is "the One judging." There is a definite article, which distinguishes God from other "judges" with no definite article. While judges were people whom God raised up, they were still under His control to carry out His purpose.

When the book of Judges opens, the children of Israel ask God who should go first into the land, and God says, "The tribe of Judah will go first." Judah would be the first tribe to fight against the Canaanites. And then God underscores something: He says, "and I will give these enemies into your hand." Why? Because they still hadn't flushed out all of the inhabitants in the land; they still hadn't done the job. In fact, there is an ironic passage in Judges 1:19. God had commissioned Judah to go, and it says, "the LORD was with Judah; and he drave out the inhabitants of the mountain; but could not drive out the inhabitants of the valley, because they had chariots of iron."

The Lord was with Judah. That should have meant that nothing was impossible for them. And yet Judah could not drive out the inhabitants of the land. Judah saw the chariots of iron and became so full of fear that they could not drive them out. That tells me Judah did not fully trust the Lord. They were looking only at the seen world—those scary chariots of iron—as opposed to looking to the Lord and declaring, "He will lead us and take us through!" This is a great demonstration of God's people not quite acting in faith, and because of their disfaith or their *apistia*, their backward momentum of not fully trusting God to deliver them, God said, "Now you are going to have to live with these people in your land, and they will stay there to prove you, to test you, to try you, to see if you will actually trust Me."

The saddest verse in the book of Judges is Judges 2:10, where it speaks of the generation that came out of Egypt that passed away, those who perished in the wilderness. But those who were born in the wilderness entered into the Promised Land with Joshua, and then that generation also "were gathered unto their fathers," that is, they died, "and there arose another generation after them, which knew not the LORD, nor yet the works which he had done for Israel." We talk about what America used to be fifty or a hundred years ago in terms of Christianity and as a Christian nation, and we see that as far as the children of Israel were concerned, it didn't take very long to see an ebbing away of God's ways. These verses describe a new generation that knew nothing about the Lord's deliverance.

I would say that this was an unfortunate lapse on the part of the parents. In Moses' day, when the Passover and certain feast days were instituted, God said, "Make sure you tell it to your children and to the generations that follow." God gave that command because He knows our frame. We can say that we know something, but we forget much faster than we learn, and it was much easier for the children of the second and third generations to fail to learn and fail to remember.

Now back in Judges, the Lord raised up people to be deliverers, and even though there was a clear pattern, the people He chose were all unique. You can safely say that no two were alike. I want us to see some very profound things about the way the Lord uses people.

The first judge we find is in Judges 3. His name is Othniel, which means "force of God" or "lion of God." We read starting from verse 7, "And the children of Israel did evil in the sight of the LORD, and forgat the LORD their God, and served Baalim and the groves. Therefore the anger of the LORD was hot against Israel, and he sold them into the hand of Chushan–rishathaim king of Mesopotamia," whose name means "double evil"; not just one evil, but double evil. "And the children of Israel served Chushan–rishathaim eight years. And when the children of Israel cried unto the LORD, the LORD raised up a deliverer to the children of Israel, who delivered them, even Othniel the son of Kenaz, Caleb's younger brother." The word translated "deliverer" again is *Strong's* number 3467.

If you want to learn about Othniel's background, you must read about Caleb in the book of Joshua. Judges is quoting from the book of Joshua, where we read starting from Joshua 15:13: "And unto Caleb the son of Jephunneh he gave a part among the children of Judah, according to the commandment of the LORD to Joshua, even the city of Arba the father of Anak, which city is Hebron. And Caleb drove thence the three sons of Anak," three sons of the giants, "Sheshai, and Ahiman, and Talmai, the children of Anak. And he went up thence to the inhabitants of Debir: and the name of Debir before was Kirjath–sepher," the city of the book or the city of law. "And Caleb said, He that smiteth Kirjath–sepher, and taketh it, to him will I give Achsah my daughter to wife. And Othniel the son of Kenaz, the brother of Caleb, took it: and he gave him Achsah his daughter to wife." Note that Othniel was not the literal son of Kenaz. But he was called the son of Kenaz according to the Levitical structure; it is clear that something had happened, perhaps someone had died, and Othniel was taken into the family. And Caleb's daughter became the wife of Othniel. "And it came to pass, as she came unto him, that she moved him to ask of her father a field," and she also wanted a place where there would be water. So it was given to her, and verse 20 says, "This is the inheritance of the tribe of the children of Judah according to their families."

Othniel was of the tribe of Judah, which was one of the first to go into the land. So he had a good pedigree, he came from a good family, and he had seen some action as a man of war. We read in Judges 3:10, "The Spirit of the LORD came upon him, and he judged Israel, and went out to war." Again we can see that the concept of a "judge" in the Old Testament does not carry with it the idea of a black robe and a gavel. But under the direction of the Lord, he led the people and they went out to war, and the Lord delivered them. That is the key here: "the LORD delivered Chushan–rishathaim king of Mesopotamia into his hand; and his hand prevailed against Chushan–rishathaim. And the land had rest forty years. And Othniel the son of Kenaz died." This begins the pattern of the judges. No matter how few verses or how many verses are devoted to each of these individuals, we see the people fall into sin, they are turned over to their enemies and they are oppressed for a time. Then they cry out, God raises up a deliverer, they are delivered, the deliverer dies—and the people go back to doing evil.

We read again and again, "The children of Israel did evil again in the sight of the LORD." If you want to know what was the evil that was repeated so often, God had said, "Go into the land and seize the land," but they would not go in and do exactly what the Lord had told them to do. In some cases they made an alliance with the people of the land and they dwelt together. Their sons and their daughters were getting married to the people who dwelt in the land, and we begin to see that they were doing everything that the Lord had said not to do. They worshiped Baalim, they worshiped Ashtoreth and they worshiped other gods.

We read in 1 Kings that Solomon loved many strange women. Why would that be an important thing to note in the Bible? There is no greater lure to draw someone away from the living God than to bring someone into their life who has no knowledge of the Lord, someone who can turn their heart away. It is very easy to see only the flesh and want to follow that person. These people were guilty of that.

The next judge was Ehud. We read, "The children of Israel did evil again in the sight of the LORD: and the LORD strengthened Eglon the king of Moab against Israel." Think about that staggering concept: *the Lord* strengthened the enemy who was oppressing the people of God, "because they had done evil in the sight of the LORD. And he gathered unto him the children of Ammon and Amalek, and went and smote Israel, and possessed the city of palm trees," that is, Jericho. Any time you read in these passages about the "city of palm trees," it refers to Jericho. Think about that. The book of Joshua records the great victory that the children of Israel had at Jericho when they did what God had ordered them to do. What is so terrible is that now they are back at the same place, but they are back at the same place in disobedience. Too bad that it did not serve to remind them. "So the children of Israel served Eglon the king of Moab eighteen years." Eighteen years! It was as though God was saying, "I've had it with your rebellion!" "But when the children of Israel cried unto the LORD, the LORD raised them up a deliverer. . . ."

There is the same word again that we saw in Nehemiah 9, where it is translated "saviours."

"The LORD raised them up a deliverer, Ehud the son of Gera, a Benjamite, a man left-handed." Why would that detail be included? There is some irony here because the word "Benjamin" means the "son of my right hand" or the "son of the right hand," and Ehud was a left-handed man. If you were reading in the Semitic frame, it might not only mean that he was left-handed. It might mean that there was something actually wrong with his right hand; his hand could have been limp or maimed. "And by him the children of Israel sent a present unto Eglon the king of Moab." The word for "present" in the Hebrew is *minchah*, which is also translated "offering" or "tribute." "But Ehud made him a dagger which had two edges, of a cubit length; and he did gird it under his raiment upon his right thigh." He was a left-handed man with a dagger strapped to his right thigh. "And he brought the present unto Eglon king of Moab: and Eglon was a very fat man. And when he had made an end to offer the present, he sent away the people that bare the present. But he himself turned again from the quarries that were by Gilgal, and said, I have a secret errand unto thee, O king: who said, Keep silence. And all that stood by him went out from him."

I am sure that King Eglon had security guards around him, and they saw Ehud and they didn't really think he was a threat because he was left-handed. They assumed that no soldier would be left-handed, so they probably didn't even check his leg. So Ehud made his way in to see the king, and the Bible says that "Ehud came unto him; and he was sitting in a summer parlour, which he had for himself alone. And Ehud said, I have a message from God unto thee." And Eglon "arose out of his seat. And Ehud put forth his left hand, and took the dagger from his right thigh, and thrust it into his belly." He left the blade because "the fat closed upon the blade, so that he could not draw the dagger out of his belly; and the dirt came out." Most likely the dagger went to the back and the fat just closed up over the handle of the knife. "Then Ehud went forth through the porch, and shut the doors of the parlour upon him, and locked them. When he was gone out, his servants came; and when they saw that, behold, the doors of the parlour were locked, they said, Surely he covereth his feet in his summer chamber." The meaning of that passage is ambiguous; it could mean they thought he was sleeping, or it could mean they thought he was doing something else that we don't want to know about.

"And they tarried till they were ashamed: and, behold, he opened not the doors of the parlour; therefore they took a key, and opened them: and, behold, their lord was fallen down dead on the earth. And Ehud escaped while they tarried, and passed beyond the quarries, and escaped unto Seirath. And it came to pass, when he was come, that he blew a trumpet in the mountain of Ephraim, and the children of Israel went down with him from the mount, and he before them. And he said unto them, Follow after me: for the LORD hath delivered your enemies the Moabites into your hand. And they went down after him, and took the fords of Jordan toward Moab, and suffered not a man to pass over. And they slew of Moab at that time about ten thousand men, all lusty," which means they were all fat, "and all men of valour; and there escaped not a man. So Moab was subdued that day under the hand of Israel. And the land had rest fourscore years."

So far we have looked at two people who are called saviors, judges or deliverers. They do not look the same, but the point is that God raised them up for a purpose. Too many people think that all the people of God should look and act the same way, as though God uses a cookie cutter. When God raises up a person, they will be unique, though they will have certain characteristics in common, because it is one Spirit that belongs to God and He gives that one Spirit severally as He wills, to give gifts to men and women.

The last judge we are going to look at today is Shamgar. Shamgar only gets one verse in the book of Judges, though he will be mentioned again in Judges 5:6 in the song of Deborah and Barak. But Shamgar was a judge and was considered a deliverer. We read, "And after him was Shamgar the son of Anath, which slew of the Philistines six hundred men with an ox goad." We are not talking about a weapon, but an agricultural tool. God didn't necessarily equip him with all the modern weapons of war, but with only an ox goad he wiped out six hundred Philistines. And it says, "and he also delivered Israel," using the same word for "delivered," *Strong's* number 3467.

Shamgar might have been from the tribe of Simeon. Thus Judges spans the twelve tribes of Israel as it chronicles the twelve judges, from the obedience of Judah to the disobedience of Samson the Danite, the last judge. Note that there is one named in the book of Judges who was not a judge, Abimelech. People often get confused and think that Abimelech was a judge, but he was not.

We can glean from these passages that God raised up saviors in every generation. Even if the people seem to be rather obscure, it is clear that God raised them up for a specific purpose in that day. Though you may not have been called to be a missionary or a teacher, if you have been enabled to receive the word of God, then you too have been called for a purpose for a certain time.

God raises up people of diverse sorts. No two of these judges looked exactly the same. It is not true that somehow Othniel was greater than Ehud, or Ehud was greater than Shamgar, simply because one of them may have had more verses devoted to him. But the Bible refers to them as saviors and people whom God raised up. We can thank God that we no longer need to have the plural concept of saviors; we have *the* Savior. 1 John 4:14 describes that Savior as the Savior of the world, and not just the savior of the children of Israel when they were in trouble.

With that being said, what can we take out of this message for us today? God is still raising up people. And while they are not "saviors" in the same sense as they are in the book of Judges, He is still raising up people to carry His message, to be a banner, to be the eyes, the ears, the light and the salt of the earth. And regardless of your condition, as long as you have an interest in hearing God's word, that indicates that He has raised you up for a purpose too.

In the New Testament, the book of Ephesians says that God gave some gifts to the church: He gave some apostles, and prophets, and evangelists, and pastoring-teachers for the perfecting of the saints. But He also gave gifts to the saints, to His out-called ones, and those gifts are not to be despised, they are not to be hid; they are not to be abused, either. I want us to understand that God through His word is saying, "I have not changed My ways. I am still raising up people."

God is still raising up people for a purpose. We should not be like the followers of Eglon, who were just fat cats taking everything in and not even thinking twice about the grace of God and the wonder of His calling. And He called us for an incredible purpose. Some of you, though you are very faithful, still do not realize that you have a purpose in God's plan. And that purpose should not be caricatured by the so-called evangelists who say, "You can be the greatest you can be." Rather, God raised you up to accomplish *His* purpose and will in your life.

Understand that God has raised you up for a time. And if you doubt what I am saying, comb through the Bible and recognize the diversity of the men and women whom He has called. Abraham was called out of a very bleak Ur of Chaldees. Moses was called out of Egypt's palaces. What I love about all of these people in the Bible is that they are relatable to you and to me. For the most part, they began as average people. They were not special people with special skills. One man had the Spirit of the Lord come upon him and he conquered a city so he could get a wife. Another man's claim to fame was that he was a left-handed man, not necessarily that he killed a fat king, but that he was left-handed. And one man wiped out six hundred enemies using only an ox goad. Do those men look like there was anything special about them when they were called? No, they look like everyday, average people. And that is exactly what God keeps doing: He keeps raising up people who are just like that.

You are not an accident; you are not just treading water. You are here for a purpose. We cannot say that we are "saviors"; we have one Savior, but we know that we have been raised up. You need to settle it concerning your own life. I have encountered people who say, "I feel like I am just passing the time." And I tell them, "Well, snap out of it! God raised you up for a purpose. It is time you start acting like it." You are children of a heavenly God, now act like it. The Lord is so gracious to give us this high calling. That does not mean that we are elevated above others, but rather that we can walk with the knowledge of the privilege and honor that we are part of something that is so great and so good, because God is saying through His word, "I raised you up as well." God is not done with His church, He is not finished with you, and He is certainly not finished with me.

God has given us this opportunity and this message to say He will keep raising up people, as long as we keep looking to Him and trusting Him, and not being like Judah getting scared of the iron chariots or whatever else is coming our way. We know that He is faithful to bring to pass what we have committed unto Him unto that day, when He brings it all to fruition.

So with that being said, let no one despise your calling. Don't let anyone suggest that you are just part of some amorphous mass. No, you are a part of something great: it is called God's kingdom! Recognize that He raised you up like the people in Nehemiah's day. He raised you up for a purpose, so be glad about that.

CHAPTER 19

JEPHTHAH: A REJECT RAISED UP BY GOD

We have been studying the prayer in Nehemiah 9 and have used one particular verse as a bridge to the book of Judges. We read in verse 27, "Thou gavest them saviours, who saved them out of the hand of their enemies." When we read the word "saviours," we normally think of *the* Savior, our Lord Jesus Christ. But this word is used of those who were raised up by God to deliver His people. In the previous message, we started with two concepts that are important to the understanding of the whole book of Judges. Judges 2:16 says, "The LORD raised up judges, which delivered them out of the hand of those that spoiled them," and Judges 2:18 says, "And when the LORD raised them up judges, then the LORD was with the judge."

We have looked at a few of the judges, including Othniel, Ehud and Shamgar. Othniel was of the tribe of Judah and his name means "force of God." Ehud was a left-handed Benjamite. Shamgar was a farmer and a mighty warrior who killed six hundred Philistines with an ox goad. There are other more well-known judges, including Deborah, Gideon and Samson. It is a tragedy that some of the best Bible commentaries seem to have missed the essence of the whole book of Judges, which is God's sovereignty in raising up people who look very much like us. Some of them are quite ordinary. Some of them are rather bizarre. Some appear for only one or two verses and then disappear off the pages of history just as quickly.

Many commentators grapple with what to do with Deborah, because she is one of the judges. There are many who have the mindset that God cannot call a woman, and therefore they deny the sovereignty of God to choose whom He will. Deborah was not only a judge, she was a warrior, a prophetess, a wife and "a mother in Israel." There is much to say about her, and interestingly, she was left off of the list of the heroes of faith in Hebrews 11, where it says, "The time would fail me to tell you about Gideon, and Samson, and Jephthah, and Barak," but not Deborah. Gideon and Samson are also recorded in the book of Judges, and both are colorful characters. But all of these people have something in common, which is that God raised them up.

People also fail to note that not every judge was described as a warrior. There are two "minor" judges recorded in Judges 10: Tola and Jair. If you combine the times that they judged, it comes to forty-five years, which is a longer period than that of some of the other judges; yet very little is said about them. We know that they produced many children and that they were prosperous. There may have been peace during their lifetimes, because no specific information is given about any wars that were waged. These two are similar to Shamgar in that they are relatively unknown; they appear on the pages of Scripture and then they disappear just as quickly. Though little is said about them, that does not take away from the fact that God raised them up for a purpose during that time. That in itself is a lesson concerning God-ordained leadership.

I often meet people who feel the need to appoint themselves as leaders, but most of those people do not understand what leadership really means. The Scripture shows that those whom God appointed were often relatively obscure and they remained obscure, even though they did mighty things for God. For example, there was Adino, one of David's mighty men, who killed eight hundred Philistines using only a spear. There are many people like that in the Bible, and we are not likely to hear a sermon devoted to them. They are probably not the people we would consider if we were choosing a leader; they are people who probably would not pass the scrutiny of a board of inspection. But they are all part of what I would call the obscure characters whom God chose to use for that particular time. The people whom God raised up as "saviours" had many flaws and great frailties, and they all had something very human about them. That is one of the reasons why, if you really want to know about God's way of doing things, you must stick with what is recorded in His book.

We looked at the reoccurring pattern in the book of Judges: The children of God sinned, which brought forth God's anger and they were subjugated to an oppressor. They cried out to the Lord, and then God raised up a deliverer who delivered them. Then that deliverer died, and a whole new cycle started over again. We read starting at Judges 10:5, "And Jair died, and was buried in Camon. And the children of Israel did evil again in the sight of the LORD, and served Baalim, and Ashtaroth, and the gods of Syria, and the gods of Zidon, and the gods of Moab, and the gods of the children of Ammon, and the gods of the Philistines, and forsook the LORD, and served not him."

Isn't it interesting that the children of Israel always had the capacity to find and worship every other god except *the* God? The lesson of this particular passage may seem simple in its form, but it is not antiquated. We are capable of doing exactly what the children of Israel did for so many years, which is finding something as a substitute for God. Even though Judaism and Christianity have been showing forth the worship of the Creator throughout the millennia, people still have the tendency to look for anything else to worship besides *the* God. Or people will gravitate toward things that are called "Christianity" that indeed are not. There is a great need for solid Bible teaching today.

"And the anger of the LORD was hot against Israel, and he sold them into the hands of the Philistines, and into the hands of the children of Ammon." Who were these enemies? The Philistines were descendants of Mizriam, the son of Ham. We learn that from the

Table of Nations in Genesis 10, specifically verse 14. The Ammonites were descendants of Lot. When Lot separated from Abraham, he took the better part of the land and ultimately went to live in Sodom. After Lot fled from the destruction of Sodom and Gomorrah, his daughters got him drunk and had incestuous relations with him, resulting in their having children who would become enemies of God's people. We read in Genesis 19 that the eldest daughter produced the line of Moab known as the Moabites, who were for the most part hostile to the people of God. The only exception might be Ruth, who became a part of the genealogy of Christ. Lot's younger daughter had a child named Ben–ammi, who became the father of the Ammonites. So the Moabites and the children of Ammon were actually distant relatives of the children of Israel by virtue of Lot.

God turned His people over to the Philistines and sold them into the hands of the children of Ammon. "And that year they vexed and oppressed the children of Israel: eighteen years, all the children of Israel that were on the other side Jordan in the land of the Amorites, which is in Gilead. Moreover the children of Ammon passed over Jordan to fight also against Judah, and against Benjamin, and against the house of Ephraim; so that Israel was sore distressed. And the children of Israel cried unto the LORD." Notice the pattern. They said, "We have sinned against thee, both because we have forsaken our God, and also served Baalim. And the LORD said unto the children of Israel, Did not I deliver you from the Egyptians, and from the Amorites, from the children of Ammon, and from the Philistines? The Zidonians also, and the Amalekites, and the Maonites," some translations read *Midianites*, "did oppress you; and ye cried to me, and I delivered you out of their hand. Yet ye have forsaken me, and served other gods." Note that the word for "delivered" is a form of the same word used in Nehemiah 9:27 for "saviour." In essence, God was saying, "Don't you remember all the things that I have done for you in the past, and for your parents before you?"

It is so easy for us to forget all the things that the Lord has done for us. Children are taught to sing the song, "Count your blessings, name them one by one," but we would do well to learn that simple lesson. God said to these people, "You have forsaken Me to go and serve other gods." The people did not have any difficulty finding the strangest gods to worship. They just had a problem finding *the* God—until they got into trouble. It is tragic, but that is the way the cycle works.

When the people cried to the Lord, His response was a little frightening. He said, "Go and cry unto the gods which ye have chosen; let *them* deliver you in the time of your tribulation." Again, this is not an archaic concept. I have met many people who make other things their god. They can find all kinds of things to do on a Sunday morning that are more important to them than being in church and listening to Bible teaching. C. S. Lewis spoke of the danger of even a good book keeping you from your prayers. There is no harm in curling up with a good book, except if it takes you away from *the* Good Book. If anything comes between you and God, it becomes an idol, which is why John says at the close of his first letter, "Children, guard yourselves from idols." We tend to think of idols in terms of Baal and Ashtaroth, but we do not recognize that there are all kinds of idols all around us.

God said, "Go and cry unto the gods which ye have chosen." Unfortunately it is all too common that we only cry out to God when we are in the worst situations. I am not saying it is wrong to cry out, but why do we have to wait until there is a crisis? "And the children of Israel said unto the LORD, We have sinned: do thou unto us whatsoever seemeth good unto thee; deliver us only, we pray thee, this day. And they put away the strange gods from among them, and served the LORD: and his soul was grieved for the misery of Israel. Then the children of Ammon were gathered together, and encamped in Gilead. And the children of Israel assembled themselves together, and encamped in Mizpeh. And the people and princes of Gilead said one to another, What man is he that will begin to fight against the children of Ammon? he shall be head over all the inhabitants of Gilead."

All of this leads us to Jephthah. Judges 11 begins, "Now Jephthah the Gileadite was a mighty man of valour, and he was the son of an harlot." I want you to notice the order in which Jephthah is described. Jephthah the Gileadite is first called "a mighty man of valour," and secondly, "he was the son of an harlot." Some people do not want to teach from these Bible passages because they are embarrassed or ashamed of the people God used. I am not ashamed; rather I am so grateful that God included these people in His book. Even though it does not specifically say in this passage in Judges that "God raised up Jephthah," we know from Judges 2:18 that God did indeed raise him up.

Before Jephthah was considered to be a mighty man of valor, his birth was memorialized with these words: he was the son of a harlot. There are many people in the Bible who come to mind when we hear the word "harlot." We think of Rahab, who put out the scarlet thread and was saved when God's people under Joshua took Jericho. In Hosea 4:15, Israel is referred to as a harlot because she chased after other gods. Even though the word may sound shocking to an English-language reader, God used this language to drive home the message, "I do not choose people from only some specific, elite group, but I choose from all kinds of people and can use whomever I choose."

Jephthah's birth, beginnings and bravery are described, and we read, "Gilead's wife bare him sons; and his wife's sons grew up, and they thrust out Jephthah, and said unto him, Thou shalt not inherit in our father's house; for thou art the son of a strange woman." Jephthah's name means "Jehovah will open." God will open up the vista of this man's life, although he did not have a very noteworthy beginning. That is the beauty of the Bible; as Paul said in the New Testament, God has chosen the base and foolish things to confound the wise. None of us would have picked Jephthah. In fact, his own brothers rejected him. We are reminded of John's words concerning Christ: "He came unto his own, and his own received him not." This has never changed.

It is difficult for some to grasp the fact that those who appear to be the world's greatest rejects are often God's most important people. Those are the ones He cares about. So if you feel like you have been rejected, know that God loves you enough to call you out of the world. Some people may think that they are a part of God's chosen elite. I once sat across from a man who confidently declared of himself, "Well, sister, I have never sinned!" I am glad I know the Bible, because 1 John says that if any man says he has not sinned, he is a liar.

Judges 11:3 says, "Then Jephthah fled from his brethren, and dwelt in the land of Tob," which means "good," "and there were gathered vain men to Jephthah, and went out with him." The word *vain* means "worthless" or "without a cause." This can happen when you get thrust out of a group that you thought you were a part of: you might join yourself to others who are like what you perceive yourself to be. "And it came to pass in process of time, that the children of Ammon made war against Israel. And it was so, that when the children of Ammon made war against Israel, the elders of Gilead went to fetch Jephthah out of the land of Tob: and they said unto Jephthah, Come, and be our captain, that we may fight with the children of Ammon." Isn't that interesting? These people were in trouble, so now they had to seek out the very one whom they had rejected. "And Jephthah said unto the elders of Gilead, Did not ye hate me, and expel me out of my father's house? and why are ye come unto me now when ye are in distress?" Jephthah said, in essence, "Wait a minute, you guys kicked me out! Why are you coming to get me now that you are in trouble?"

"And the elders of Gilead said unto Jephthah, Therefore we turn again to thee now, that thou mayest go with us, and fight against the children of Ammon, and be our head over all the inhabitants of Gilead. And Jephthah said unto the elders of Gilead, If ye bring me home again to fight against the children of Ammon, and the LORD deliver them before me, shall I be your head?" Will I really be your leader? "And the elders of Gilead said unto Jephthah, The LORD be witness between us, if we do not so according to thy words."

Most Bible commentaries say that Jephthah could not have been a believer in the Lord. We do not know whether or not Jephthah was born of a believing mother; the Bible simply says that she was a harlot. But when we read what Jephthah said, we can see that he was not only a believer, he also knew the history of God's people. Those two concepts go hand in hand. If you know the history of God's past deliverances in the Bible, in the church and in your own life, you know the God you are dealing with; therefore you can have the confidence that He will deliver you in your present circumstances. We must have that mindset in order to understand Jephthah.

"Then Jephthah went with the elders of Gilead, and the people made him head and captain over them: and Jephthah uttered all his words before the LORD in Mizpeh. And Jephthah sent messengers unto the king of the children of Ammon, saying, What hast thou to do with me, that thou art come against me to fight in my land? And the king of the children of Ammon answered unto the messengers of Jephthah, Because Israel took away my land, when they came up out of Egypt, from Arnon even unto Jabbok, and unto Jordan: now therefore restore those lands again peaceably. And Jephthah sent messengers again unto the king of the children of Ammon: and said unto him, Thus saith Jephthah, Israel took not away the land of Moab, nor the land of the children of Ammon."

Here is where you find out who Jephthah really was. He was a man who knew the history of his people. He did not have to go and consult with anyone, and he knew enough history to set the king straight. He sent messengers again to the king of Ammon, saying, "When Israel came up from Egypt, and walked through the wilderness unto the Red sea, and came to Kadesh; then Israel sent messengers unto the king of Edom, saying, Let me, I pray thee, pass through thy land: but the king of Edom would not hearken thereto. And in like manner they sent unto the king of Moab: but he would not consent: and Israel abode in Kadesh. Then they went along through the wilderness, and compassed the land of Edom, and the land of Moab, and came by the east side of the land of Moab, and pitched on the other side of Arnon, but came not within the border of Moab: for Arnon was the border of Moab. And Israel sent messengers unto Sihon king of the Amorites. . . ." Jephthah was telling this king, "You need to get your facts straight." And Jephthah will not say, "Moses and Joshua won a victory in that day," but he will very clearly say, "It was the Lord who gave us the victory." Jephthah was a man who not only knew history and knew who God was, he knew who *his* God was.

"And Israel sent messengers unto Sihon king of the Amorites, the king of Heshbon; and Israel said unto him, Let us pass, we pray thee, through thy land into my place. But Sihon trusted not Israel to pass through his coast: but Sihon gathered all his people together, and pitched in Jahaz, and fought against Israel. And the LORD God of Israel delivered Sihon and all his people into the hand of Israel, and they smote them: so Israel possessed all the land of the Amorites, the inhabitants of that country. And they possessed all the coasts of the Amorites, from Arnon even unto Jabbok, and from the wilderness even unto Jordan. So now the LORD God of Israel hath dispossessed the Amorites from before his people Israel, and shouldest thou possess it? Wilt not thou possess that which Chemosh thy god giveth thee to possess?" In other words, "Since God gave us the victory and the land, why do you think this land should be yours? If your god is so great, then just take what he gives you. But he has *not* given you this land that our God has given us." The last part of verse 24 reads, "So whomsoever the LORD our God shall drive out from before us, them will we possess." We now see Jephthah as a man of faith, saying, "Whatever God does, He does it well."

"And now art thou any thing better than Balak the son of Zippor, king of Moab?" You can read about him in the book of Numbers. "Did he ever strive against Israel, or did he ever fight against them, while Israel dwelt in Heshbon and her towns, and in Aroer and her towns, and in all the cities that be along by the coasts of Arnon, three hundred years?" In other words, "If you really had a claim to this land, then why did you wait three hundred years to make this an issue?"

Now Jephthah's faith is clearly displayed. He says, "The LORD the Judge be judge this day between the children of Israel and the children of Ammon." Jephthah is saying that God knows what is going on and that God is going to decide who has the victory.

"Howbeit the king of the children of Ammon hearkened not unto the words of Jephthah which he sent him." There will always be enemies in the world who will come around and tell the people of God how they should do things. But Jephthah knew who his God was and he had faith. And not only did God raise up Jephthah, but like Gideon and Samson, God gave Jephthah His Spirit. "Then the Spirit of the LORD came upon Jephthah, and he passed over Gilead, and Manasseh, and passed over Mizpeh of Gilead, and from Mizpeh of Gilead he passed over unto the children of Ammon." Gilead means "a rough place," Manasseh means "causing to forget," and Mizpeh means "the place of the watchtower" or "place of the watch." To restate this in its pictorial sense, once the Spirit of the Lord came upon Jephthah, he passed through the rough places and through the places that cause to forget. He was a man who understood his mission and he went past the place of watch, passing over all of these places until he came to the children of Ammon.

"And Jephthah vowed a vow unto the LORD, and said, If thou shalt without fail deliver the children of Ammon into mine hands, then it shall be, that whatsoever cometh forth of the doors of my house to meet me, when I return in peace from the children of Ammon, shall surely be the LORD'S, and I will offer it up for a burnt offering."

Some have called Jephthah's vow a rash vow. We will read in Judges 11:34 that it is his daughter who comes out of his house when he returns. This has been a point of contention for some because they wrongly assume that Jephthah sacrificed his own daughter as a burnt offering. That is not what happened at all. But let's think about Jephthah's vow analytically for a moment and recognize that the vow would not have been honored by God if it was displeasing to God. God could have said, "Seeing as you have made this rash, unrealistic vow, I will *not* deliver the children of Ammon this day to you." But God gave Jephthah the victory.

Read Jephthah's vow carefully. He said, "Whatsoever cometh forth of the doors of *my* house. . . ." Jephthah must have known that the options were limited. While it is possible that it would be an animal that came forth from his house, most likely it would be either his wife (who is not mentioned here) or his daughter. Jephthah's vow revealed his priorities. He was a man who preferred God and the victory for God's people over himself and his family. To make a New Testament application, I think of Jesus' words in Luke 14: "If any man come to me, and hate not his father, and mother, and wife, and children, and brethren, and sisters, yea, and his own life also, he cannot be my disciple."

"So Jephthah passed over unto the children of Ammon to fight against them; and the LORD delivered them into his hands." It is important to see that it was God who gave the victory. In Judges 7–8, God also gave Gideon the victory, though Gideon had been full of fear and he constantly questioned God. God is the same and does not change. He is saying, "I have one Spirit and it is the Spirit of truth." That one Spirit will inhabit people who are diverse, and Jephthah is a prime example of this diversity. In verse 33, we read of how God subdued the children of Ammon across vast territories. And after the victory, "Jephthah came to Mizpeh unto his house, and, behold, his daughter came out to meet him with timbrels and with dances: and she was his only child; beside her he had neither son nor daughter."

Many have erroneously thought that Jephthah sacrificed, that is, slaughtered, his daughter. But notice what Jephthah's daughter says: "Let me alone two months, that I may go up and down upon the mountains, and bewail my virginity, I and my fellows." We can see from this verse that Jephthah's daughter was preparing for a life of service to the Lord, which would mean that she would never marry. That is why she went to lament her virginity with the other maidens. Jephthah's vow was similar to Hannah's vow in 1 Samuel when she dedicated her child to the Lord. In Jephthah's case, it is clear that his daughter was to be dedicated wholly unto the Lord in service, and not burnt with fire as the pagans did with their children.

Jephthah's vow was not a rash vow. It was a vow that showed he valued God above everything else in his life. This same type of mindset should permeate the church. Like the prophet Elijah, people should care about the things of God more than their own personal needs. God will take care of those people who put Him first, trust Him and have faith in His word. When you put God first, He will take care of the rest. When you are fretting over the cares of your life, remember Jesus said in Matthew 6, "Don't be anxious. Consider the birds and the flowers. Who takes care of them? And aren't you more important than these?" Trust that the Lord will take care of you. God has called you out of the world and has given you a spirit that recognizes you belong to Him. Trust that the Lord will see you through.

Jephthah made a vow and declared, "I have opened my mouth unto the LORD, and I cannot go back." There is a passage in Ecclesiastes 5 that speaks of making vows. It says, "Better is it that thou shouldest not vow, than that thou shouldest vow and not pay." In other words, you should keep your word to your own hurt. We see this quality in Jephthah and in any person who cares more about the things of God than anything else.

We read in Judges 12, "And the men of Ephraim gathered themselves together, and went northward, and said unto Jephthah, Wherefore passedst thou over to fight against the children of Ammon, and didst not call us to go with thee?" They said, in essence, "Why did you go out to fight the children of Ammon without calling us?" The Ephraimites did virtually the same thing to Gideon, and Gideon appeased them and they backed off. Here the Ephraimites threatened Jephthah, saying, "We will burn thine house upon thee with fire." But Jephthah responded, "I and my people were at great strife with the children of Ammon; and when I called you, ye delivered me not out of their hands. And when I saw that ye delivered me not, I put my life in my hands, and passed over against the children of Ammon, and the LORD delivered them into my hand: wherefore then are ye come up unto me this day, to fight against me?" Jephthah said, "It was God who delivered me. I called on you to help me but you didn't come."

When you read this passage, don't simply think of Ephraim criticizing Jephthah. This can and does happen to any God-ordained leader. There will always be people who come around and say, "You should have done this!" and "You should have done that!" I have encountered this for many years. Those same people will never lift a finger to help when the call is put forth for people to come into the church, to start giving and to start acting in faith. And when a victory is won, they will complain that they were not consulted first.

Now if Jephthah were a man like Absalom, he would have boasted about winning the victory in his own strength. Instead, Jephthah said, "The LORD delivered them into my hand," giving God all the credit and all the glory for the victory. In my own life, I know for a fact that everything is of God, because on my own I can do nothing. The Lord must get all of the credit.

"Then Jephthah gathered together all the men of Gilead, and fought with Ephraim: and the men of Gilead smote Ephraim, because they said, Ye Gileadites are fugitives of Ephraim among the Ephraimites, and among the Manassites." They were saying, "What business do you have here? You are nothing but a bunch of renegades!" I want you to put flesh and blood on these Bible passages. There will always be people in the church who will say, "You didn't consult me!" But Jephthah didn't take his orders from the people. Jephthah was following his God.

Again, it was God who raised up Jephthah. The Spirit of the Lord came upon Jephthah. The elders of Gilead asked Jephthah to be their head, but Jephthah did not appoint himself of his own accord. The people didn't decide; God decided. I do not mean that God wound up history like a clock and determined the outcome in advance. In this case, He raised up Jephthah for a purpose that these Ephraimites were too proud to see. The Bible says many times that the Ephraimites were a very prideful people.

"And the Gileadites took the passages of Jordan before the Ephraimites." The Ephraimites would have to cross over the Jordan to get back into their own territory. "And it was so, that when those Ephraimites which were escaped said, Let me go over; that the men of Gilead said unto him, Art thou an Ephraimite? If he said, Nay; then said they unto him, Say now Shibboleth: and he said Sibboleth: for he could not frame to pronounce it right." The Ephraimites spoke with a recognizable accent, and it was possible to determine who was an Ephraimite just by listening to them speak, the same way that we can tell what part of the country someone is from by the way they pronounce certain words. These Ephraimites could not properly pronounce the *sh* sound and it came out sounding like an *s*. And like Peter in the New Testament when he sat by the fire, those who stood by said, "Surely you are one of them; your speech gives you away!"

So if a man could not pronounce the word *shibboleth*, "Then they took him, and slew him at the passages of Jordan: and there fell at that time of the Ephraimites forty and two thousand. And Jephthah judged Israel six years. Then died Jephthah the Gileadite, and was buried in one of the cities of Gilead."

When we read in Nehemiah 9, "God gavest them saviours, who saved them," I want you to think of this man. We do not read anywhere that Jephthah had a formal education or that he was from a prestigious family. In fact, right after Jephthah is called "a mighty man of valour," he is called "the son of an harlot." When whoever prayed the prayer in Nehemiah said, "God gavest them saviours," it was spoken with the knowledge of the types of people God works with. Jephthah is included in the list of heroes of faith who are memorialized in Hebrews 11, and Jephthah's victories were all to the glory of God. God would ultimately give us *the* Savior, Jesus Christ. As it says in 1 John 4:14, Jesus is the Savior of the world. He paid it all.

God used some very interesting and diverse individuals to deliver His people. God's sovereignty allows Him to choose people like Deborah and Gideon and Jephthah. Don't forget the sovereignty of God in your own life. People can walk around with their eyes closed not understanding that they have been called and chosen. Recognize that God has chosen you, raised you up and brought you into the awareness that you are one of His called ones, which is a precious thing in His sight. Perhaps you fit into the category of Jephthah and you don't *look* like what the world has determined a Christian should look like. Perhaps you are a second generation Christian, but remember what David du Plessis said, "God has no grandchildren." In other words, growing up in a Christian home does not determine anything about your relationship with God. You must be born again from above. A deposit of God must be placed in you, and you become a new creature in Christ Jesus. We were all base creatures and children of darkness, but God has raised us up and has brought us into His glorious light!

It is memorialized for us that God uses ordinary, base men and women to do His work. Recognize that there are probably more Jephthahs, Gideons and Baraks in the church than there are perfect, pristine people. The ones who think they are perfect can stay in their pharisaical towers, but I live for the message that God raised up ordinary people. This makes no sense to the "wise" ones in the world. But it makes perfect sense to those of us who understand that we are being saved. Woven into the gospel of grace is the fact that God takes the broken, the frail, the rejects, the downcast and the downtrodden, and lifts them up to place His nature and His life in them to become new creatures in Christ Jesus.

It is a great comfort to know that God loves sinners just like you and me. He raised up saviors in the days of the judges, and He has given us *the* Savior, Jesus Christ, in our day and for eternity. Praise God and rejoice in that knowledge!

Chapter 20

WHY ON EARTH DOES GOD FORGIVE?

We have been journeying through the extraordinary prayer in Nehemiah 9, and we will be using Nehemiah as a launching pad to take us into a psalm that will contrast the Lord's goodness with Israel's wickedness. And from that context, we will examine the question, "Why on earth does God forgive?"

We read beginning at Nehemiah 9:26, "Nevertheless they were disobedient, and rebelled against thee, and cast thy law behind their backs, and slew thy prophets which testified against them to turn them to thee, and they wrought great provocations." God would use different means to reach His people, but the people would not listen. "Therefore thou deliveredst them into the hand of their enemies, who vexed them: and in the time of their trouble, when they cried unto thee, thou heardest them from heaven; and according to thy manifold mercies thou gavest them saviours."

We have previously looked at that word "saviours," which is used here of those whom God raised up because they indeed delivered the people. But make no mistake about it, that word is linked inextricably to God, who is *the* Savior. God used people as instruments to deliver throughout history, from Moses, the greatest prophet of them all, all the way to Malachi, the last prophet of the

Old Testament. He could have done it another way, but this is the way He did it. That word "saviours" will also be important in this message because at the heart of everything, God is the One who delivers. He is the Deliverer.

"Thou gavest them saviours, who saved them out of the hand of their enemies. But after they had rest, they did evil again before thee: therefore leftest thou them in the hand of their enemies, so that they had the dominion over them: yet when they returned, and cried unto thee, thou heardest them from heaven; and many times didst thou deliver them according to thy mercies." This is a cycle that is typical of the children of Israel, but also tends to be our human nature. We get ourselves in a pinch and suddenly we find out how to talk to God. Have you ever noticed how much easier it is to talk to God when your back is against the wall?

"Many times didst thou deliver them. . . and testifiedst against them, that thou mightest bring them again unto thy law: yet they dealt proudly, and hearkened not unto thy commandments, but sinned against thy judgments, (which if a man do, he shall live in them;) and withdrew the shoulder, and hardened their neck, and would not hear. Yet many years didst thou forbear them," You warned them, "and testifiedst against them by thy spirit in thy prophets." The purpose of God's sending His prophets was to tell the people, "Turn back to God. If you turn back to God, God will turn back to you." And each time the prophets would proclaim the message, it would fall on deaf ears. The people would "not give ear: therefore gavest thou them into the hand of the people of the lands. Nevertheless for thy great mercies' sake thou didst not utterly consume them, nor forsake them; for thou art a gracious and merciful God."

Notice verse 26 says, "Nevertheless they were disobedient," and verse 31 says, "Nevertheless for thy great mercies' sake." Those two *neverthelesses* will serve as bookends to highlight the contrast between the people's rebellious spirit and the Lord's goodness and mercy. These verses reveal the concept of sin at work and the pattern of God's people constantly getting themselves into trouble. The tumultuous history of the children of Israel serves as a looking glass for us. It is not as though there was only one occasion where the people simply had bad judgment or made poor decisions; rather, these verses describe something that is innate in mankind's fallen nature. And no matter how critical we would like to be of the children of Israel, we are in many ways just like them. But we have the record in front of us that they did not yet have.

Milton, in *Paradise Lost*, called the fall of Satan the "foul revolt." And from that foul revolt, Lucifer, the chief musician, brought a third of heaven down with him and caused the next step: the fall of humankind. When God said, "Let us make Adam in our image," He created man with a purpose and design. We are not some kind of random creation. But God's creation was marred by the fall, and considering the record of His people in constant rebellion throughout history, the question may be asked, why would God forgive these people?

That question is not meant to be judgmental. When you read the Scriptures it is a logical question to ask. And perhaps there is an answer to this question, though it is not a simple one. In Deuteronomy, when God spoke to the people through Moses, He said, "Look, I didn't choose you because you were great in number." He chose to put His love on a people and to deliver them because it is His nature to deliver, to save and to help His fallen creation.

When I refer to the love of God, I do not mean *love* in the sweet, syrupy sense that some people use. I mean the love of God expressed by the fact that He would even try to work with His fallen creation. And it was "work" indeed. God continued to send His prophets throughout the millennia, from Moses all the way down to Malachi. But never at any given time did the people completely turn to Him, nor were they inclined to listen to Him. So the concept expressed between the two *neverthelesses* is, as Jonah said, that salvation is of the Lord, and also that we cannot save ourselves. So the question remains, why would God forgive these people? I take you to another "nevertheless" to find the answer, in Psalm 106.

I want to travel through this psalm to look at twelve things that the children of Israel were guilty of, and undoubtedly we may be guilty of the same things. We could call them the twelve shades of sinning man. These things do not exhaust the concept of sinning man, for as Isaiah said, "All we like sheep have gone astray," each of us has gone our own way and done what is right in our own eyes. But these twelve things even surpass what is described in Proverbs 6, which says, "six things doth the LORD hate: yea, seven are an abomination unto him." And as we survey this list, I want us to remember that God still chose to work with these people.

Number 1: Psalm 106:7 reads, "Our fathers understood not thy wonders in Egypt; they remembered not the multitude of thy mercies; but provoked him at the sea, even at the Red Sea." They "understood not" and they "remembered not." I labeled this verse "a lack of gratitude, and a poor understanding of their condition or state." Many people in Christendom today do not understand the state they were in before they came to know the saving power of Jesus Christ, who took us from the curse to the cure for humanity. They will come into the church with a works-oriented mindset: as long as you can show that you have some inherent good in you and that you can do some good works, you are okay. But that contradicts what is said everywhere in the Scriptures. Ephesians 2 says it plainly: "By grace are ye saved through faith; and that not of yourselves: it is the gift of God: not of works, lest any man should boast. For we are his workmanship. . . ." Salvation is God's work in us.

The people had a lack of gratitude and did not understand nor remember all the things the Lord had done. Do not think that this only applies to the children of Israel; I want you to think of yourself. I never preach in a condemnatory way, but if we are going to be honest with ourselves before God, we have to take a look in the mirror at our own lives. A lack of gratitude, a lack of understanding, and not remembering the things that the Lord has done is a common disease, especially in the church.

Number 2 on our list is really a whole cluster of things. Verses 13 and 14 read, "They soon forgat his works; they waited not for his counsel: but lusted exceedingly in the wilderness." I would label these verses "not remembering God's works" and "unrestrained appetite."

They did not remember God's works and did not wait on Him. That is also a description of many of us. We can become impatient and want to see results, but the greatest things happen *within* you, if the word of God has been richly planted in your heart. You may know that the word of God has been planted in your heart by faith, and that "faith comes by hearing, and hearing by the word of God," yet you still cannot *see* your salvation. Have you ever grappled with your salvation because you could not see it or because you did not feel different? I am not ashamed to say that I wrestled for many years with trying to understand that concept. One day it became clear to me that this concept of "by faith" means exactly that. I must take God at His word. His word says He died, hung on the cross in open shame and spilt His precious blood for me, a sinner. My salvation is not dependent upon how clean I feel, because I sin daily, hourly and sometimes minute-by-minute. I am made clean because of what Christ did for me.

Verse 14 says that they "lusted exceedingly in the wilderness, and tempted God in the desert." They lusted, or had an unrestrained appetite. Too many people in the pulpit love to misinterpret this verse and say, "It's all about sex," but it is not all about sex. Unrestrained appetites can be anything that lures you away from questing after the Bread of life and the living Water. But people still go questing after other things. I spent many of my years chasing after other things. They were like the proverbial brass ring that disappears when you try to grab hold of it; there was really nothing there to grab hold of. So don't simply think of the children of Israel lusting for the food of Egypt to fill their bellies. God's response was that He "gave them their request; but sent leanness into their soul." He gave them outward prosperity, but they had inward poverty. I would rather have the inward riches of Christ. Let me die without a penny in my pocket, but let me die with the riches of Jesus Christ by His shed blood. I have learned that it is easy to tell God what I desire, but ultimately I must come back to "not my will, Lord, but Thine."

Number 3: Verse 16 reads, "They envied Moses also in the camp, and Aaron the saint," or the holy one, "of the LORD." I would label this verse "the sin of envy or jealousy." Remember when Miriam said to Moses, "Hey, you're not the only one God speaks to!" And there were others, like Korah and his band who said, "Moses isn't doing his job right!" Miriam was smitten with leprosy and the ones who criticized Moses were swallowed up when God opened up the earth. We are always capable of being envious and jealous. Sometimes it is a spiritual envy, which is what I believe is being described here.

As we survey these things in Psalm 106, remember that Romans 3:23 says, "*All* have sinned, and come short of the glory of God," and that means *all*, not some, not a few; it means *all*. God said, "I will give you the law, and if you can keep it perfectly and not miss one jot or tittle, then by that law you will be saved." But no man could keep the law, and therefore all have sinned.

Number 4: Verse 19 reads, "They made a calf in Horeb, and worshipped the molten image." I would label this "the sin of idolatry." It is so easy for us to exempt ourselves and say, "Well, I don't bow down to a statue, and I don't worship a stained glass window." No, but idolatry can take the form of many things. I am not saying you had better act like some fundamentalist who doesn't live life. There are some people who think that if you are a Christian, you have to be miserable all the time and never live life. What I am saying is that the sin of idolatry is very subtle and no one is immune from it. It can be a form of idolatry to sleep in on a Sunday morning instead of going to church. Going to church does not make you "saved," but we put ourselves at risk any time we start to think, "It is more important for me to do *this*, than it is for me to open up the Bible, and talk about and listen to the things that pertain to my eternal position with God." It is very easy to slip into many different kinds of idolatry.

Number 5: Verses 21 and 22 read, "They forgat God their saviour, which had done great things in Egypt; wondrous works in the land of Ham, and terrible things by the Red Sea." I would label these verses "forgetting." If you were a slave in Egypt, how could you ever forget the labor, the terror and the monstrosity of Egypt? But they forgot. And you and I can forget as well. After you have been a Christian for a while, it is possible to forget that you were once in darkness; you were once outside the realm of God's great light. The danger of forgetting is always there.

Number 6: Verse 24 reads, "Yea, they despised the pleasant land, they believed not his word." I would label this verse "unbelief" or "disfaith." Look at the great contradiction in this psalm between verse 12 and verse 24. Verse 12 says, "Then believed they his words; they sang his praise," and verse 24 says, "Yea, they despised the pleasant land, they believed not his word." Were the children of Israel just a very fickle people, or does this show us that ebbs and flows are a part of living? I do not preach the doctrine "once saved, always saved." I believe that it is entirely possible for people who have come to the faith to disconnect themselves. You must remain connected to the power source in order for the power to flow. And the power source is Christ. That is why I have camped out for many years in John 15: abide in His word, and His word will abide in you. That is the principle of staying connected through the word of God.

Number 7: Verse 28 reads, "They joined themselves also unto Baal–peor, and ate the sacrifices of the dead." I would label this "apostasy." There may not be such a thing today as "Baal–peor," but people can still join themselves to things in our world other than Christ. You may even join yourself to a church, but if it is disconnected from the Scriptures, if it is disconnected from worshiping the Lord Jesus Christ, or if it is disconnected from an understanding of salvation by faith, then you are either engaged in works or you are engaged in a social fellowship program. Apostasy occurs whenever people join themselves to something other than Christ.

Number 8: Verse 32 reads, "They angered him also at the waters of strife, so that it went ill with Moses for their sakes." That is a very polite way of putting it. It went a little bit more than *ill;* it cost him the Promised Land! Let's label this "insurrection." God told Moses to speak to the rock, but when the people murmured, he struck the rock. The insurrection of the people ultimately resulted in Moses' being denied entrance into the Promised Land. Again, do not make the mistake of thinking that these verses only apply to the children of Israel in that day. We are in danger of all these things. There are people who want something other than what God wants. It is common in the church for people to think that they are anointed and appointed as the rightful decision-makers in matters of church conduct. The spirit of insurrection is common to the people of God throughout the ages.

Number 9: Verse 34 reads, "They did not destroy the nations, concerning whom the LORD commanded them." Let's label this "disobedience." God said, "Go in and attack these people. Wipe them out." But they did not, and in some cases they befriended them. When we look at these labels, somewhere on these pages we will see ourselves to some degree.

Number 10: In verses 35 and 36, we read that they "were mingled among the heathen, and learned their works. And they served their idols: which were a snare unto them." I have labeled this "conforming to the world." Too many people want to go to a church and say, "We want to do what they do over there, because they have a nice café where you can get a latte to sip while you listen to the sermon, and maybe you can play a little video game in-between when you get bored." I would like to imagine for a moment what their reaction would be if God were to visibly materialize before them while they sipped their lattes and decided whether or not to mentally tune in to what the preacher was teaching! The New Testament says, "Be not conformed to the world, but be ye metamorphosed; be ye transformed." We were called out of that darkness into His precious light.

Number 11: Verse 38 says that they "shed innocent blood, even the blood of their sons and of their daughters, whom they sacrificed unto the idols of Canaan: and the land was polluted with blood." I labeled this "murder." Let's take this into a New Testament realm. Jesus said, "If you hate in your heart, you are as guilty as a murderer." The thought is as bad as the deed. There are too many people today who claim to be Christians and boast of their standing with the Lord, but all they do is spread hatred and vitriol when they talk about others.

Number 12 is the last on our list. Verse 39 reads, "Thus were they defiled with their own works, and went a whoring with their own inventions." I labeled this "the motive of self." They sought after their own works and their own inventions. This is the besetting sin of our current generation. It typifies the ego of a self-serving generation who can only ask, "What's in it for *me?*"

We have looked at these twelve different shades or dimensions of sinning man as described in this psalm. It is certainly not an exhaustive list, but it paints a picture for us. When I read the Bible, sometimes I get angry at those children of Israel who saw all of those wondrous things: the plagues on Egypt, the hail and the frogs. They stood at the edge of the Red Sea and saw God part the waters. How could they forget all of those things and turn from God? Yet if we are honest, we will also find ourselves in these verses. The question remains, "Why would God forgive these people?" We asked it earlier when we were reading from the prayer in Nehemiah 9 and looked at the two *neverthelesses* in verses 26 and 31. The answer is found after another *nevertheless* in this psalm, amidst these twelve different shades of sinning man that God knew about His people.

Psalm 106:8 reads, "Nevertheless he saved them for his name's sake, that he might make his mighty power to be known." God saw His people's sinning nature, nevertheless He saved them for His name's sake. When we speak of God's forgiveness of His people, it encompasses the concept of His saving them, rescuing them and delivering them. And this message hinges on that concept, not just for the children of Israel, but for us as well.

Nestled in Nehemiah 9, we read all about God's goodness, God's mercy, God's forgiveness, God's care, as well as God's provision and healing for His people. And while God does all these things for His people, there are people who say, "Yeah, okay, that's great. What else are You going to do for us? Are we there yet? We don't really feel like doing what You told us to do, so can You figure out some other way?"

It is easy to become angry at those people because we think that if we had lived in those times, we would have done things differently. But if we are really honest, we know that we would probably be just like them. After seeing the first miracle, you would think the people would quit complaining and get on God's side. But they witnessed miracle after miracle, including the greatest of them all: the death angel passing over their home when they obediently put the blood on the doorpost. That was a very simple test of obedience: If you applied the blood on the doorpost, your firstborn lived. If you did not, they died.

God did not save the children of Israel in response to their moral rectitude. We have seen the fatal flaw in man, thanks to Adam and Eve and the fall, nevertheless "He saved them for his name's sake." This is a concept that is repeated throughout the Scriptures. And each time it says that God did something for His name's sake, it is usually connected to the forgiveness of sins or the saving of the soul.

That is why we are looking at this psalm with the background of the prayer in Nehemiah 9, which chronicles the span of time beginning with God's calling Abram out of Ur and continuing up until Nehemiah's day. That covers thousands of years, and we learn that the people had not changed. Their nature was still the same. But God also does not change. I love what it says in Malachi: "I am the LORD, I change not." Thank God for that and thank God this psalm says, "Nevertheless he saved them for his name's sake."

Let's look a little more closely at this verse in the Hebrew. It says, "Nevertheless he saved them. . . ." Interestingly enough, the word "nevertheless" in English does not appear in the Hebrew. It is understood by the presence of the Hebrew letter, *vav*. It takes only one letter in the Hebrew to explain the idea, which we could translate "and yet." Next it says, "he saved them," and the word "saved" is from the same Hebrew word that means "saviour," which is *Strong's* number 3467. The root of that word is *yasha*, from which we get the name *Yehoshua* or *Joshua*. The Greek translation of that name is *Jesus*.

But the word I want to focus on is a small Hebrew word that is translated "for the sake of." It means "for the sake of," "on account of," "to the intent" and "in order that." The undercurrent of the use of this word is that God saved in order to maintain His reputation or character, because it is God's nature to save and to forgive. When we talk about why God saved these people, why He forgave them and why He delivered them, it brings us back to the creation. It brings us back into the book of Genesis.

When the creation is described in the book of Genesis, it says, "In the beginning God," using the name *Elohim* for God. It is a plural majestic name that represents the Triune God. But in Genesis 2, we read, "the LORD God formed man," and we find the compound name "LORD God," which is *Yahweh Elohim.* As you read through the Bible, you begin to see a relationship between *Yahweh* and mankind.

The name *Yahweh* or *Jehovah* is the covenant name of God. There is another Hebrew word for Lord, *adonai.* It is a lesser name for Lord, as it can also be used regarding man. Dr. Gene Scott used to describe the name Jehovah by using a word picture. Imagine taking a water hose and pinching the hose so that you can feel the water pressure building up. He would say that the name Jehovah is like that: it is like a force seeking to be released. That is a wonderful way to explain it. The name Jehovah is often paired with other names that reveal a dimension of God's nature. For example, *Jehovah–rapha* means the "Lord who heals," and *Jehovah–nissi* means the "Lord is our banner." But the foundation of all these names is Jehovah, the covenant name.

When God spoke to Moses in Exodus 3, He said, "Tell the people, 'I Am that I Am' sent you." And in Exodus 6, He clearly said to Moses, "In the old time before you, they didn't know Me by the name *Yahweh*. I am revealing Myself to you in this way to show a part of My nature." And the revelation of that name began the process of saving and delivering the people out of Egypt's bondage. The name is tied to the delivering and redeeming nature of God. Although we cannot fully define this side of God, we can glimpse an aspect of His nature. The name *Yahweh* represents the substance of His existence that has always existed, that will always be, and that is yet to be revealed.

In the New Testament, Christ said, "I am the bread of life, I am the water, I am the way and the truth." He was declaring that

He was the same "I am" who said to Moses, "I am that I am. And as you continue on your journey, I will unfold for you a revelation of who I am." Later, God will say to the children of Israel, "I am the Lord your God who delivered you out of Egypt." We read in Psalm 23:3 that God restored and led His people "for his name's sake." Psalm 25:11 says, "For thy name's sake, O LORD, pardon my iniquity; for it is great." God is saying, "I did all these things for My name's sake, for My honor is at stake."

The Westminster Shorter Catechism contains a list of questions and answers that was designed to help people learn the doctrines of the Bible. It poses the question, "What is the chief end of man?" and correctly gives the answer, "Man's chief end is to glorify God, and enjoy Him forever." But man could not do that because of his disconnectedness from God. And it is in the name Jehovah that we begin to encounter the relationship of God to man, where God is the Deliverer and Savior. Even in Ezekiel's day, at a time when God's people were so far off the track, God still said, in essence, "I will deliver you for My name's sake, for the nations will see and they will know. They will see My power and they will know who I am."

It is easy to see ourselves in what I have called the twelve shades of our sinning ways in Psalm 106. Find one or all of them that belong to you. But remember that verse 8 says, "Nevertheless he saved them for his name's sake." Let's break this down a little more and talk about the Savior, the Lord. First I want us to see that *He* saved them. And all mankind needs to be saved. You don't have to do something mystical or special in order to be saved, but you must understand that it is His nature to save. The God of the Old Testament is revealed in the New Testament. As John said, "Behold the Lamb of God, who takes away the sin of the world." In the book of Revelation, we read, "Worthy is the Lamb," as those who were washed by His blood rejoice around the throne and sing His praises.

It might sound like a simple concept, but it is necessary to first understand that it is the Savior who saved them. They did not save themselves. We *cannot* save ourselves. It is such a basic, fundamental concept that you might think, "Well, surely everyone knows this."

You might be surprised by the number of people I speak to who still think they can go out and do something good to save themselves. There are many who believe that if you do something good, you can live like a son of a gun the rest of the time. They think that God must be so pleased with whatever good deed they have done that they can then get off the hook.

So it may seem self-evident, but we must remember that the Savior, the Lord Jesus, Jehovah, the "I am" is the one who saves. I want us to think not only of God's declaration that He saved them, but also of how He has saved throughout time as evidenced throughout the Old and New Testaments. God has always provided a way. He has saved through His prophets and He saved through His Spirit. And in Nehemiah we read about the judges whom He raised up, who are referred to as saviors.

Imagine what God has long endured. Have you ever found yourself in the impossible situation of loving someone so deeply and completely only to have them reject you? And isn't it a horrible feeling? We are merely human flesh experiencing that pain, yet imagine what God has long endured. That is why we call Him "long-suffering." He goes through rejection after rejection, generation after generation. This is why we are without excuse.

Most of the church world lives in some kind of delusion that you are either okay as you are, or that you can fix things by yourself if you would just perform and jump through their hoops. That is why I highlighted the issues in this psalm, to show that there is no one who does not grapple with something. Every single person, right now at this moment, is dealing with something that they wish they could just be rid of, whether it is cancer, drug addiction, psychological issues, family problems or other issues. You just wish it would go away! But it won't; it is still there.

Remember that our Savior does not change, and His name is holy. He said, "I am a holy God." Many in the church misinterpret this to mean that they shouldn't smoke, drink, breathe or do much of anything because they think they are "holy" people. But God said, "My *name* is holy." And we know He did not change between the Old

Testament and the New. In the New Testament, Jesus taught His disciples to pray "hallowed be thy name." His name has not changed and His word is settled in heaven. It is still holy and separate. It is still the purest and greatest name that could ever roll off of our lips. People say that God is so holy that He cannot stand sin. This is true, but if you understand the real meaning of holiness, you will also understand the concept of His love, and that for His name's sake, He had to send His only begotten Son to earth to die for our sins. He loved the people that much.

Judges 10:16 says that God was grieved within His soul when He saw how deeply the people had fallen. That is the love of God grieving over His fallen creation. God's holiness and love are wrapped up in the concept of the Savior saving for His name's sake. He said, "I have loved you with an everlasting love," which is a love that cannot be broken, cannot be damaged and cannot be altered. You and I may change, but He does not.

In the book of Hosea, we see God's lament when He cries, "Ephraim, Ephraim," speaking of that lost love of the children of Israel and also of all the people throughout the ages. He cries, "If only you would hear My voice, if only you would turn back to Me. . . ." God is still weeping bitterly for His people.

This is not a message of perfectionism. It is a message of grace: God saved the people for His name's sake, for His holiness, His love and His righteousness. All the dimensions of God are wrapped up in His name's sake, in the name which is above every name. And yet people will come into the church and because they say a couple of "amens" and "hallelujahs," they think that settles the matter, but it does not.

"He saved them for his name's sake, that he might make his mighty power to be known," that He might reveal Himself. From the beginning until the end of time it will be that way. Jeremiah speaks of a day when people will know the Lord; they will know Jehovah. They will know Jesus, the Savior. Zechariah says they will look upon Him whom they have pierced and they will mourn. They will weep with the knowledge that this indeed was and is the Savior of the world.

What does it mean "to make his mighty power known"? Many churches have "testimony" services where people stand up and testify that the Lord delivered them from something. They believe that their testimony is a revelation of God's power, a means "that he might make his power to be known." And most of those testimonies are from people who say they have been delivered from something visibly obvious, something that the church has categorically defined as sin. But that is not what the Bible teaches. The reality is that each and every child of God has a testimony, and you are a hypocrite if you deny it. A testimony does not mean you were delivered from being a whore, a drug addict, a chain smoker or a crackhead. The testimony is that you heard the word and although nothing may have visibly changed right away, in reality everything changed. That is the testimony. That is God's power being made known.

People like to talk about someone they know who was "converted" under So-and-so's ministry. I have heard people talk about someone being "led to the Lord." Let me tell you that a man leading another man usually results in nothing more than a man-made conversion, not a God-made conversion. Real conversion can only occur as Jesus describes it in John 3: you must be born from above. It is not something you are born into because your parents were Christians. As David du Plessis said, "God has no grandchildren."

Conversion is not a change of your appearance, or getting "cleaned up" in the eyes of some fundamentalist who does not like your hairstyle or the way you dress. There are some things that God may heal you of or deliver you from, but there is really nothing special about that: God does those kinds of things every day. The greatest thing to occur is that God translates you from the kingdom of darkness into the kingdom of His light. That is the greatest thing: God making His power known! There are many who say of themselves, "Well, I'm basically a good person," but they are living a godless life without Christ. The concept of God's power being made known unto you is so simple on the surface, yet so very deep and profound.

The most wonderful gift is the ability to respond, the ability to hear! God did not save you because you possessed something inherently good. Even if you think that the worst thing you have ever done isn't really that bad, God sees what goes on in the darkness of our minds. He knows. Perhaps when you see that reality, you will be able to look in the mirror and say, "I see myself there: I see not only the possibility, but the reality of sin."

In Psalm 106:6, the children of Israel made a confession and said, "We have sinned with our fathers, we have committed iniquity, we have done wickedly." Those are words that come out of the mouth of anyone who comes into the light, no matter how bad or how good they thought that they were. Despite the wickedness of the children of Israel and the wickedness of fallen man, the goodness of God is that He is still saving people today, and He is still doing it for the same reason. Not only can we look into the Old Testament and say, "He saved me for His name's sake," but we can look into the New Testament and realize that He sent His only begotten Son. He was named Jesus, for He shall save His people from their sins. The message is simple. It is basic Christianity. You do not have to say any special prayer and you do not need an "altar call," because the response is something that happens in your heart as you hear the message.

I cringe every time I hear some modern evangelist try to make someone come up to an altar and recite some words. If you are really honest, you are going to look at these shades of sinning man that are catalogued in Psalm 106 and say, "That's me. I see myself there." You are going to be touched to your core with the understanding that you and I are no different than these rebellious people in the Old Testament. And suddenly this verse, "Nevertheless he saved them for his name's sake," should come alive for you. His power is "being made known" the moment we turn from our way to His way.

The whole church world will tell you that you just need to stop sinning, which is an impossibility. You will frustrate yourself right into the grave if you think you can somehow stop sinning. I have even heard people say, "Well, I don't sin anymore." And they are the same people who will make you believe that there is something wrong with you. Nonsense!

I am preaching a message of grace straight out of the pages of the Old Testament. God did not save His people for any reason other than for His name's sake. Philippians 2 says that the eternal person, the Son of God, took on the form of a servant. When we read that passage, we understand that the name, which is above any and every name that could be named on earth, under the earth or above the earth, is the name of Jesus Christ.

And that brings me to a pivotal point. We are not left to wonder, "What should I do?" We know that we are to act in faith, to *faithe* in His finished work. When I think of Calvary, I remember that "God so loved the world that he gave his only begotten Son." You can substitute your own name for "the world" and say, "God so loved *me* that He laid down His life and was resurrected, so that *I* may live in that resurrected power, and have life more abundantly!" That is the beginning of the breath of eternity upon each and every individual who comes to the faith and the saving knowledge of Jesus Christ.

My prayer is that someone among you will hear, and not just hear the words between the *neverthelesses* of Nehemiah and the *nevertheless* of Psalm 106, but between the empty pages of your own life, which for some are very empty indeed. Some may say, "I'll get to it at some point," or "I'll deal with it later," but there is a right-now moment. I am not saying, like some people say, that a moment comes when you must "make a decision." But there is a right-now moment when you realize you are in a serious state, and you can say from your heart, "I know that I am trusting God, Yahweh, Jehovah, my Savior, Jesus Christ." And for that simple faith, for that simple trust, He has promised to give you life eternal. As Romans 5 says, He has taken us from the curse to the cure. He has taken me from where I once was, living without Him, to being washed and cleansed by the blood of the Lamb.

When we read, "He saved them for his name's sake," we stand on the knowledge of all that His name means. The Jewish people to this day refuse to pronounce the name Yahweh, or Jehovah, because it is too sacred for them. But in Exodus 6, God plainly said, "This is the name by which I want to be known. My name is Jehovah," and He began to reveal His salvation, which would ultimately be revealed in the flesh in its fullness in our Lord and Savior Jesus Christ.

Use this knowledge as a looking glass, not to abase yourself and say, "Look at how bad I have been," but to see God's goodness more clearly. I have met many people who say, "But I don't know how I could ever be forgiven." I call that frustrating the grace of God. Understand that God did not save you because of something that you merited or some good work that you could do, but He saved you and me for His name's sake, wrapped up in the person of Jesus Christ. And He saved us with no works or strings attached. He saved us for the simple faith that says, "This is my Savior. He took me from the condition I was in, and brought me into this moment now."

God is making His power known through the preaching of the gospel message of the grace of God, as opposed to a "testimony" that only makes God's power known in an individual life. Can anyone come in response to the gospel message? The Bible says, "Whosoever shall call upon the name of the Lord shall be saved." When Jesus prayed His high-priestly prayer, He said, "Father, I have revealed Your name. I have declared You. I have made Your power known." He also said, "There are other sheep that I have not yet brought in."

Quit frustrating the grace of God. Quit trying to figure out if there is some merit in your life that deserves His grace. None of us deserve it, but thanks be to God for what He did for us. I am unworthy. You are unworthy. Yet for our simple act of faith we are saved, cleansed and delivered. The breath of eternity is upon those who understand that. Rejoice in the knowledge that He saved us for no other reason than what we have declared, which is the name of Jesus Christ. We are saved by our simple act of faith.

Chapter 21

THE PRIVILEGE OF SERVICE

Whatever you do for God, do it one hundred percent. Don't do it with lip service, and don't say, "I will get around to it." Commit your way to the Lord and do it fully. Commit your way, delight yourself in the Lord, and He will give you the desire of your heart. That means if the delight of your heart is the Lord, then the Lord will give you Himself. That is not complicated.

2 Timothy 3:16 says that all Scripture is given by the inspiration of God. Other translations say, "All Scripture is God-breathed." So someone might ask, "Was God holding His breath when Nehemiah 11 was written?" Because it looks like it is nothing but a list of names, including many that are difficult to pronounce. Lists are important in God's book. Most of us when we read the Bible tend to skip over the lists of names. After a while they all look like "So-and-so begat So-and-so, and the son of So-and-so begat So-and-so, etc." But the lists are there for a good reason. There are five different lists in the book of Nehemiah, and they are all relevant; we can glean something from each of them.

The first list is in Nehemiah 3. It is comprised of the names of the people who rebuilt the walls and the gates. I believe this list was deliberately included to show just how few people did that work, which they miraculously did in such a short period of time in spite of all the things that came against them. The second list is in Nehemiah 7. It is the genealogical record of the people who returned from captivity. It includes some overlap of the family names from the first list, because it reflects the different generations of people who returned to Jerusalem in successive waves. Again, it shows how few people returned.

Those who study the books of 1 Chronicles, Ezra and Nehemiah will discover that there are some differences in the lists of names and the number of people. I want to give you an approach for dealing with such apparent discrepancies. When you consider that these people were carried into captivity and that there was no real restoration until the time that Ezra came and read the law, it is really quite miraculous that any of these records survived. It is as if God were saying, "This is what I am preserving in perpetuity."

There are some who say, "Well, if the records do not exactly match up one hundred percent, that means there is something wrong with their authority." No, it does not mean that at all. Let me make a simple analogy. Suppose that you had lived in ten different places during your lifetime. And suppose that two or three generations pass and someone then tries to reconstruct the records from your lifetime. I am not talking about recordkeeping in the digital age, but imagine your papers and photographs being passed on to your children and your children's children. Would all of the records survive? I do not think so. I believe it is quite a miracle that some of these lists in the Bible survived as well as they did. It is a miracle that they were even preserved for us at all. And a few discrepancies in the names do not destroy the validity and authority of these records.

The third list is at the beginning of Nehemiah 10. These are the names of the people who, after hearing the law read, had a great wave of repentance and sorrow, and they signed a firm covenant, essentially agreeing to do and to carry out all that they had heard written in the law. The fourth list occurs in Nehemiah 11, which is the focus of this message. This is a list of the names of the people who returned to live in the city. For what good would it have done to have rebuilt the altar, the temple and the walls if there were no people to live in the city? This list also tells of what the people did, their privilege of service. The last list is found in Nehemiah 12. It is a list of the priests and Levites. It may seem to be an overwhelming amount of unnecessary information, but all of these lists were preserved for us for a purpose.

Nehemiah 11 begins, "And the rulers of the people dwelt at Jerusalem: the rest of the people also cast lots, to bring one of ten to dwell in Jerusalem the holy city, and nine parts to dwell in other cities." There are a few things that I would have you notice. The first thing to notice is the percentage of the people who would dwell in the city. People normally think of the "tithe" in terms of money; but here, they cast lots to select a tithe of the people, one in ten, who would dedicate themselves to the service of the Lord and go and populate the city. They applied the principle of the tithe when they selected the people to live in the city.

The next thing to notice is that the rulers were already dwelling in the city, but the total number of people available must have been very small indeed if they had to cast lots to determine who would live within the city. Casting lots was a common practice. We tend to caricature the casting of lots and imagine that maybe they tossed dice, but that is not at all what was meant. In Leviticus 16:8, it says that Aaron cast lots to see which goat would fall to the Lord and which would be the scapegoat. The casting of lots was a common practice all the way into the New Testament days. In Acts 1:26, the lot was cast to select a replacement for the dead disciple Judas, and Matthias was chosen by lot. I have not heard many sermons about Matthias, so the casting of the lot in that case did not accomplish much. But the lot was used as a means to determine God's will. Many people have speculated that the casting of lots had much to do with the Urim and the Thummim, which the high priest held in the breastplate of his ephod.

If we pause right here on the first verse of Nehemiah 11, we see something profound going on: the rulers were already there, and they realized the necessity for people to dwell in Jerusalem.

Again, what good was it to reestablish and rebuild the temple and the altar, to make preparations for service, and for there to be walls to secure the city, without having people there? When we take this concept into the present day, we see that the same principle applies. I have heard many people say, "Why should I go to church?" You do not have to go to church to be a Christian. You may live out in the middle of some sparsely populated area and have church in your home. You may live in a city with fifty churches around you and still have church in your home. But the idea portrayed here in Nehemiah is very clear: Jerusalem, the place referred to more than once as "the holy city," was a city set apart to bear God's name. We are the church of Jesus Christ; the church bears His name and we are His body. We see the importance of making a testimony by gathering together in one place. But when people do not take their opportunity and responsibility seriously, they are basically saying, "I don't feel the need to become a part of the population of the family of God."

I am not throwing rocks at those who don't go to church, because as I have just said, going to church doesn't make you any more saved or less saved. In fact, in Jeremiah's day, before the children of Israel were carried away into bondage, when the temple was still standing there were plenty of people coming and going. But they did not serve with their heart, and it was for that very reason, their wayward and wicked ways, that they were carried away. So I think that by Nehemiah's day, the people would have viewed it as a high privilege and honor to be associated with anything concerning the holy city.

Can you imagine what it might have meant for the people living in that day to go and live in the holy city? Think of the connotations. To live in the holy city meant to be at the very center of everything that was happening, because Jerusalem was the epicenter for the people of God. Everything revolved around the city, the temple and the activities of worship, and everything else flowed from that. People would pour into the epicenter of worship in that day, but today we see the reverse is happening. That is why I said you can glean something important out of every single verse in this book.

It says that the people cast lots, though I do not believe that the lot was cast to conscript people who did not want to go. I believe that they cast lots because so many of the people wanted to be chosen that they had to determine the divine will concerning who would have the privilege. The resulting initial population would probably have been around 5,000 people. It is a little sad to think that the entire city would be comprised of only 5,000 people.

There was something more going on here, because we read in verse 2, "The people blessed all the men, that willingly offered themselves to dwell at Jerusalem." The passage is self-explanatory: they did not go under coercion. The root of the Hebrew word for "they willingly offered themselves" is *nadav*. You will find the exact same English translation in the book of Judges in the Song of Deborah, where it says two times that the people willingly offered themselves to go into battle and they knew the risk. Likewise, the people who were chosen to live in the city not only offered themselves willingly, they also knew the risk. This same word for "willingly offered themselves" occurs in other places, including Leviticus, Ezekiel, and the closing of 2 Chronicles. Most of the time this word is used with regard to the offering of things, but many times it describes a person offering themselves when there is possible danger.

This city had danger written all over it. Nonetheless these people willingly offered themselves. Some have suggested that the only reason people went to live in the city was to provide a garrison, but I do not believe that. When you read from verse 25 to the end of the chapter, you can see that the surrounding villages were populated by relatives who could have served as the garrison and the guard. I believe that the people went to live in the city primarily because of their sense of duty and privilege. They knew about the danger, but there is something about duty and danger that go hand in hand.

Many people erroneously think that serving the Lord is without peril. There is danger that comes with proclaiming God's word because you will come under attack not only from Satan and his minions, but also from people who are on a mission to stop the word of God from going out.

Nehemiah 11 speaks to us first and foremost about the repopulation of the city as the epicenter of worship. I do not want us to think of these passages only in their historical light; I want us to consider what it means with regards to repopulating the church. It is the congregation's responsibility to repopulate the church. I am not saying that every church should become a mega-church. If that is what God decides, that is His business. But when people talk about how to make better communities, it starts with a recognition that their community lacks an epicenter. Communities are failing for lack of a place where a pulse beats, a place where the people are able to gather to face, as it were, their vital statistics, as opposed to a place that only offers a salve, where the people are told, "Heal thyself; you are doing great."

But here in Nehemiah, we are dealing with the repopulation of Jerusalem, and we read, "Now these are the chief of the province that dwelt in Jerusalem: but in the cities of Judah dwelt every one in his possession in their cities, to wit, Israel, the priests, and the Levites, and the Nethinims," the temple servants, "and the children of Solomon's servants. And at Jerusalem dwelt certain of the children of Judah, and of the children of Benjamin." The first emphasis is chiefly on those who would be dwelling at Jerusalem: the children of Judah and the children of Benjamin. The territory of those two tribes falls in the general area of this city, but you have to study Genesis to find out why it was important that the children of Judah were preeminently mentioned before the children of Benjamin. The list continues, "the children of Judah; Athaiah the son of Uzziah, the son of Zechariah, the son of Amariah, the son of Shephatiah, the son of Mahalaleel, of the children of Perez." It says "Perez," but it is referring to the children of Pharez of the line of Judah.

Pharez was in the genealogy of Shealtiel, who are both part of the genealogy of Christ. In Genesis 38, we have the story about Judah and Tamar, whose descendants will become known as the tribe of Judah. Judah had promised to give Tamar a husband to give her children, but Judah did not keep his promise. In that day, a woman's sole function essentially was to produce children. And when the last surviving son of Judah was not given to her, she disguised herself as a harlot and waited by the roadside in a place where she knew that Judah would visit. Judah saw her and thought that she was a prostitute. He wanted to sleep with her, but he did not have anything to pay her with, so she asked for a pledge of his signet ring, bracelet and staff. Judah later sent his friend with a goat to pay her, and when his friend inquired after her, he was told, "There wasn't any harlot in the streets here. What are you talking about?" And out of that relationship, two children were produced: Pharez and Zarah.

Pharez's name means "the breach" because when the two children were about to be born, his hand came out first. God had promised that "the scepter shall not depart from Judah," and all of these passages are like a hidden diamond, covered in dust but still there and shining; God is saying, "This is what I said I would do." Here is the line that will ultimately bring us to Christ. But there are multiple dynamics at work in this passage. God was concerned with preserving both the lines of Pharez and Zarah.

Nehemiah 11:24 says, "And Pethahiah the son of Meshezabeel, of the children of Zerah," which is Zarah, that is, Pharez's brother, "the son of Judah, was at the king's hand in all matters concerning the people." This particular descendant of Zarah must be related to Zimri, because all the other children of Zarah are accounted for in Chronicles. These people are recorded in Nehemiah as though God is saying, "I did not forget." But the most important one that we are focusing on is Pharez, because he is in the line that descends to David and Solomon and ultimately to Christ.

We read in verse 6, "All the sons of Perez that dwelt at Jerusalem were four hundred threescore and eight valiant men." There were only 468 of these men. That is not very many. The chapter began by mentioning the rulers, but we don't know how many rulers there were. Next were "the sons of Benjamin; Sallu the son of Meshullam, the son of Joed, the son of Pedaiah, the son of Kolaiah, the son of Maaseiah. . . . And after him Gabbai, Sallai, nine hundred twenty and eight." There were 928 of them, but that was still not very many.

Behind all of this is not just the fact that the people were carried away into captivity and then an edict was given for them to return. Remember that when Joshua was leading the people into the Promised Land, many of God's people were killed. So it is a miracle that there were still so many living descendants, who were then carried away, who survived the captivity and then came back to the land. And they will become the seed to repopulate the city. God took the time to record the names of these descendants, first because He wanted us to know, "I have preserved My seed; I have preserved what I have promised." Second, He wanted to show us the repopulation of the city, because without all of these people coming to live in the city, the city would have had no pulse. It would just be brick and stone, inanimate nothingness. It took people to bring the city to life.

Now we are going to move from the people to some of their tasks. Verses 9–11 say, "And Joel the son of Zichri was their overseer: and Judah the son of Senuah was second over the city." We see that there was a command and a sense of order. "Of the priests: Jedaiah the son of Joiarib, Jachin. Seraiah the son of Hilkiah, the son of Meshullam, the son of Zadok, the son of Meraioth, the son of Ahitub, was the ruler of the house of God."

You are going to see that everything here was focused on the house of God. Every single activity had a purpose and a function. The privilege was not only to live in the holy city, the city set apart, but also to have a part in performing some duty, any duty. This is the other missing ingredient today when I tell people what a great privilege it is to serve God. Now, not everybody is going to be a pastor, and I am not saying that you should be, but in any capacity in your everyday life, you have the ability to serve God with all of your heart, one hundred percent. That is not lip service. That means in whatever you do, as Paul said to the Colossians, you give thanks. You see God in everything around you and in every person, and you look for the opportunities of faith. People will often say, "Well, that was the Old Testament and these people had specific tasks to perform in the service of the temple." That is true, but there are still specific tasks that need to be performed in the church today.

There are people who have administration skills, there are people who have artistic skills, there are those like Bezaleel with craftsmanship skills, and those with musical skills. When you start thinking about all of the things that are a part of the body of Christ, it is really quite staggering. The people in the church that I pastor are living epistles who embody that very principle of diversity in service.

This list of names is not merely a dry record, it is a memorial. Malachi 3:16–17 speaks of a book of remembrance that was written before God, for them that feared the Lord. And on the day when He makes up His jewels, He will remember those people. I love that passage because it tells me that God is not looking for perfection, and indeed He cannot find perfection on this earth; rather, He is looking for people who will trust Him. The ones who fear the Lord are simply those who will recognize Him in all that they do.

Now let's continue from verse 12: "Their brethren that did the work of the house were eight hundred twenty and two." There were 822 people who did the "work of the house," whatever it was. There had to be maintenance work going on. There were not just the Levitical and priestly responsibilities, there had to be someone doing the equivalent of KP duty. God made a provision to memorialize everyone who served, from the greatest to the least. This record serves as a memorial for us to look at and understand that God still expects the population of His people to assume the responsibility of the work. He could do it without us, but He has chosen to do it through us and with us. That ought to strike a chord in our hearts of the recognition of what a privilege we have been given, just like these people.

"And Adaiah the son of Jeroham, the son of Pelaliah, the son of Amzi, the son of Zechariah, the son of Pashur, the son of Malchiah, and his brethren, chief of the fathers, two hundred forty and two: and Amashai the son of Azareel, the son of Ahasai, the son of Meshillemoth, the son of Immer, and their brethren, mighty men of valour." These were men who were ready for battle, and there were 128 of them. "And their overseer was Zabdiel, the son of one of the great men. Also of the Levites . . . the chief of the Levites, had the oversight of the outward business of the house of God." Somebody had to take care of the outside. They had people to take care of the inside, and they had people to take care of the outside.

I believe that all of these people looked at the opportunity with honor, with respect and with reverence. I am sure that some of them thought, "Wow! I can do this?" I think many Christians today live their lives like a book that has been put on the shelf, because they don't feel like they are doing something that can be seen or that matters. Let me tell you that there is still a book being written, even if you removed yourself or perhaps God removed you for a time. This Bible is closed, but your book is still being written; it is not finished. That is why when you read these passages, they should inspire you to say, "I can do something too. Lord, I will do whatever You would have me to do." Be careful when you pray that prayer. Believe me, when you pray a prayer like that, God will say, "Okay, I got you now."

There was something for everyone to do in this city. "Mattaniah the son of Micha, the son of Zabdi, the son of Asaph, was the principal to begin the thanksgiving in prayer." It is believed that his role might have been to read the psalms, in essence to "prime the pump" to begin the praise and thanksgiving in prayer. "Bakbukiah the second among his brethren, and Abda the son of Shammua, the son of Galal, the son of Jeduthun. All the Levites in the holy city were two hundred fourscore and four," that is, there were 284 of them. "Moreover the porters," were the gatekeepers. There were 172 of those.

There are many different duties at a church, and God cares about the details. If you are picking up debris on the sidewalk for God, you are doing an important work. I do not care about the world's ideas. You would be surprised by how many people think that they should have an important position and title in the church. I suppose that as the pastor my title could be janitor, because the pastor is always the one who is called when someone makes a mess of things and wants to know how to clean it up!

We have the Levites and the gatekeepers, and then it says in verses 20–21, "And the residue of Israel, of the priests, and the Levites, were in all the cities of Judah, every one in his inheritance. But the Nethinims," the temple servants, "dwelt in Ophel," which was an outside area just beyond the gates, "and Ziha and Gispa were over the Nethinims." So there were even overseers over the temple servants. Everything had a structure.

Verse 22 begins, "The overseer also of the Levites. . . ." The Hebrew word for "overseer" is *paqeed,* which is translated with the Greek word *episkopos* in the Septuagint. "The overseer also of the Levites at Jerusalem was Uzzi the son of Bani. . . . Of the sons of Asaph, the singers were over the business of the house of God." Music in the church can be a way to help connect the people to the pulse and get them focused, which is a good thing. But music in the church ceases to be a good thing when it becomes entertainment. And it ceases to be a good thing when the church tries to emulate what the world is doing, in an attempt to attract people simply by offering a contemporary sound without meaningful or even intelligible lyrics.

The singers were included "over the business of the house of God. For it was the king's commandment," that is, the king of Persia, "concerning them, that a certain portion should be for the singers, due for every day." And here we have "Pethahiah the son of Meshezabeel, of the children of Zerah," it says, "Zerah," but it was Zarah the son of Judah, who "was at the king's hand in all matters concerning the people."

In Nehemiah 11, we have seen the people populating the city, and we have seen the privilege of service. We have seen how God has used man and memorialized people on the pages of His book. We have seen that the lists of names were recorded for a number of reasons. They show us that the line was preserved right there in the city leading up to Christ who would come more than 400 years later. They show us that not only was everybody doing their part, but also that there was variety and diversity within one ministry. Not everybody was doing the same thing, but all of their activities focused on the priority of worship, and God was at the center.

We could easily take these pages out of the Old Testament and bring them into the New Testament. At the close of Romans, Paul begins by saluting Phoebe, who was his fellow worker, and then he goes on to name a long list of people, saying, "Salute Priscilla and Aquila, salute the church that is in their house, and salute those who are fellow laborers; salute this person over here, and those who labor over there." Every book in the Bible names people and tells us that God's work has always been performed with people involved. We know that God can do anything without us, but He chose to use us, flawed and marred vessels. That is what I love about God.

There is another New Testament lesson in Nehemiah 11. We could go to 1 Corinthians 12, where Paul tells the people that there are diversities of gifts, there are diversities of operations, there are diversities of administrations, but all the same Spirit. In other words, all of these gifts bring you back to the same place.

I have seen many ministries overtaken by a fatal flaw, where an auxiliary activity is introduced and starts to expand and gain popularity, and then everyone jumps on the bandwagon and says, "That's great! Let's all do that!" And suddenly everyone forgets about the main thing, the reason for gathering together, which is to open up the word of God and bring the Bible passages to life.

There are chapters in the Bible that you may have passed by many times, thinking, "Who cares about the sons of this person and the sons of that person, and who dwelt over here and who dwelt over there?" Yet these passages are memorials left for us that serve a similar function as the memorials that Paul recorded in his letters.

1 Corinthians 12 shows that the ministry still needs a variety of people to do a variety of tasks, and not everybody can do just any task. You might think that you are called to do a certain thing, but you must understand that the work of the ministry is not like doing an ordinary job. There is a mindset that should accompany everything we do in the ministry, and it is a mindset that follows God's way of doing things. If people are left on their own, which is the way much of the church world behaves, they will revert back to man's ways of doing things. Most of the church world uses man's

methods to bring people into the church and to motivate people to give money.

There is a way to do God's work. One of the first lessons you have to learn is that it is much easier to get a job done than it is to do the job God's way. And when we are doing something that is for God, we want to consider exactly what it is that we are trying to achieve. Are you just trying to get a result? Then just get out there and do it. That is not how to do God's work, which should be done with the desire that it be something well-pleasing to God. The goal of the people who cast lots and committed to repopulate the city was not to serve themselves. And they did not go to Jerusalem to hang out at a coffee counter near the altar.

Nehemiah 11:25–36 tells us about the people who lived outside of the city in their villages and all of the far-flung corners, but these people were still vitally important. They undoubtedly made their living from the produce that came from the land, which would become the food for the city itself. So everything here is important, including the list of the priests and the Levites. But the whole focus of the activity centered on one thing. The people did not come back to take some time off; they came back to work for God, they came back for the ministry. They came back to reestablish the priority of worship in their lives.

A long time ago in this country, whenever a city was being planned, the first thing that was considered was the location of the church. Now by today's standards, it would be considered divisive to take into account the location of a church when planning the design of a city. Most people would say, "Who cares about the church?" But years ago in this country, all the major cities, especially on the eastern seaboard, were built around the church; the church was the epicenter. The church was where people felt their connectivity, even though they had Christian homes and prayed in their homes.

The people who came back to Jerusalem, came back for a purpose. They came back to work, they came back to worship; they had God in their hearts. They had a fixed purpose; it wasn't for some random activity and it wasn't ambiguous. Each person had a job and a responsibility. And I love the fact that it says, "They gave of themselves willingly," they offered themselves.

I am earnestly praying that people will understand that there is still work to do in the church today. As these people were memorialized in this book, we are memorialized in the Lamb's book as children of Christ. The people who will overcome, the people who will stay with the stuff right until the end are written in His book. Some of you may have had the devil whisper in your ear, "It is just not worth it." But God's word says that our labor is not in vain.

We only have to read two chapters further in Nehemiah to see that the people did not stay committed. Nehemiah had to return to Babylon for a time, and in his absence, the people let the house of God become profaned. They began to do things that he spoke against, which is why you will find Nehemiah often talking about keeping the Sabbath, keeping it holy, keeping the people set apart. To be holy simply means to be set apart. By that definition, anything can be made holy. We can say that something is holy, but until it is holy unto the Lord God, our Savior, it is not truly set apart. The people in Nehemiah's day committed the very sin that the people in Jeremiah's day committed. Just because they lived in the holy city did not make them holy people.

The Bible says that we are now the habitation of God. That is the beautiful thing. We are no longer looking for a city that can be touched with hands; we are waiting for the New Jerusalem to descend. Our focus is no longer on things that we can touch; our focus is on our stewardship of the things of God. You will find that when you read the Bible, the same principle is repeated over and over again. Nehemiah was not only a preacher of reformation, he was preeminently a preacher of order and stewardship in the temple, so that the integrity of God's work and His people would be maintained. Although it could not be maintained after he left, as long as he was present, he would make sure to his last breath that it was.

That is the dilemma of the church today. There is no dedication. There are many who will read a chapter like this in the Bible and make no application to themselves. There would be a grand celebration in Nehemiah 12 when the wall was dedicated. People will always come out to celebrate, but this group was celebrating what God had done, crying, "Glory to God! Look what the Lord has done! He delivered us; He brought us back to be able to participate in His work!" Now in our day and age, people forget. That is what we said in the previous message about the twelve shades of sinning man: it is easy for people to forget what it was like when they first started their walk and their journey.

If you are in the church for a long enough time, there is the danger that you might become a "religious" person. You can think that you are so far away from where you started that you no longer remember the days of crying out in the darkness, the days when you didn't have any hope and when you didn't know if you were going to make it.

I pray that I never forget those days. I live day by day with that remembrance. But the church is in terrible peril for that reason. Sin is no longer considered sin. We ought to understand that God has taken care of that by the shed blood of Jesus Christ, but that does not lighten the reality of the condition we are born into. And when those ideas become just ideas and are no longer a living embodiment in our lives, when they are not conveyed through our expression of faith in our Lord and Savior Jesus Christ, then the church becomes only a place of routine and ritual, and the pulse is gone.

Nehemiah 11 speaks to me about the privilege of being a child of God. These people had the honor of being memorialized on a page in the Bible. Some of them are well-known, some are less known, and some we do not even know their names. We have an even greater opportunity and responsibility than they did. This is not to say, "You are not doing enough; do more." This is to make us consider that each and every day God gives us opportunities. And while you might think that they are insignificant, God doesn't see it that way.

There are some who have never committed to do anything, who have never said, "This is my time with God" and commit to do it one hundred percent, such as setting aside a time to pray or to gather together to listen to the word being taught. We don't need to have our names recorded on a page in the Bible. God has already taken care of that. He looks at each and every one of us and He sees our faltering and our failures, and He sees the fact that some of us act like a closed book that is just collecting dust on a shelf. But if the heart is willing to turn back, we can say, "I know I can be of service, even if it appears to be just a little service. I know I can be of service like those who took care of the outside, or like those who took care of the inside." And neither the outside people nor inside people were saying, "Well, I have a more important job than you have. I work on the inside and you work on the outside, so I am better than you!"

We read in 1 Corinthians 12, beginning at verse 4, "Now there are diversities of gifts, but the same Spirit. And there are differences of administrations," or service, servicing, services or servanthood, if you will, "but the same Lord. And there are diversities of operations," the Greek word is *energama*, of energies, of things that are working, "but it is the same God which worketh all in all. But the manifestation of the Spirit is given to every man to profit withal. For to one is given by the Spirit the word of wisdom; to another the word of knowledge by the same Spirit; to another faith by the same Spirit; to another the gifts of healing by the same Spirit; to another the working of miracles; to another prophecy; to another discerning of spirits; to another divers kinds of tongues; to another the interpretation of tongues: but all these worketh that one and the selfsame Spirit, dividing to every man severally as he will." That means God decides. He decides; you do not.

As you read on in this passage, you will start to realize that you are a part of something bigger than any of the activities you do. And those activities may seem small in your eyes, but they may be that crucial cog that moves something else into position or enables someone else to do their job, like a vital organ in the body. Paul says, "For as the body is one, and hath many members, and all the members of that one body, being many, are one body: so also is Christ. For by one Spirit are we all baptized into one body, whether we be Jews or Gentiles, whether we be bond or free; and have been all made to drink into one Spirit. For the body is not one member, but many."

I highly doubt that the servants in the temple said, "Well, you pick up the stuff in the street and I clean the altar, so I am much more important than you," like that ludicrous illustration of the people on the inside chiding the people on the outside. Paul goes on to say, "If the foot shall say, Because I am not the hand, I am not of the body; is it therefore not of the body? And if the ear shall say, Because I am not the eye, I am not of the body; is it therefore not of the body? If the whole body were an eye, where were the hearing?"

I have heard people say, "I've been thinking that maybe I've been called to the ministry." If you really feel that is your calling, I will not try to talk you out of it. But I would caution you that the ministry may not be what you think it is. If you are ready to commit your way and really turn your life over, it means you turn your life over completely. You are not your own, you turn it all over. That doesn't mean there will be no striving with God at the first, but eventually, if it is God who is going to do something and get the glory, then you will have to turn it all over. And that means whatever time you have is not your own time; it is His time. He will use it as He sees fit.

There are many opportunities for service in the body of Christ. Paul goes on to say, "If the whole body were an eye, where were the hearing? If the whole were hearing, where were the smelling? But now hath God set the members every one of them in the body, as it hath pleased him." There is something for everybody to participate in; there is the privilege of serving. And no, your name won't be written on a page in the Bible, but it will be written in His book; and whether it is a little or a lot, it doesn't matter. God says, "This is all unto Me, and it is all for Me and about Me." 1 Corinthians 12:27 sums this all up, "Now ye are the body of Christ, and members in particular." Think about that. You belong to the body and the body is always moving and progressing forward, and that is the church you are a part of.

God did not have the people rebuild Jerusalem so they could say, "Hey, now we have a nice building." He said, "You must bring the people." So likewise with the church: people must be brought so that the word can be spread and planted in the people's hearts, so that the service can be performed, and so that the service may be carried out in a manner pleasing to God. These people in Nehemiah 11 are memorialized for us to show that God cares about the details.

There is something for everybody to do in the church. It takes people to populate, people with a willing heart. I am praying that the heart of servanthood be renewed and revived because there is a very big work to do. That requires people saying, "I will help. Tell me what you need done; I am available and I am malleable. I will learn. I may not do the job perfectly, but my heart is focused on God and I know that I can do something, even if it is a little something, even if it is sweeping the floors; use me." It takes people with a heart that is focused like these people in Nehemiah's day. They were delighted to have the opportunity to answer the call and return to Jerusalem to rebuild. They must have felt like free men, even though they were still under the king of Persia. We are free men and women in Christ, but we have a lot of work to do. When that spirit is fully revived in the church, we will be a mountain-moving people.

The work of the ministry is an abundant grace that will probably never be exhausted in our lifetime. So roll up your sleeves and enjoy the fact that God has called you and given you the opportunity to have the joy of serving. My prayer is that you are inspired today and can say from your heart, "Yes, I am called to do something great, and the Lord will enable me," because in the great words of Dr. Gene Scott, "Whom the Lord calleth, He enableth."

CHAPTER 22

THE SPIRIT OF NEHEMIAH: RESTORATION OF GOD'S WAYS

Reformation is necessary in every age. We are not immune. We like to think of ourselves as being immune, but we are not immune to slipping into things that quite frankly do not belong in the church. Most people do not understand what the church exists for, and there are some who think that people don't really need to go to church. That whole mindset is wrong, and I will tell you why it is wrong.

The church, first of all, is a people who belong to the Lord, God's "out-called ones." They are called out from among other people who have not been called to belong to a part of the body of Christ, not an independent body, but the body of Christ. And if we want to know why the church exists, we must start with what was in the mind of its Founder. We want to know what purpose He had in mind when He declared, "I will build *my* church, and the gates of hell shall not prevail against it." People love to talk about the Great Commission, but the Great Commission is not an end in itself. Jesus said, "Go and teach," but that is not all that He said. He said, "Teach them to observe all things whatsoever *I have commanded you.*"

In other words, the reason the church exists is to propagate the teaching of Jesus Christ, the message that He is risen and all the things that He taught His disciples, who then gave us the epistles, of which the apostle Paul wrote two-thirds. It was the apostle Paul who gave us direction concerning what the church should and should not look like.

We are looking at Nehemiah 13, starting with a general overview of this epilogue to the book of Nehemiah. There are lessons for the church in Nehemiah 13 that are neither archaic nor strictly Judaic. It doesn't take much for the people of God to come up with things that seem good in their own eyes, like the people who were selling doves and changing money in the temple when Jesus drove them out. Jesus had to contend with it in His day, so I do not want us to think that it is anything new or that the church has come so far that it is no longer an issue.

Nehemiah had returned to Jerusalem after having to go back to his official duties in Babylon for a time. We do not know how long Nehemiah was gone. It seems very tenable to me that, just like at the beginning of the book, a new message came to him while he was serving the king, informing Nehemiah that the things that he had put in place were now coming undone. That seems plausible, otherwise we see no reason why he would have returned. We read starting from verse 4, "And before this, Eliashib the priest, having the oversight of the chamber of the house of our God, was allied unto Tobiah." Remember that Tobiah was an Ammonite. He was the enemy who, along with Sanballat and Gashmu, or Geshem, had ridiculed the people and tried to stop the work.

Then we read of the terrible thing that Eliashib had done to help this enemy, Tobiah. "And he had prepared for him a great chamber, where aforetime they laid the meat offerings, the frankincense, and the vessels, and the tithes of the corn, the new wine, and the oil, which was commanded to be given to the Levites, and the singers, and the porters," the gatekeepers, "and the offerings of the priests. But in all this time was not I at Jerusalem: for in the two and thirtieth year of Artaxerxes king of Babylon came I unto the king, and after certain days obtained I leave of the king: and I came to Jerusalem, and understood of the evil that Eliashib did for Tobiah, in preparing him a chamber in the courts of the house of God. And it grieved me sore: therefore I cast forth all the household stuff of Tobiah out of the chamber. Then I commanded, and they cleansed the chambers: and thither brought I again the vessels of the house of God, with the meat offering and the frankincense."

We are going to catalogue four evils that Nehemiah encountered, and we are going to characterize them using four key words that begin with the same letter to help you remember them. The first one is the misuse of God's house, which we will call the violation of the *sanctity* of the house of God. Now you might think it was crude of Nehemiah, having just come back into town, to take Tobiah's stuff and essentially throw it to the curb. But this is what needs to happen in many churches in America today. There are way too many "Tobiahs" abiding in the churches.

Now I certainly do not mean that we should throw people out of the church because they do not conform to some fundamentalist's standard, nor am I suggesting that we throw people out because they are different. Rather, I am saying that something has come into the church that does not belong there. I believe that we as the church of Jesus Christ should show forth and radiate the love of Christ, but that does not mean we must homogenize all doctrines and live in a syncretistic society where everything is equal. I am speaking about Christendom, not about race, age or gender. These evils that Nehemiah exposed had to be dealt with, because they caused a number of trickle-down effects.

You see, that chamber that Tobiah was living in was formerly the place where they brought the tithes and offerings and all of the things that would have been for the Levites. You can read about that in Nehemiah 12. At least the priests could live off of the portion of the offerings that was theirs to take, but the Levites could not. So the consequence of Eliashib's decision to misuse God's house was pretty grave.

It sounds ludicrous, but someone actually asked me, "Would you ever consider opening a coffee shop in your church?" My answer was that if you want a good cup of coffee, go find a coffee shop. You come to church to listen to the good word of God, not to have coffee and sit back and chill out. You come to church to be spiritually filled up with God's word. You come to church because Christ is here among us. Now, He is with you when you get into your car and wherever you go; but the Scripture says that where two or three are gathered in His name, He is in our midst. I do not believe that Jesus would be opposed to sitting down with you at a bar or in a coffee shop and having a drink or a cup of coffee, but not in a place that bears His name.

Now, you might say, "What's the big deal?" There isn't a big deal, until you start messing with the sanctity of the church. Once you open up the door and say, "Okay, let's do this," then a month or a year later we are doing something worse and then pushing it a little bit more, and a little bit more, until suddenly you can no longer recognize God's house. That is the way it works. That is equally the way backsliding occurs; it doesn't happen in one fell swoop. These things occur imperceptibly over time.

But the first evil here is the misuse of God's house. And upon uncovering this evil, Nehemiah set out to make it right. He threw out Tobiah's stuff, and he cleansed and purified the chambers. That is very reminiscent of what will happen a few hundred years later, when Christ would enter the temple and confront the money changers there. There is a popular idea that Christians should be mealy-mouthed and never get angry. But there is such a thing as righteous indignation. You can get angry when it concerns the things of God, and that is just how Nehemiah reacted.

So this first evil snowballed into the second evil, the failure to take care of God's servants, which I am labeling as the failure to provide for *service*. Beginning in verse 10, "And I perceived that the portions of the Levites had not been given them: for the Levites and the singers, that did the work, were fled every one to his field." Think about the ramifications of the Levites not getting their portions. If they did not get what they needed to survive, they would have to go back to the fields. They did not own their own land, but they would have to go out and work in whatever fields they were allowed to work in. And when that happened, other things would suffer. The word of God would not go forth; the singing and the praise worship would not go forth. So there was a trickle-down effect that had an impact beyond the storage room where Tobiah was living. Other people suffered, starting with the Levites and the singers.

We read what happened next in verse 11, "Then contended I with the rulers, and said, Why is the house of God forsaken?" Didn't we hear them make a pledge at the end of chapter 10? Read again the final words of Nehemiah 10:39: *"and we will not forsake the house of our God."* They all said that. Now Nehemiah is asking, "Why is the house of God forsaken?"

I do not believe that it took very long for this forsaking to occur. We do not know exactly how long Nehemiah was away. Most people speculate that it could have been any time up to twelve years, but it was enough time for everything that had been put in place to fall apart. It was only a relatively short time after that grand procession and celebration and the voice of the people saying, "We will not forsake the house of our God." And now Nehemiah has to deal with these people.

How does this apply to the church today? Paul said, "They which preach the gospel should live of the gospel." That means they should be taken care of by the gospel. Paul was a tentmaker; he had a trade, and that is wonderful. But in the structure of the growing church, at some point, being a tentmaker would not remain a practical activity if you became an overseer, if you were responsible for what snowballed into a great number of churches all over Asia, which would require Paul's full-time attention. The ramifications of not taking care of the Levites extend into today's realm. I have encountered many churches where the pastor is not properly taken care of. There are two sides to the matter, because it is also the pastor's responsibility to teach the people and show them what God says in His word about giving. It is true that there have been abuses that have occurred throughout the ages, where the person of God goes beyond the pale. That is not something new, and it goes all the way back to Judas. But when the pastors are not taken care of, of course they have to go out and do something else, and the worship suffers and everything else in the church suffers. Pastors need to immerse themselves in the word of God and then share what that immersion has brought forth, but they cannot do that when they are doing twenty other things to support themselves.

Some have the mindset that the pastor must drive an old clunker, with the door barely attached and the muffler hanging down. Then the onlookers can approve and say, "There goes a humble leader, who looks so spiritual." And then you have the opposite extreme, like a pastor who boasts that he has three private planes. I am not someone's fruit inspector to judge what is too much and what is too little. But I will say that there is a practical balance to all things. I just want us to recognize that the person of God should be taken care of. In Nehemiah's day, when the teachers of God's word were not taken care of, they all went back to the fields, and the teaching of God's word suffered and worship suffered.

Verse 12 says, "Then brought all Judah the tithe of the corn and the new wine and the oil unto the treasuries," into the storehouse. "And I made treasurers over the treasuries, Shelemiah the priest, and Zadok the scribe, and of the Levites, Pedaiah: and next to them was Hanan the son of Zaccur, the son of Mattaniah: for they were counted faithful, and their office was to distribute unto their brethren." These were people whom Nehemiah counted as faithful and trustworthy to assist in financial matters.

I meet people all the time who say, "Don't even talk to me about church. They just want your money; that is all they care about. They're all a bunch of crooks." I believe that if a person in the ministry turns out to be a fraud, God will deal with that person. It may not happen in this lifetime, but I believe it will happen in the next when they appear before the Lord. If they expect a reward, they will certainly get their reward. Every time there is some new scandal in the church, the onlookers always say, "How could anyone have supported that ministry?" I do not believe that the contributors will lose their eternal reward if they supported innocently. But the flip side is that everyone still has the responsibility to open up their Bibles and learn what is contained therein, so that they will not be duped. That will sort out the people who are too lazy or who say, "I'll let the pastor do that for me. It is too complicated for me." What kind of relationship can you possibly be having with God when you do not even know what His word says?

Nehemiah's exceptional qualities as a person of God are seen in this chapter. He restored what had been set in place: he restored the sanctity of the house, he restored the service in the house, and he restored God's method of taking care of His servants. That is why I call him a reformer. Then in verse 14, he said, "Remember me, O my God, concerning this, and wipe not out my good deeds that I have done for the house of my God, and for the offices thereof." Nehemiah said several times, "Remember me," and one time he said, "Remember them." When he said, "Remember me," he meant "Remember me, O God, please don't wipe out my heart towards You in this house for what the people in their decline and their laxity have done. Don't wipe it out; don't count it as nothing."

Since Nehemiah knew the Scriptures, I can imagine that in the back of his mind were echoes of what he knew about Moses, and how the sins and the grumbling of the people provoked Moses to do what he should not have done. Every leader faces the challenge of sometimes being provoked. If you care about God's work so much, it can be like protecting your baby. You can be offended by the way people treat that same work.

Further, "In those days saw I in Judah some treading wine presses on the sabbath, and bringing in sheaves, and lading asses; as also wine, grapes, and figs, and all manner of burdens, which they brought into Jerusalem on the sabbath day: and I testified against them in the day wherein they sold victuals." This third evil was a failure to submit to the Sabbath, which I will simply label *submission.* Let me say that I am not advocating legalism. There is a principle involved here that applies to our walk of faith in any age.

We read, "There dwelt men of Tyre also therein, which brought fish, and all manner of ware, and sold on the sabbath unto the children of Judah, and in Jerusalem. Then I contended with the nobles." We had read in verse 11, "Then contended I with the rulers," and in verse 17, he was contending with the nobles. Nehemiah contended with everybody. The Hebrew is somewhat ambiguous here and it could mean that he argued in the sense of having a legal cause, or it could mean he argued in the sense of having a fight. Either way, Nehemiah took a stand for what was right. He "contended with the nobles of Judah, and said unto them, What evil thing is this that ye do, and profane the sabbath day? Did not your fathers thus, and did not our God bring all this evil upon us, and upon this city? yet ye bring more wrath upon Israel by profaning the sabbath." Nehemiah showed that he knew both history and Scripture.

There are lessons to be gleaned out of every verse. Today there are certain organizations that have appointed themselves to be watchdogs over Christian churches. They monitor churches and decide whether a church is doing good or bad, in their view. The problem with those types of entities is that all they are interested in is "exposing." But that is only one-half of the job. If you are going to engage in that type of activity, if all you do is go around "exposing" things and you never bring the light of God's word into the equation, then all you are doing is exposing darkness. You are just exposing someone's evil, and nothing is ever done about it. But Nehemiah took action. He identified the problems and he addressed those problems immediately. And that is what any pastor should do. If someone asks, "What should I look for in a leader?" I say look no further than this, because here is a man who didn't just point out the evil, he appealed to history and to Scripture and said, "That is not the way you will do this."

Here is the action that Nehemiah took: "It came to pass, that when the gates of Jerusalem began to be dark before the sabbath, I commanded that the gates should be shut, and charged that they should not be opened till after the sabbath." Can you imagine the shock of the merchants in that day? I am sure that some of them said, "Are you kidding me? Who does he think he is?" But Nehemiah said, "Some of my servants set I at the gates, that there should no burden be brought in on the sabbath day. So the merchants and sellers of all kind of ware lodged without Jerusalem once or twice. Then I testified against them. . . ." This is the second time that he had to testify against something. "I testified against them, and said unto them, Why lodge ye about the wall? if ye do so again, I will lay hands on you." Most people today would say, "Well, that is not very Christian. I want my leader to be more Christian!" But Nehemiah asked them what they were doing there, and he said, "If you do that again, I will lay hands on you!" And it worked, for it says, "From that time forth came they no more on the sabbath."

There is no question that Nehemiah knew the Scriptures, and that he understood the concept of the Sabbath from Exodus 20. It was the Lord's Day and He had commanded, "Remember the sabbath day, to keep it holy." But Nehemiah also remembered the historical consequences of not keeping the Sabbath. In Jeremiah 17, the prophet warned the people saying, "If you don't keep the Sabbath, God is going to bring doom upon this city like you have never seen before." Did that come to pass? The answer is yes. You might ask, "What kind of a God is that?" He is the God who says, "I am looking for people who will listen to Me." But these people wouldn't listen, so Nehemiah said, "Isn't this what your fathers did? And look at the evil that was brought upon this city." Nehemiah then "commanded the Levites that they should cleanse themselves, and that they should come and keep the gates, to sanctify the sabbath day." And again, he prayed, "Remember me, O my God, concerning this also, and spare me according to the greatness of thy mercy."

So far we have looked at three evils that Nehemiah exposed and took action on. In the New Testament realm, it is the pastor's responsibility to address such matters and to take action. The problem with the church in this generation is a lack of care, a lack of enthusiasm and a lack of commitment. There is a great work to do, which is to keep the word of God going forth for those who have heard and those who have not yet heard. It is important; it matters. There has never been a greater matter at hand.

Let's look at the fourth evil that Nehemiah uncovered, which we will call a blatant disregard of God's *standards*. I would like you to write these four key words in the margin of your Bible, to help you remember what this chapter is about. The first was a misuse of

God's house, a violation of its *sanctity*. The second was a failure to provide for its *service*. The third was a failure of *submission* to God's word and God's way. And this fourth evil was a disregard of God's *standards*, which in their case had to do with the problems caused in that day by intermarriage.

"In those days also saw I Jews that had married wives of Ashdod, of Ammon, and of Moab: and their children spake half in the speech of Ashdod, and could not speak in the Jews' language, but according to the language of each people." Isn't that interesting? Remember that these people all made a vow, and Nehemiah 9 culminates with the people coming together to sign a covenant. They made that covenant after hearing the law of Moses and they all agreed to what they would do and would not do. Let's read it starting from Nehemiah 10:29: "They clave to their brethren, their nobles, and entered into a curse, and into an oath, to walk in God's law, which was given by Moses the servant of God, and to observe and do all the commandments of the LORD our Lord, and his judgments and his statutes; and that we would not give our daughters unto the people of the land, nor take their daughters for our sons: and if the people of the land bring ware or any victuals on the sabbath day to sell, that we would not buy it of them on the sabbath, or on the holy day: and that we would leave the seventh year, and the exaction of every debt."

That was the covenant they had made. And in the absence of Nehemiah, every vow they had made was broken! Again, my point is not about keeping the law. I do not preach law; I preach grace. I want us to see how easy it is for people to open their mouths and make a commitment. These were the same people who had said, "We will not forsake the house of our God." There are people who were once in the church and who said, "You can count on me," who are no longer there. It is very easy to back off from something you have said. That is why the Scripture says, "It is better not to make a vow." We can get giddy in the moment and say, "I am going to do this." It is like a New Year's resolution. Someone gets motivated for a moment and says, "This is the year I am going to quit smoking" or anything else you can think of, but it only lasts for about three hours.

It is important to not twist what is being said here in Nehemiah, and to not view it legalistically as a prohibition against marrying people from another race or culture. There were many practical reasons for avoiding mixed marriages in that day. First of all, the woman's primary role in those days was to have children, and the mother would be the one to raise and educate them. The mother would have to pass on the oral tradition concerning the things of God. But now a new generation was coming up that did not speak the Hebrew language. That meant they could not understand the liturgical, religious practices. That was the first disconnect. The second one was the fact that these people had made a vow. Nehemiah was not arbitrarily saying, "You can't do this." The people had broken their vow.

We read in Ezra 9 and 10 that Ezra confronted the same problem, and this may have occurred earlier than these events recorded in Nehemiah. When Ezra heard that the children of Israel had married the daughters of the Canaanites, the Ammonites and other enemies, he plucked his hair off of his head and his beard, he rent his clothes and he sat down, the King James Version says, "astonied" at what he had heard.

Nehemiah contended with the rulers, he contended with the nobles, now he "contended with them" over the issue of mixed marriages, "and cursed them, and smote certain of them, and plucked off their hair, and made them swear by God, saying, Ye shall not give your daughters unto their sons, nor take their daughters unto your sons, or for yourselves."

The reason for the prohibition against mixed marriages was not solely to preserve the line to Christ. Nehemiah said, "Did not Solomon king of Israel sin by these things? yet among many nations was there no king like him, who was beloved of his God, and God made him king over all Israel: nevertheless even him did outlandish women cause to sin." Nehemiah wanted them to see the consequences of what had happened in Solomon's day, because they changed the future from a united kingdom to a divided kingdom. This one thing that God had expressly prohibited is what had caused the kingdom to be torn in two.

We read in 1 Kings 11, "But king Solomon loved many strange women, together with the daughter of Pharaoh, women of the Moabites, Ammonites, Edomites, Zidonians, and Hittites; of the nations concerning which the LORD said unto the children of Israel, Ye shall not go in to them, neither shall they come in unto you: for surely they will turn away your heart after their gods: Solomon clave unto these in love. And he had seven hundred wives, princesses, and three hundred concubines: and his wives turned away his heart. For it came to pass, when Solomon was old, that his wives turned away his heart after other gods: and his heart was not perfect with the LORD his God, as was the heart of David his father. For Solomon went after Ashtoreth the goddess of the Zidonians, and after Milcom the abomination of the Ammonites. And Solomon did evil in the sight of the LORD, and went not fully after the LORD, as did David his father. Then did Solomon build an high place for Chemosh. . . ." He went from loving strange women to building places for their gods, including "Chemosh, the abomination of Moab, in the hill that is before Jerusalem, and for Molech, the abomination of the children of Ammon. And likewise did he for all his strange wives, which burnt incense and sacrificed unto their gods. And the LORD was angry with Solomon, because his heart was turned from the LORD God of Israel, which had appeared unto him twice, and had commanded him concerning this thing, that he should not go after other gods: but he kept not that which the LORD commanded. Wherefore the LORD said unto Solomon, Forasmuch as this is done of thee, and thou hast not kept my covenant and my statutes, which I have commanded thee, I will surely rend the kingdom from thee, and will give it to thy servant."

The kingdom stayed united until the death of Solomon in 931 B.C., and then it split apart into a northern kingdom and a southern kingdom, and became fragmented as well. God had said that this is what would happen. He had mercy on Solomon and kept the kingdom together until his death, but it was Solomon's actions that brought forth God's anger. Nehemiah was saying, "Isn't this what King Solomon did? Isn't this how he sinned, by these many women? There was no king like him, and yet he did this thing."

There are some who have twisted this Scripture and coupled it with Paul's admonition in the New Testament, "Be not unequally yoked." They make it into a prohibition against mixed marriages in the modern day, and apply it to race, skin color, age or whatever else they want to apply it to. First of all, I would point out that there were exceptions even in the Old Testament. God enters in to many strange situations. Look at Ruth, the Moabitess. She turned from going her own way and she said, "I will serve your God, the living God." So you cannot say that God forbids relationships with other races. We are talking on a spiritual level in the spiritual realm. The issue Nehemiah was dealing with had to do with marrying someone who would draw you away from your relationship with God.

I have seen this happen to couples in the church, where one of them decides they no longer want to attend because they want to pursue something else. But then the other person decides they must also go, because they don't want to risk offending or losing their boyfriend or girlfriend, husband or wife. They have their eyes focused on the flesh and they say, "I cannot live without that person." But the reality is that they have taken their eyes off of the very lifeline that we truly cannot live without. Although I do not give dating advice, I always tell young people that if you walk with the Lord and stay committed to Him, He will provide a helpmate for you. And while they may have all kinds of strange quirks and oddities, it will be someone who loves what you love. If you commit your situation to the Lord, He will enter in and He will work it out right.

In the case of these people in Nehemiah's day, Nehemiah admonished the people, saying, "Don't you know what happened in history? This is the very thing that resulted in the kingdom being divided." He made his appeal using history and Scripture, and said, "Shall we then hearken unto you to do all this great evil, to transgress against our God in marrying strange wives? And one of the sons of Joiada, the son of Eliashib the high priest, was son in law to Sanballat the Horonite: therefore I chased him from me."

This final chapter should be interpreted for the ages as the record of a man who had the spirit of a reformer. When I think of the spirit of Nehemiah, the name of Martin Luther immediately comes to mind. This chapter displays a person with the love of God and the courage to declare, "This is what the truth looks like." And he did not just say, "Let's expose it," he said, "Let's take action and correct the problem." I love the fact that that is exactly what Nehemiah did. He wasn't the kind of man who would just talk about things. He was a man who took action and implemented the cleansing of the temple and the restoration of everyday worship.

Nehemiah prayed two times, "Remember me," and then he prayed, "Remember them, O my God, because they have defiled the priesthood, and the covenant of the priesthood, and of the Levites. Thus cleansed I them from all strangers, and appointed the wards of the priests and the Levites, every one in his business; and for the wood offering, at times appointed, and for the firstfruits. Remember me, O my God, for good." That was the third time he said, "Remember me, O my God." Nehemiah was not boasting, "Look at what I have done!" Rather, he was imploring God from a sincere heart, saying, "Lord, please don't forget me in spite of the calamity that has happened here, the collapse of respect for the things of God."

Let's bring this prayer into the New Testament frame:

"Lord, in spite of the insanity of this world, in spite of a church that wants convenience and fast-food Christianity and instantaneous problem-solving, please don't hold all of this to my account. I still love You, God, and I still love Your work so much that I will clean house and stay by the stuff. And if I have to, I will throw Tobiah's garbage out into the street and restore the proper service and respect and standards and dignity to Your house and to Your worship, for Your sake."

I pray this for many of you; I pray it for myself. This study in Nehemiah has encouraged me to look at an example, not only of a man of faith, but also of how quickly people fall away. Even though there may be a strong leader who says, "Come on, follow me as I follow Christ," people can quickly fall away when they forget the very reason why they came to the kingdom in the first place and why they came to the church.

You do not go to church to be entertained, you do not go to have coffee, you do not even go to church because you have nowhere else to go. You go to church because Christ has called you out from darkness into the light, to be part of the family of God, and to rejoice and connect in fellowship.

May the spirit of Nehemiah rest on your pastor, to never allow people to slip things into the church under the guise of convenience or making our lives easier. And may the spirit of Nehemiah rest on the congregation, that as you go about your everyday business, you will know the difference between a straight stick and a crooked stick. You will know the difference between what saith the word of God, and the garbage that is peddled that may deceive the multitudes; but at least you will not be deceived.

The Scripture says that we should not be tossed and turned with every new wave of doctrine, but that we should stay the course. For this time and for this generation, the church of Jesus Christ needs people with the spirit of Nehemiah. That does not mean you should go out and pick fights and think that your whole mission in life is to expose other people's garbage; rather it means that you should simply stand on the word of God. Let this be our prayer:

"Lord, remember us. Not as though we have made any great sacrifice or any great contribution, but remember us in the midst of this tumult, what I call this strange moment in time when people seem to be unaffected by the word of God and unsympathetic to the cause of Christ and what the church stands for."

May the Lord remember us, and let the spirit of Nehemiah be upon everyone who can hear and who knows that, no matter what, we are not being conformed to the image and likeness of this world, but we are being conformed to the image and likeness of Jesus Christ. That is my prayer.

Appendix I

The Wall of Jerusalem in Nehemiah's Day

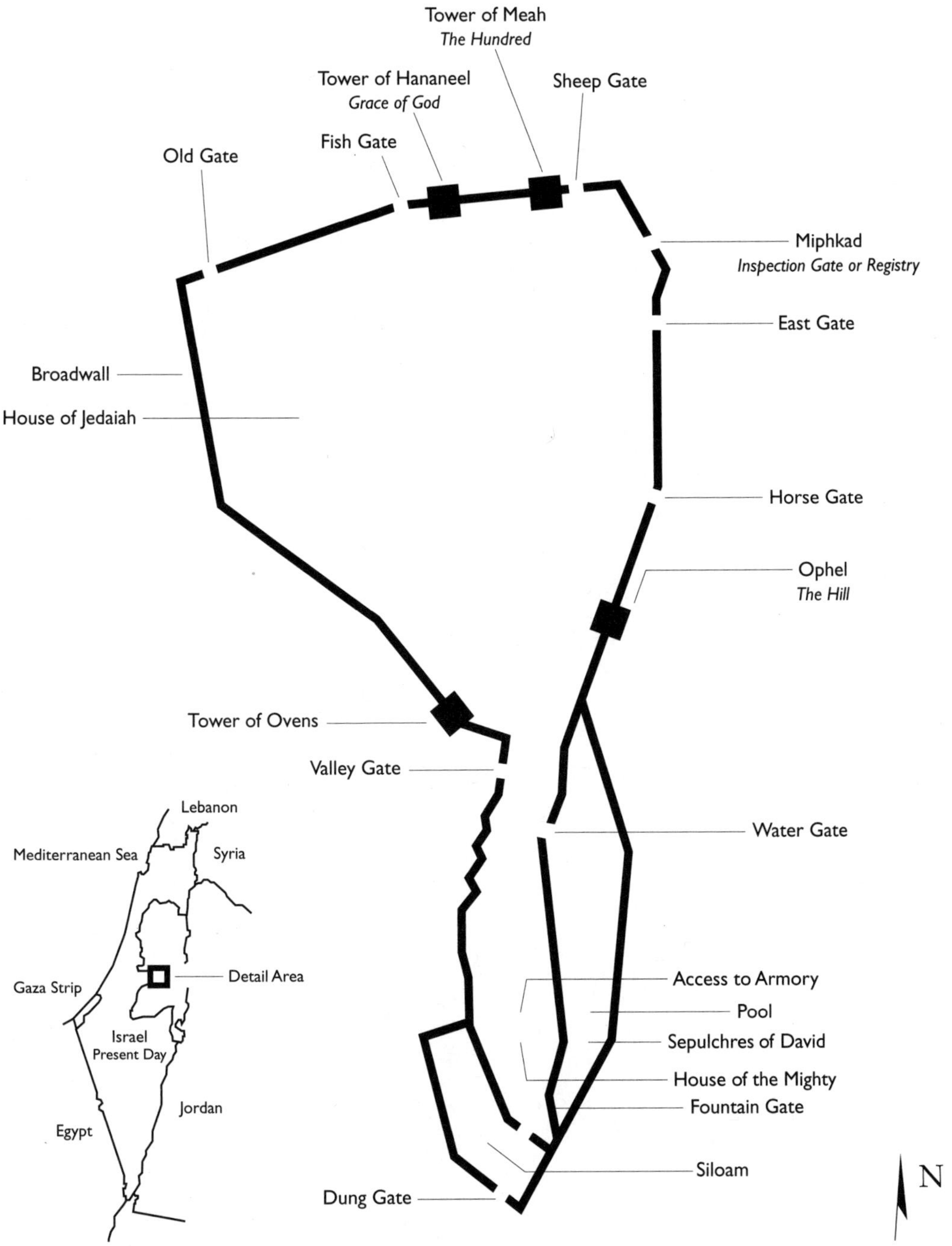

Appendix II

Time Line of the Events Surrounding the Rebuilding of Jerusalem

All dates are B.C. Dates in italics are approximate or uncertain.

590 – 530	Cyrus' lifetime. Prophecies concerning Cyrus were given 120–150 years earlier as recorded in Isaiah 41, 44, and 45.
539	Cyrus conquers Babylon.
539 (*538*)	The edict of Cyrus in the first year of his reign, as recorded in 2 Chronicles 36:22–23 and in Ezra 1:1–4.
536 (*537*)	The first wave of returnees to Jerusalem under Zerubbabel and Jeshua (Joshua) as recorded in Ezra 2 (though there are questions regarding the date and identity of Sheshbazzar mentioned in Ezra 1 and Ezra 5). Essentially the same list is recorded in Nehemiah 7. The first wave did the bulk of the temple construction.
530	Cyrus dies. Cambyses rules.
522	Cambyses dies. "False Smerdis" is the temporary successor. The construction work at Jerusalem stops. Smerdis will be succeeded by Darius.
520	Darius is reigning. Haggai and Zechariah prophesy. Darius' decree as recorded in Ezra 6. Temple construction resumes.
515	Temple completed as recorded in Ezra 6:15.
465	Artaxerxes I rules.
458	Artaxerxes' edict. The second wave of returnees under Ezra as recorded in Ezra 7–8. Ezra 8 records the names of the people who returned with Ezra.
445	Nehemiah goes to Jerusalem.
444	The wall is completed.
432	Nehemiah goes back to Babylon for a time, and then returns to Jerusalem. Nehemiah 13:6.

Appendix III

THE UNDERSTANDING THAT COMES FROM GOD

A WORD STUDY

The word "understand," its origin and certain cognates

Our English word "understand" is comprised of two parts, "under" and "stand." The word "under" in this context does not mean the same thing as the preposition *under*, which means "beneath." Rather, it comes from the Proto-Indo-European root **nter*, which can represent "between" or "among." The word "stand" comes from the Proto-Indo-European root **sta*. If you are familiar with Latin words, you will recognize its cognate *stare*, "to stand." The verb form has the sense of "exist or present." Those who have worked in copy editing or printing will recognize the cognate *stet*, meaning "let it stand," which is an editor's instruction to a printer to disregard a correction made to a text.

In the Greek, we have the words *histémi* and *stasis*. The word *histémi* means "to put, to place, or to stand." This word is used repeatedly in Ephesians 6, where we are told to "stand," "withstand" and "stand therefore." The word *stasis* is found in many English words; it can mean "with stillness" or "standing still." A multiplicity of words descend from *histémi* and *stasis*, including *station*, *status* and *stall*, which is the German word for a stable. In Old Irish, the word *seasamh* means the "act of standing." This is only a brief survey of the origin and cognates of our English word "understanding."

The use of the word "understand" in Nehemiah 8

Now let's turn to the book of Nehemiah to see the use of the word "understand" in its context. Notice the number of times that this word occurs in Nehemiah 8:

Verse 2: "And Ezra the priest brought the law before the congregation both of men and women, and all that could hear with *understanding*."

Verse 3: "and those that could *understand*; and the ears of all the people were attentive."

Verse 7: "caused the people to *understand* the law."

Verse 8: "and caused them to *understand* the reading."

Verse 9: "and the Levites that *taught* the people." The word "taught" is a form of the same Hebrew word "to understand."

Verse 12: "because they had *understood* the words that were declared unto them."

The Hebrew word *been*

In every one of these instances in Nehemiah 8, it is the same Hebrew root word that is translated "understand" or "understanding." The word is *Strong's* number 995. The basic root of this verb in Hebrew is comprised of three letters: *bet, yod, nun*. We could transliterate it using the letters *b-y-n* or *bîn*. In Hebrew, reading from right to left, it is בִּין. It may be pronounced like the English word *been*, with a long *e* sound.

Hebrew verbs and the Hiphil stem

Hebrew verbs are built up like building blocks: to a given verbal root, various prefixes, suffixes or infixes may be added that indicate person, number, gender, etc. A verb may appear in a number of different "stems," which indicate voice (e.g., active, passive, reflexive) and aspect (e.g., intensive, causative, etc.).

The simplest stem is known as *Qal*, which normally represents a simple, active voice. The simple passive stem is called *Niphal*. It is noteworthy that all of these instances of the word *been* in Nehemiah 8 save one are in what is called the *Hiphil* stem.

The Hiphil stem has at least five uses, which are classified as *causative*, *inner-causative* (or *stative*), *nominative*, *declarative* and *miscellaneous.* Our focus is on the causative usage. The word *been* in the Hiphil means "to *cause* to understand." Its Greek equivalent in the New Testament is *sunesis*. If you look at Nehemiah 8 in the *Septuagint*, the Greek translation of all the *been* words are a form of *sunesis*, except for one instance.

The use of *been* in the book of Daniel

We find a consistent use of this word in the book of Daniel, which was written in a similar timeframe as Nehemiah. When studying word meanings, it is important to take into consideration the relative dates of authorship of the various texts, since a word might undergo some shift in its meaning over time. Also, we know that the Hebrew is ambiguous and is not as precise as the Greek. Nonetheless, the greater part of the occurrences of the word *been* in Daniel carry a similar connotation.

We read in Daniel 1:17, "As for these four children, God gave them knowledge and skill in all learning and wisdom: and Daniel had understanding in all visions and dreams." Again in the Hebrew the word for "understanding" is in the Hiphil; and in the Septuagint, the Greek word is *sunesin*. Note that it says, speaking of Daniel and the three Hebrew children, "God gave them knowledge and skill in all learning and wisdom: and Daniel had understanding," that is, we could say, "Daniel was caused to understand in all visions and dreams."

Daniel 8:15–16 says, "And it came to pass, when I, even I Daniel, had seen the vision, and sought for the meaning, then, behold, there stood before me as the appearance of a man. And I heard a man's voice between the banks of Ulai, which called, and said, Gabriel, make this man to understand the vision." Here the verb *been* is in the form of a Hiphil imperative; it is a command. In the Septuagint, it is the Greek word *sunetison*. "So he came near where I stood: and when he came, I was afraid, and fell upon my face: but he said unto me, Understand, O son of man: for at the time of the end shall be the vision." This is not the best rendering, but again it is a Hiphil imperative: "Understand!" In this particular instance, it could be a declarative Hiphil, but it would still carry a causative force with it.

Daniel 8:23 says, "And in the latter time of their kingdom, when the transgressors are come to the full, a king of fierce countenance, and understanding dark sentences, shall stand up." In this instance, the word *been* is a Hiphil participle, and the Greek is *sunion*. A participle has a different function than a verb, and I would translate this word as "a master of darkness" or "one who understands riddles."

Daniel 9:21–22 says, "Yea, whiles I was speaking in prayer, even the man Gabriel, whom I had seen in the vision at the beginning, being caused to fly swiftly, touched me about the time of the evening oblation. And he informed me. . . ." The word "informed" is a form of *been*. Then the angel Gabriel said, "O Daniel, I am now come forth to give thee skill and understanding," that is, "He made me understand."

Daniel 9:23 is a bit more complicated. "At the beginning of thy supplications the commandment came forth, and I am come to shew thee; for thou art greatly beloved: therefore understand the matter, and consider the vision." The Masoretic Text swaps two clauses, "so consider therefore the message and understand the vision." In the Hebrew, the first instance of our word is a Qal imperative: "Consider therefore"; and the second is a Hiphil imperative: "Understand the vision."

After this, the prophecy is unfolded to Daniel: "Seventy weeks are determined upon thy people and upon thy holy city, to finish the transgression, and to make an end of sins, and to make reconciliation for iniquity," and so forth. "Know therefore and understand" means that what follows is an unfolding of the prophecy. Again, verse 23 reads, "therefore understand the matter, and consider the vision."

This understanding does not come from within Daniel; it comes from God. Daniel is the recipient of this understanding.

Perhaps the clearest illustration is found in Daniel 10, beginning in verse 10: "Behold, an hand touched me, which set me upon my knees and upon the palms of my hands. And he said unto me, O Daniel, a man greatly beloved, understand the words that I speak unto thee, and stand upright: for unto thee am I now sent. And when he had spoken this word unto me, I stood trembling. Then said he unto me, Fear not, Daniel: for from the first day that thou didst set thine heart to understand, and to chasten thyself," literally "to humble thyself before thy God, thy words were heard, and I am come for thy words." My translation from the Masoretic Text reads, "From the first day that you set your heart to gain understanding and humbled yourself before your God, your words have been heard, and I have come because of your words." Daniel prayed to gain understanding. And the angel was sent to give him that understanding. Our word *been* is used all the way through this passage. Not all knowledge and understanding is from within; rather, God must give it to us.

Now turn to Daniel 12:8–10: "And I heard, but I understood not: then said I, O my Lord, what shall be the end of these things? And he said, Go thy way, Daniel: for the words are closed up and sealed till the time of the end. Many shall be purified, and made white, and tried; but the wicked shall do wickedly: and none of the wicked shall understand; but the wise shall understand."

It is important that this passage be rendered correctly, because it uses reflexives that are not indicated in the King James Version. The King James Version simply says, "Many shall be purified, made white, and tried." The Hebrew says, "Many shall purify *themselves*, and make *themselves* spotless and be refined." The only passive verb is "be refined," because it is God who will do the refining. It is quite clear that the majority of these examples in Daniel, most of which are in the Hiphil, represent an understanding that is given by God.

The use of *been* in Psalm 119

There are seven instances of *been* that I would like us to look at in Psalm 119:

Verse 27: "Make me" or *cause* me "to *understand* the way of thy precepts." Here is the psalmist petitioning to receive understanding.

Verse 34: "Give me *understanding*, and I shall keep thy law."

Verse 73: "Give me *understanding*, that I may learn thy commandments."

Verse 125: "I am thy servant; give me *understanding*, that I may know thy testimonies."

Verse 130: "The entrance of thy words giveth light; it giveth *understanding* unto the simple."

Verse 144: "Give me *understanding*, and I shall live."

Verse 169: "Give me *understanding* according to thy word."

Psalm 119:130 is the most important to our study. I have translated this verse: "The unfolding or opening of your words causes light; it imparts understanding to the simple," those whose eyes and ears are open. It is saying that the opening up of God's word illuminates.

In Nehemiah 8, the people gathered themselves together as one man, which is analogous to the people who were gathered together on the day of Pentecost. In both cases, the people were hearing, and they were hearing with understanding. Nehemiah 8:12 says, "they had understood the words that were declared unto them." Now, not all have the capacity to receive; and therefore not all have the capacity to understand. That is why in Isaiah 6:8–9, when God says, "Who will go for us?" and the prophet says, "Send me," God says, "Well, they will not hear. They will not see. They will not understand. Your preaching will fall on deaf ears."

We know that not everybody is called or chosen; not everybody can hear. But if you have even a small desire to listen and to hear the word opened up, and if it has some impact, that means you are a recipient of God's word. You are like those Paul described in Ephesians 1:4, whom

God chose for Himself. That knowledge should have a momentous impact on your life, perhaps in contradistinction to those who have no interest. That does not mean that at some point God will not illuminate and open the minds of those without interest, it simply means that God chose you to hear.

If you are interested in studying the word of God, that interest can only come from God. That does not mean you belong to some kind of elite group that can boast, "Hey, I am one of those!" But it brings to mind a reality of your calling and the grace of God's operating in you. We have all known people who are completely disinterested. Pray for those people. You do not know what God will do. There is a season for everything, and everything is in His perfect time. The book of Ecclesiastes says that God "has placed eternity in their hearts." When we speak of eternity, I do not want you to only think of heaven; think also of hell because both of those places are eternal. We cannot "lead someone to make a decision for Christ." If a person leads another person to Christ, it may be only the flesh or a momentary emotional response. But if such a conversion has any real staying-power to it, it will be God who gives the eyes of understanding and the appetite for His bread. And if a person is hungry, they will want that bread regardless of how it is delivered. That is why Psalm 119:130 is so powerful: it is the unfolding or opening up of God's word that gives illumination.

Jesus' use of the equivalent Greek word *sunesis*

We now turn our attention to how Jesus used the Greek word *sunesis* and its various forms, to gain a fuller understanding of why some may understand while others will not. The word *sunesis* is a cognate of *suniémi*, which is a compound word meaning "to put together" or "to comprehend." By implication it means to act piously, to consider, to understand, and to be wise.

In the parable of the sower in Matthew 13, Jesus concluded with these words: "Who hath ears to hear, let him hear. And the disciples came, and said unto him, Why speakest thou unto them in parables?

He answered and said unto them, Because it is given unto you to know the mysteries of the kingdom of heaven, but to them it is not given." In today's society, that would not be considered fair. "For whosoever hath, to him shall be given, and he shall have more abundance: but whosoever hath not, from him shall be taken away even that he hath. Therefore speak I to them in parables: because they seeing see not; and hearing they hear not, neither do they understand," this final word being *suniousin* in the Greek.

Then Jesus quotes from Isaiah 6:9, saying, "And in them is fulfilled the prophecy of Esaias, which saith, By hearing ye shall hear, and shall not understand," again, *sunesis* or *been*, "and seeing ye shall see, and shall not perceive: for this people's heart is waxed gross, and their ears are dull of hearing, and their eyes they have closed; lest at any time they should see with their eyes, and hear with their ears, and should understand with their heart, and should be converted, and I should heal them." To "understand with the heart" implies that the heart must first be opened to receive. So we can see how these words are connected.

Jesus went on to say, "But blessed are your eyes, for they see: and your ears, for they hear. For verily I say unto you, That many prophets and righteous men have desired to see those things which ye see, and have not seen them; and to hear those things which ye hear, and have not heard them."

Many people think that they are hearing, but they have no hunger and their hearts are not open to receive illumination. They only desire man's words that are flattering and pleasing to the ears. This was foretold in the New Testament when Paul wrote to Timothy about people with "itching ears," people who want only smooth words.

Now we go on to read the explanation of the parable: "Hear ye therefore the parable of the sower. When any one heareth the word of the kingdom. . . ." Pause right there and notice that it is the word of the *kingdom*, not the word of self-help, not the word of feeling good and telling you that you are okay. When anyone hears "the word of the kingdom, and understandeth it not, then cometh the wicked one, and catcheth away that which was sown in his heart. This is he which received seed by the way side. But he that received the seed into stony places, the same is he that heareth the word, and anon with joy receiveth it; yet hath he not root in himself; but dureth for a while: for when tribulation or persecution ariseth because of the word. . . ." Because of the word! When tribulation or persecution arises because of the word, "by-and-by he is offended." The Greek word translated "offended" has a cognate in English, the word "scandalized." The seed has not taken root; the person is scandalized, and they are gone.

"He also that received seed among the thorns is he that heareth the word; and the care of this world, and the deceitfulness of riches, choke the word, and he becometh unfruitful. But he that received seed into the good ground is he that heareth the word, and understandeth it; which also beareth fruit, and bringeth forth, some an hundredfold, some sixty, some thirty." That tells us that not everybody who hears with understanding yields fruit in the same way or in the same dimension: some yield a little and some a lot; but they all yield fruit. And that fruit is fruit unto the Lord, not fruit that someone comes to inspect.

A parallel concept found in the writings of the apostle Paul

There is a parallel concept expressed in Romans 10. The apostle Paul had been addressing the Gentiles, but he turned his attention to Israel beginning in Romans 9 and continuing through Romans 11. And in the middle of that discourse, he says, "For there is no difference between the Jew and the Greek: for the same Lord over all is rich unto all that call upon him. For whosoever shall call upon the name of the Lord shall be saved. How then shall they call on him in whom they have not believed?" That is, how can they call the One whom they have not trusted or *faithed* in. "And how shall they believe (or *faithe*) in him of whom they have not heard? and how shall they hear without a preacher? And how shall they preach, except they be sent?" All of these concepts come back to one place. Paul says in Ephesians 4 that God gave gifts to the church, and all of those gifts come back to the word of God. Whether it is an evangelist who heralds the good news, or a prophet who is bubbling forth with the word of God, or whether it is a pastoring-teacher—all of these gift ministries come back to the word of God.

No one who is truly called of God for that task will appoint themselves; they must be sent by God. That is why the first ministry on the list in Ephesians 4 is "apostle," meaning "sent one." All of these gifts revolve around the word. The person who opens up the word is performing scriptural exegesis. But before exegesis occurs to the hearers, God must do something to their hearts, which brings us back to the Greek and Hebrew words for understanding, *sunesis* and *been*. God enables that understanding, and I do not believe that it happens all at once. I do not believe that everything makes sense on your first day in church. I believe it is a progressive revelation. And the more a person stays in the word of God, the more understanding comes.

The gift of *been*

While there are different facets being presented here, they all come back to the same idea: God must do the stirring. He has to enable someone to teach and open up the word of God, and He also has to open up the heart of the hearers. The Bible says that some were created to honor, and some to dishonor and shame. 1 Corinthians 1:18 says that the preaching of the gospel is the greatest gift to those who are being saved, but to those who are in the process of being destroyed, it is foolishness. We should celebrate the capacity to be responsive to God's word. We are conduits of the Spirit and we can bring people to the church, but we cannot force the people we bring to be interested in or desire the word. That must come from God. It is prevenient grace. It is a gift of God, in the same manner that *been* or *sunesis* is a gift of God.

Now if you have that gift, praise God for it. Be grateful and do not abuse that gift or treat it lightly. God does turn people around, giving them the ability to become children of light even as they once were children of darkness, as you and I once were. But God help us to never get so settled in and become so comfortable that we forget the grace that has been bestowed upon us. And that grace—amazing grace—should make each and every one of us want to press in closer to Him and to the place where His word is being taught.

If your understanding is not crystal clear, do not think that is a fault. No person has perfect understanding of God's word, because we are imperfect vessels; we are flawed; we are sinful. I do not think we can ever have perfect understanding; but you should continue to press in and listen to the teaching of God's word. If you keep staying in the word, clarity will come. And you will have perfect vision when you stand before Him and He says, "Well done, good and faithful servant." Until then, we need a little help in our understanding. That help comes from Him. Praise God for it!

Isaiah talks about God giving His Spirit to give understanding: to give *been*. We know that God gives us His Spirit. We see in Nehemiah that though the people were given understanding, they still fell away when Nehemiah was absent for a time. This proves that just because God gives people the capacity to understand, that does not prevent them from sinning. Having this type of gift from God does not make you perfect. Some people think that once you reach a certain place, you can relax and say, "That's that!" But look at Solomon. He is a perfect example of a man who prayed for wisdom and received it, but he did not use the wisdom that was given him, and he fell into sin.

The use of *been* in Proverbs

Solomon spoke about wisdom and the rewards of wisdom and understanding. In Proverbs 2:4–8, he said, "If thou seekest her as silver, and searchest for her as for hid treasures; then shalt thou understand," *been*, "the fear of the LORD, and find the knowledge of God. For the LORD giveth wisdom: out of his mouth cometh knowledge and understanding. He layeth up sound wisdom for the righteous: he is a buckler to them that walk uprightly. He keepeth the paths of judgment, and preserveth the way of his saints." If you could sum up this advice, it essentially says that to seek, to receive and to gain wisdom and understanding from God, is more precious than any other gift you can ever give or receive. It is life-giving. It is the way of righteousness and the way of life. At least two and a half chapters in Proverbs are devoted to this idea. "Happy is the man that findeth wisdom, and the man that getteth understanding."

It is possible to have wisdom, knowledge and understanding, and still fall down. What was Solomon's besetting sin? He took up with strange women who turned his heart away from God. So receiving the gift does not prevent you from falling. But you should recognize it as a gift, treat it as such and never become casual about it.

Conclusion

Our love of the Lord should keep on increasing. Nonetheless, there will be ebbs and flows in our relationship with God. Thank God for the gift of eyes, ears and heart. Even Solomon said that wisdom and understanding are to be treasured above all, because they come from Him. It is His gift operating in your life, the gift of His presence. Moses said, "Lord, if Your presence does not go with me, I do not want to go." Likewise, we can pray, "Lord, if You are not going to give me understanding, how can I even connect?" But God has already opened up the channels of our understanding. You do your part, which is abiding in the word, and He will abide in you.

Bibliography

The Amplified Bible, Containing the Amplified Old Testament and the Amplified New Testament. Grand Rapids: Zondervan, 1987. p. 550.

Bíblia King James Atualizada (Português). São Paulo: Abba Press, 2012.

Boyd, James. *The Westminster Shorter Catechism.* Philadelphia: Presbyterian Board of Publication, 1854. p. 19.

Bunyan, John. *The Works of John Bunyan.* Ed. George Offor. Vol. 1. Glasgow: Blackie and Son, 1855. p. 65.

Du Plessis, David. *The Spirit Bade Me Go: The Astounding Move of God in the Denominational Churches.* Gainesville: Bridge-Logos, 2004. p. i.

The Genuine Works of Flavius Josephus, the Jewish Historian: Containing Twenty Books of the Jewish Antiquities, Seven Books of the Jewish War, and The Life of Josephus. Trans. William Whiston. Vol. 1. New York: William Borradaile, 1823. p. 37.

The Histories of Herodotus. Trans. Henry Cary. New York: D. Appleton, 1904. pp. 43–75.

The Holy Bible, English Standard Version. Peabody: Hendrickson, 2009. p. 490.

The Holy Bible, New Living Translation. 2nd ed. Wheaton: Tyndale House, 2004. p. 374.

Kierkegaard, Søren. *The Prayers of Kierkegaard.* Ed. Perry D. LeFevre. Chicago: U of Chicago P, 1956. p. 214.

Lewis, C. S. *The Great Divorce.* New York: Simon, 1996. p. 72.

——. *The Screwtape Letters.* New York: Harper, 2001. p. 59.

Luther, Martin. *D. Martin Luthers Werke: Kritische Gesamtausgabe, Briefwechsel.* Vol. 5. Weimar: Hermann Böhlaus Nachfolger, 1934. p. 420.

Milton, John. *Paradise Lost: A Poem in Twelve Books.* 2nd ed. Vol. 1. London: J. and R. Tonson, 1750. p. 12.

Murray, Andrew. *With Christ in the School of Prayer: Thoughts on our Training for the Ministry of Intercession.* London: Nisbet, 1887. p. 170.

La Sainte Bible, qui Comprend L'Ancien et Le Nouveau Testament. Trans. Louis Segond. Paris: Delessert, 1899. p. 556.

Scott, Dr. Gene. "Building the Wall: Zechariah's Fifth Vision." *The Pulpit.* Vol. 9. Glendale: Dolores Press, 2015. pp. 4–19.

——. "God Shall Arise." *The Pulpit.* Vol. 7. Glendale: Dolores Press, 2013. p. 238.

——. "The Resurrection: A Factual Basis for the Christian Faith." *The Pulpit.* Vol. 9. Glendale: Dolores Press, 2015. pp. 207–230.

——. "The Resurrection of Jesus Christ." *The Pulpit.* Vol. 10. Glendale: Dolores Press, 2017. pp. 155–175.

——. "Run to the Name of the Lord." *The Pulpit.* Vol. 9. Glendale: Dolores Press, 2015. p. 188.

——. "Tough Shoes for a Tough Trip." *The Pulpit.* Vol. 3. Glendale: Dolores Press, 2009. pp. 265–273.

The Septuagint Version of the Old Testament, with an English Translation. Trans. Lancelot Charles Lee Brenton. London: Samuel Bagster and Sons, 1879.

Spurgeon, C. H. *The Metropolitan Tabernacle Pulpit.* Vol. 36. London: Passmore & Alabaster, 1890. p. 275.

Strong, James. *Strong's Exhaustive Concordance of the Bible: Updated and Expanded Edition.* Peabody: Hendrickson, 2015.